Grid and Cloud Computing

Katarina Stanoevska-Slabeva • Thomas Wozniak
Santi Ristol

Editors

Grid and Cloud Computing

A Business Perspective on Technology
and Applications

 Springer

Editors

Prof. Dr. Katarina Stanoevska-Slabeva
Thomas Wozniak
University of St. Gallen
Institute for Media and
Communications Management
Blumenbergplatz 9
9000 St. Gallen
Switzerland
katarina.stanoevska@unisg.ch
thomas.wozniak@unisg.ch

Santi Ristol
Atos Origin S.A.E.
C/ Albarracín, 25
28037 Madrid
Spain
santi.ristol@atosorigin.com

ISBN 978-3-642-05192-0   e-ISBN 978-3-642-05193-7
DOI 10.1007/978-3-642-05193-7
Springer Heidelberg Dordrecht London New York

Library of Congress Control Number: 2009939830

Cover design: WMXDesign GmbH, Heidelberg, Germany

Printed on acid-free paper

Springer is part of Springer Science+Business Media (www.springer.com)

Foreword

In 2004, at the early stage of the IST-FP6 programme, during an industrial panel organised at the Launch of the first FP6 projects on Grid Technologies, the need for industrial evidence of the benefits brought by the adoption of Grid Technologies became explicit.

High-level representatives from industry discussed how to exploit the European strength in Grid. A few critical topics emerged: the weak industrial take-up of Grid technologies as well as the technological challenges to be addressed for this take-up to happen. Security and privacy were deemed to be essential factors, but performance and quality of service, easy manageability and low deployment costs were also considered as key. However, technology was not seen as a major risk as the real one laid in the deployment and management of the Grids and in their commercial uptake, since the area was not mature enough for widespread adoption by industry. What was critical was to take the Grid to the market.

This is the story of the foundations of BEinGRID, which is essentially addressing the issue on how to bring the Grid to the industry and builds a series of industrial cases of adoption of Grid Technologies.

At the time of FP6 Call5, a consortium of 75 partners[1] from across the European Union, led by Atos Origin, put forward a proposal. The consortium was composed by leading Grid research organisations committed to its business use, and by a broad spectrum of companies keen to assess the benefits to their productivity, competitiveness and profitability from their use of Grid solutions. The project was selected out of the competitive call, started its activities on 2006 and this year it will complete its activities. As planned, it has helped several European industries to introduce the Grid into their business. This has resulted in a fabulous load of experience, in technical, economical, business and last but not least legal terms. A broad spectrum of companies has assessed the benefits to their productivity, competitiveness and profitability from their use of Grid solutions. The technical solutions found, the economic research, the legal boundaries and constraints in which they operate constitute an extremely interesting knowledge which is there to be reused.

The originality of BEinGRID findings and proposed solutions is that they have already been tried out. The project is not about theories or frameworks, but about real, tested, experimented, adapted solutions and the experiences gained by their use. The case studies that BEinGRID proposes are real, conducted by a broad spectrum of European businesses which operate in the real world. RoI has been examined, the legal context has been worked out, technical problems have found a solution and all of this has been packaged and made available on the repository the project has created: Gridipedia.

And at last, it has to be noted that it is not just about Grid. The adoption of Grid technologies was the triggering factor for the project, and the context around the

---

[1] Extended to 97 with the Open Call of November 2007.

project has evolved since. However it is quite clear that the problems addressed are also of more generic nature, and many if not all of the solution found are of interest for anybody who wishes to approach a distributed solution for its business, being that SaaS, Clouds or Grid. This book contains loads of information, coming from real cases. I am sure that the extremely valuable experiences of the early adopters of Grid based solutions will motivate several other organizations to do the same.

Annalisa Bogliolo
European Commission
Project Officer
DG Information Society and Media
Unit Software and Services Architectures and Infrastructures

The opinions expressed above are those of the author and do not necessarily reflect those of the European Commission

To be, or not to be: that is the question:
Whether ›tis nobler in the mind to suffer
The slings and arrows of outrageous fortune,
Or to take arms against a sea of troubles,
And by opposing end them? ....

    Hamlet, Act three, Scene one. (William Shakespeare, 1564-1616)

Foreword

The idea to set up such a practical project like BEinGRID was born in early 2005 after realising that the commercial exploitation of Grid technology was lagging behind what we knew could be done.

Since 2000, Atos Origin had taken part in the development of a number of European Grid architecture solutions for enabling the management of distributed resources across multiple enterprises' boundaries and creating collaborative environments (also known as Virtual Organisations) that were completely transparent to the users. There had been a significant number of software middlewares as a result of FP5 IST Grid research (GRIA, GRASP, CROSSGRID, GAT, etc.), but they were too unconnected to achieve their full potential. In the first calls of FP6, Grid projects were pooling their research efforts using open standards to guarantee the interoperability and taking advantages of existing synergies to design and develop underlying Grid technologies that enable a wide variety of business applications. The promised architecture for a Next Generation Grid (NGG) is in line with "OGSA and beyond" that was already under design and development.

For some reason, the benefits of global Grid Computing had not yet caught on with most businesses, and the promise of delivering almost limitless computing power to any user, anywhere – and the many benefits this would bring - was still little more than a dream. There appeared to be a clear threat that industry and commerce would not accept the middlewares on offer simply due to a lack of knowledge and/or a lack of confidence in their maturity and reliability.

At that moment, despite a significant investment, Grid was at a critical phase in its transition from use in research and academia, to adoption across all enterprise sectors. An unawareness of the benefits brought by the use of Grid technologies and the lack of reference business cases (to demonstrate the benefits to potential users) was leading to a weak commercial exploitation of results and so of the general deployment of this technology into the market, failing to exploit the EU's competitiveness and leadership in this technological area. It was time to establish effective routes to push this technology adoption and to stimulate the research into innovative business models. A take-up project to transfer the benefits of the Grid to business scenarios was needed. It was the right moment to be or not to be in Grid.

BEinGRID, Business Experiments in Grid, was presented to FP6 ICT Call 5, and started in June 2006 with a clear mission to exploit European Grid middleware by creating a toolset repository of Grid services from across the Grid research domain and to use these services to deliver a set of successful Business Experiments that stimulate the early adoption of Grid technologies across the European Union. A Business Experiment was defined as a real Grid pilot application that addresses a concrete business case and in which the main actors of the economic sector are represented: the end-user, the service provider, and the Grid service integrator. The involvement of the full value chain was considered a catalysing aspect to demonstrate Grid potential and to capitalise on the derived benefits.

BEinGRID has produced a series of 25 Business Experiments from key business sectors such as chemistry, engineering, environmental, finance, gaming, health, logistics, multimedia, science, telecom, tourism, etc. on different Grid middleware solutions. Most of the findings of the project and these Business Experiments can be found in the repository created by the project initially named Gridipedia (http://www.gridipedia.eu/), and currently available as IT-Tude.com (http://www.it-tude.com or www.it-tude.eu).

Today, four years later, we are facing the last months of the BEinGRID project, in a global context in which new terms like Cloud Computing have emerged to build on the ideas originally raised by Grid Computing. I am sure that most of the findings of BEinGRID will be very relevant and helpful for those thinking to be or not to be in the Cloud.

Santi Ristol
BEinGRID Project Coordinator
ATOS ORIGIN Business Director

Contents

PART III: Grid Business Experiments

Part IV: Practical Guidelines

PART I: Introduction

1 Introduction: Business and Technological Drivers of Grid Computing

Katarina Stanoevska-Slabeva, Thomas Wozniak

1.1 Introduction

> *The Grid is an emerging infrastructure that will fundamentally change the way we think – and use – computing. The word Grid is used by analogy with the electric power grid, which provides pervasive access to electricity and, like the computer and a small number of other advances has had a dramatic impact on human capabilities and society. Many believe that by allowing all components of our information technology infrastructure – computational capabilities, databases, sensors, and people – to be shared flexibly as true collaborative tools, the Grid will have a similar transforming effect, allowing new classes of application to emerge.*
>
> (Foster and Kesselman 2004)

The vision of using and sharing computers and data as utility has been inspired by constantly increasing computing needs faced by researchers in science and can be traced back in the 1960s to the Internet pioneer Licklider (see Berman and Hey 2004). Licklider wrote in his groundbreaking paper (Licklider 1960)[1] that computers should be developed

> "to enable men and computers to cooperate in making decisions and controlling complex situations without inflexible dependence on predetermined programs."

But, it was only in the mid 1990s when this vision became reality and the term "Grid Computing" was coined in order to denote a new computing paradigm (Foster et al. 2001).

Explained from the user perspective in the most simplest way, Grid Computing means that computing power and resources can be obtained as utility similar to electricity – the user can simply request information and computations and have them delivered to him without necessity to care where the data he requires resides or which computer is processing his request (Goyal and Lawande 2005). From the technical perspective Grid Computing means the virtualization and sharing of available computing and data resources among different organizational and physical domains. By means of virtualization and support for sharing of resources, scattered computing resources are abstracted from the physical location and their specific features and provided to the users as a single resource that is automatically

---

[1] According to citation in Berman and Hey (2004)

K. Stanoevska-Slabeva et al. (eds.), *Grid and Cloud Computing: A Business Perspective on Technology and Applications*, DOI 10.1007/978-3-642-05193-7_1,
© Springer-Verlag Berlin Heidelberg 2010

allocated to their computing needs and processes. At the core of Grid Computing therefore are virtualization and virtual centralization as well as availability of heterogeneous and distributed resources based on collaboration among and sharing of existing infrastructures from different organizational domains which together build the computing Grid.

Since the mid 1990s the concept of Grid has evolved. Similar to other infrastructure innovations – for example the Internet – the Grid was first introduced and adopted in science for the support of research in various scientific disciplines that require high performance computing (HPC) together with huge amounts of data stored in dedicated databases. Examples of such sciences are Earth Science, Astroparticle Physics and Computational Chemistry. They are summarized under the term eScience. To support eScience many national and international initiatives have been started by governments in many countries in order to leverage existing investments in research infrastructure and to enable sharing and efficient use of available computational resources, data and specialized equipment. Examples of national initiatives are: Austrian Grid (http://www.austriangrid.at), D-Grid – the German Grid initiative, DutchGrid (http://www.dutchgrid.nl) and others.

One example of an international initiative is the Enabling Grid for E-SciencE (EGEE) project supported by the European Commission (http://www.eu-egee.org). The EGEE involves over 50 countries with the common aim of building on recent advances in Grid technology and developing a service Grid infrastructure which is available to scientists 24 hours-a-day (EGEE 2009). Another international initiative has been initiated by CERN. CERN is building a Large Hadron Collider (LHC) Computing Grid to manage and support the analysis of data generated by LHC experiments. The largest experiment is generating over one petabyte of data per year and around 2000 users and 150 institutions are involved in the analysis of the experiments' data. The analysis of such large quantities of data exceeds by far the available computing capacities of one single organization. All involved research institutions are joining their resources in the LHC Computing Grid.

The Grid Computing paradigm based on resource sharing was brought to broader public by the popular project (http://setiathome.berkeley.edu) SETI@HOME. The goal of the Search for Extraterrestrial Intelligence (SETI) project is the detection of intelligent life outside earth. The project uses radio telescopes to listen for narrow-bandwidth radio signals from space. As such signals are not known to occur naturally, it is expected that a detection of them would provide evidence of extraterrestrial technology. The analysis of radio telescope signals involves huge amounts of data and is very computing-intensive. No single research lab could provide the computing power needed for it. Given the tremendous number of household PCs, the involved scientists came up with the idea to invite owners of PCs to participate in the research by providing the computing power of their computers when they are idle. Users download a small program on their desktop. When the desktop is idle, the downloaded program would detect it and use the idle machine cycles. When the PC is connected back to the Internet, it would send the results back to the central site. The SETI initiative recently celebrated the 10th anniversary (it was launched

17th of May 1999) and has at present more than 3 million users that participate with their PCs.

Inspired by the success of Grid Computing in eScience and driven by current business and technological developments in companies there is increasing interest for Grid Computing in industry.

1.2 Business Drivers for Grid Computing in Companies

At present, companies have to survive and develop competitive advantage in a dynamic and turbulent environment of global competition and rapid business change. Companies are under constant pressure to simultaneously grow revenue and market share while reducing costs. To meet these requirements, companies have been changing and three major trends can be observed that have impact on company requirements upon Information Technology (IT) support:

- Striving towards high agility,
- Globalization of activities to be able to take advantage of opportunities provided by a global economy, and
- Increased mobility.

In dynamic business environments agility is considered the key success factor for companies. Only companies with high agility can be successful in today's rapidly changing business environments. In literature, there are various definitions for the term agility: from general ones as for example *"the ability of firms to sense environmental change and respond readily"* (Overby et al. 2006) to more specific ones as for example *"...an innovative response to an unpredictable change"* (Wadhwa and Rao 2003). A comprehensive and summarizing definition is given by van Oosterhout et al. (2007):

> "Business agility is the ability to sense highly uncertain external and internal changes, and respond to them reactively or proactively, based on innovation of the internal operational processes, involving the customers in exploration and exploitation activities, while leveraging the capabilities of partners in the business network."

Business agility is therefore the ability to swiftly and easily change businesses and business processes beyond the normal level of flexibility to effectively manage unpredictable external and internal changes.

One basic obstacle for achieving agility is the prevailing IT infrastructure of enterprises. Despite of efforts to increase flexibility of corporate IT, most prevailing corporate IT still involves hardwired processes and applications that cannot be changed quickly and easily. This results in long lead times before the IT infrastructure can follow and support new business process and product concepts. Thus, an agile company is only possible with an agile IT infrastructure that can quickly and efficiently be adjusted to new business ideas. Enterprises would like to have an IT infrastructure that can realign itself expeditiously to new business priorities. They require rapid and predictable turnaround times for provisioning computing power, storage, information, and application flows. Virtualization of resources (computers and data) and their flexible integration and combination to support changing business concepts has the potential to increase IT and business agility in companies.

Another development trend affecting the requirements upon the IT infrastructure in companies is the increasing globalization of companies. Companies are increasingly acting as global companies with activities spread over many locations worldwide. The globalization of companies resulted in globalisation of their IT. To support the activities of remote company parts, IT resources and data as well as data centres are also scattered worldwide. Despite of the global spread of activities companies strive to use the competitive advantage of the involved regions in a synergetic way and to create a "Global One Company" (see for example Stanoevska-Slabeva et al. 2008). Thus, there is growing need for IT support of global processes in an integrated and "follow-the-sun" principle[2] (for example global supply chains) by relying on and integrating globally scattered IT resources. Virtualization and virtual centralization of available resources in computing and data Grids could provide the necessary integration of resources by keeping at the same time their physical distribution.

The third trend in companies that has impact on requirements upon their IT infrastructure is increasing mobility of employees and resources. Due to globalization an increasing number of employees is mobile and requires mobile support. At the same time, with the maturity of ubiquitous computing and the Internet of Things, an increasing number of external devices is expected to be involved as sensors in the IT infrastructure of companies. Mobile computing resources and data as well as data sources as sensors need to be supported remotely in an efficient manner and at the same time need to be integrated into the existing infrastructure in a flexible way.

Figure 1.1 summarizes the impact of the three factors on company IT-infrastructure. In order to support agility flexible infrastructure is required that can fast be adopted to new processes.

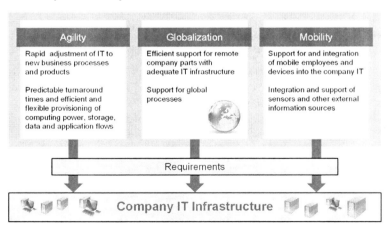

Fig. 1.1: Main factors impacting requirements upon company IT infrastructure

---

[2] As IT resources are in many cases used over night, also the term "follow-the-moon" is used.

Virtualization and abstraction of the physical location of resources, support for services and their flexible bundling as well as higher scalability and flexibility through inclusion of external resources based on Grid and emerging Cloud Computing have the potential to provide an IT infrastructure that addresses the demands of business while utilizing the IT resources most efficiently and cost-effectively.

1.3 Technological Drivers for Grid Computing in Companies

IT in companies has been constantly changing its shape in the last decades (see also fig. 1.2). This is driven by the changes in the way how companies conduct business described in section 1.2 and by technological developments and innovation. At the beginning, there were centralised data centres with mainframes. More than a decade ago, a shift from large centralized mainframe computers towards more distributed systems started to transform corporate IT. First, PCs were added to support each single user in addition to mainframes that increasingly became distributed. Recently, mobile end devices have been added to support and enable greater mobility of employees. Initially, computing power and storage of mobile devices were limited and mobile devices were mainly used for voice communication. Today, they have caught up and increasingly compete with PCs. A new trend is ubiquitous computing and the enhancement of the environment as well as products with sensors.

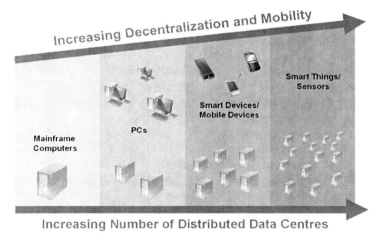

Fig. 1.2: The Evolution of IT in companies

Overall, there is a trend towards distribution and decentralization of IT resources that at the same time is confronted with the need for consolidated and efficient use of IT resources. This results in several problems:

- Ever increasing demand for storage and computing power at each data centre
- Many and scattered data centres with underutilization of their resources
- Increasing maintenance costs of data centres

Business changes as globalization and mobility resulted in an increasing number of distributed data centres. At present, prevailing practice is to optimize each data centre mostly independent of other data centres. This means that each data centre is designed to accommodate high peak demand for computation power and data. As a result, there is an ever increasing demand for storage and computing power. For example, the volume of digital content is constantly increasing. In 2007, the amount of information created exceeded available storage capacity for the first time ever (Gantz et al. 2008). Although around 70% of digital information is created by individuals, "enterprises are responsible for the security, privacy, reliability, and compliance of 85%" (Gantz et al. 2008). The total amount of information, including paper and digital content, in enterprises, governments, schools, and small businesses is estimated to grow 67% per year until 2012 (Gantz et al. 2009). This implies technological challenges as well as challenges with regard to information governance for businesses.

The increasing number of data centres resulted in overproportional increase in their maintenance costs, in particular with respect to power and cooling costs (Belady 2007). Energy efficiency of IT is a concern that becomes increasingly important. The continuously increasing amount of digital information requires increasing compute power, bigger storage capacities and more powerful network infrastructure to transmit information. This ultimately results in increasing carbon footprint of IT. By 2020, ICT are estimated to become among the biggest greenhouse gas emitters, accounting for around 3% of all emissions (Boccaletti et al. 2008). Growth in the number and size of data centres is estimated to be the fastest increasing contributor to greenhouse emissions (Boccaletti et al. 2008).

Grid computing has been among the first attempts to manage the high number of computing nodes in distributed data centres and to achieve better utilization of distributed and heterogeneous computing resources in companies. Advances in virtualization technology enable greater decoupling between physical computing resources and software applications and promise higher industry adoption of distributed computing concepts such as Grid and Cloud. The continuous increase of maintenance costs and demand for additional resources as well as for scalability and flexibility of resources is leading many companies to consider outsourcing their data centres to external providers. *"Cloud computing has emerged as one of the enabling technologies that allow such external hosting efficiently"* (AbdelSalam et al. 2009).

1.4 Towards Grid and Cloud Computing in Companies

The business and technological drivers of Grid and Cloud Computing described in sections 1.2 and 1.3 provide a strong business case for Grid and Cloud Computing in companies. To meet this demand, different types of commercial Grid and Cloud offerings have evolved in form of utility computing, Grid middleware, and applications offered in the Software-as-a-Service manner based on Grid infrastructure.

Clouds are the newest evolutionary step of Grid market offerings and provide new opportunities and challenges.

However, a broad adoption of Grid Computing cannot be observed yet, due to various reasons:

- Grid technology is complex and there is still no sufficient understanding of how to best apply it. Also, there is a lack of best practices for its commercial application.
- The requirements for Grid Computing in companies are different compared to eScience and already developed concepts and technologies cannot be directly transferred to industry. Companies have higher security and reliability requirements. In addition, companies have many processes and applications different from HPC that cannot easily be adjusted to a Grid infrastructure.

1.5 The Goal and Structure of This Book

Against the background of the developments described above, the present book aims at providing industry practitioners with a thorough understanding of how businesses can benefit from Grid Computing, and how such solutions are related to what is commonly referred to as Cloud Computing. The target audience of this book is industry practitioners interested in Grid and Cloud as well as potential buyers of Grid solutions. This may be IT decision makers in Small and Medium-sized Enterprises (SMEs) as well as in large enterprises, e.g. Chief Technology Officers (CTOs), IT department heads, or – in the case of rather smaller companies – actual management staff. In addition, this book well serves as a base for further research on Grid/Cloud and its commercial application. Thus, academic researchers and higher education are considered as secondary target audience. The contents of this book have purposely been selected and compiled with a business focus in mind. Technical details are only provided where necessary. This book is divided into four main parts:

- Part I: Introduction
- Part II: Grid and Cloud Basics – Definition, Classification, Business Models
- Part III: Grid Business Experiments
- Part IV: Guidelines for Practice

Part I sets the context and motivates this book. The main business and technical drivers for Grid and Cloud Computing are described together with the project BEinGRID (chapter 2) where most of the results presented in this book were created.

Part II starts with a definition of terms, a description of phenomena relevant for Grid and Cloud Computing and an explanation of the relationships among them (chapters 3 and 4). In chapters 5 and 6, Grid business models and Grid value chains are described respectively. An understanding of Grid value chains and business models is needed not only to understand the Grid industry but also in order to understand what a Grid solution is. A Grid solution typically involves different actors on the supplier side. Grid value networks describe the relationships between the different Grid actors. The final chapter of Part II (chapter 7) is dedicated to the most relevant legal issues that a typical customer should take into consideration when reviewing the terms for the provision of Grid/Cloud services from a technology provider.

Part III summarizes practical results from the BEinGRID project and provides concrete examples of how Grid can be applied commercially. The first chapter deals with technical features important for the commercial uptake and practical implementation of Grid and Cloud computing (chapter 8). Each of the remaining 4 chapters (chapters 9, 10, 11 and 12) covers one Business Experiment (BE) of the BEinGRID project and follows the same general structure. After a general description of the respective BE, the BE will be described from the perspective of the technology provider and from the perspective of the user, particularly considering the added value. The description from the perspective of the technology provider will comprise a detailed description of the Grid solution and its technical features as well as how it can be integrated into existing company infrastructures. The description from the perspective of the user will point out the benefits and findings from the user perspective. Finally, the findings of the respective BE will be summarized and lessons learnt will be provided. Chapter 13 concludes the third part of this book by summarizing the organizational and governance challenges associated with the adoption of Grid and Cloud Computing in organizations.

In Part IV, key findings are summarized and concrete steps for the practitioner on how to act are derived.

1.6 Acknowledgments

A book like this cannot be done without the collaboration of many people and institutions. First of all, the editors would like to thank all people and institutions involved in the BEinGRID project – the size of this book would not be enough if everyone's contribution was to be individually commended.

The actual production of the individual chapters took considerable effort and involved several iterations between editors and authors. The editors wish to take this opportunity to thank all contributing authors. We also thank Alan Readhead, Mark Sawyer and Adrian Mouat for proofreading, and Isabella Hoffend for proofreading and administrative support.

The European Commission and organizations in the BEinGRID consortium must also be acknowledged for realizing the opportunity, accepting the risk and financing an initiative of this scale. In particular, we would like to thank the BEinGRID Project Officers Annalisa Bogliolo and Maria Tsakali, and the project reviewers for their continuous support in implementing this large project as well as the head of units Jesús Villasante and Wolfgang Boch for sharing the vision that research in Service Oriented Infrastructures and their embodiment as Grid or Cloud Computing is important for Europe.

The authors involved in Part II of this book would also like to acknowledge the work of colleagues involved in Activity 2 of the BEinGRID project who contributed to the results presented in Part II: Olivier van de Werve, Damien Hubaux, Roland Dohmen, Alan Readhead, Perian Moors, Belen Serrabou Clemente-Alloza, and Csilla Zsigri.

Some of the Business Experiments described in Part III of this book rely on results from previous projects. The author of chapter 9 would like to acknowledge the use of results produced by the Enabling Grids for E-sciencE project, a project also co-funded by the European Commission (under contract number INFSO-RI-031688) and the support of Xunta de Galicia (Project R&D Grant PGIDT05SIN00101CT). He furthermore is indepted to Dr. S. Naqvi for providing his Monte Carlo C/S dose calculation code and to the medical physics group of University of Sevilla for the helpful discussions on Monte Carlo treatment verification.

The author of chapter 8 would like to thank the technical theme leaders of the BEinGRID project, who produced the results described in this paper under the author's direction. The technical theme leaders are: Angelo Gaeta (VO Management and B2B collaborations), Ivan Djordjevic and David Brossard (Security, Identity and Access Management), Christian Simmendinger (License Management), Igor Rosenberg (SLA management), Craig Thomson (Data Management), Stathis Karanastasis (Portals), Ana Maria Juan Ferrer (Common Capability coordination), Srijith Krishnan Nair, René Heek, Robert Piotter and Horst Schwichtenberg (integration scenarios).

2 The BEinGRID Project

Theo Dimitrakos

2.1 Introduction

Most of the results presented in this book were created within the BEinGRID project. BEinGRID, Business Experiments in GRID, is the European Commission's largest integrated project funded by the Information Society Technologies (IST) research, part of the European Union's sixth research Framework Programme (FP6). This consortium of 96 partners is drawn from across the EU and represents the leading European organizations in Grid Computing and Service Oriented Infrastructures (SOI) and a broad spectrum of companies covering most vertical markets keen on assessing the benefits to their productivity, competitiveness and profitability from using Grid and Cloud Computing solutions.

The mission of BEinGRID is to generate knowledge, technological improvements, business demonstrators and reference case-studies to help companies in Europe and world-wide to establish effective routes to foster the adoption of SOI technologies such as Grid and Cloud Computing and to stimulate research that helps realizing innovative business models using these technologies. In terms of technology innovation BEinGRID has defined and steered the technical direction of Business Experiments (BEs) in all vertical market sectors by offering them best-practice guidance in each of the stages (requirements, design, prototyping, demonstration), thought-leadership in tackling innovative problems and technical advice for improving the BE solution.

Teams of technology and business experts achieved this mission by eliciting common technical requirements that solve common business problems across vertical markets, by defining innovative generic solutions, called *common capabilities*, that meet these requirements, by producing design patterns that explain how these solutions can be implemented over commonly used commercial and experimental platforms and by producing best-practice guidelines demonstrating how these solutions can be applied in exemplar business scenarios.

2.2 The BEinGRID Matrix

To meet the project's objectives described above, BEinGRID has undertaken a series of targeted Business Experiments (BEs) designed to implement and deploy Grid solutions across a broad spectrum of European business sectors including the media, financial, logistics, manufacturing, retail, and textile sectors. The consortium conducted 25 Business Experiments that have been summarized at the BEinGRID project Web site (http://www.beingrid.eu/) and described in the BEinGRID Booklet (BEinGRID Booklet 2009). Each one of these 25 BEs is a showcase of a real-life

K. Stanoevska-Slabeva et al. (eds.), *Grid and Cloud Computing: A Business Perspective on Technology and Applications*, DOI 10.1007/978-3-642-05193-7_2,
© Springer-Verlag Berlin Heidelberg 2010

pilot application focusing on a specific business opportunity and addressing current customer needs and requirements. The involvement of all actors in a representative value chain including consumers and service providers has been considered crucial for producing successful case studies that build on the experiences of early adopters. Consequently participation of representative consumers and providers able to take a solution to the market has been ensured in each of the BEs. The BEinGRID Business Experiments have been classified according to their main vertical market, the business model they exploit, and the technological innovations they validate. These classifications are discussed in the next sections.

2.2.1 Vertical Market Sectors

Each BE addresses concrete business issues in a particular vertical market. Each of the main actors of a grid value network was represented. From this perspective, the 25 BEs of BEinGRID cover the following sectors:

- *Advanced Manufacturing*. This class comprises BEs that apply Grid technology to the design of products or components that are later manufactured, or to optimize some part of the production processes.
- *Telecommunications*. This sector covers the BEs that use SOI in order to improve existing or offer new innovative services that can improve the operational efficiency and the quality of services offered by network operators. These include services for sharing data and services among network operators and detecting fraud.
- *Financial*. This sector includes the solutions used by financial organizations to optimize existing business activities or to produce new and innovative services to their customers.
- *Retail*. This sector includes BEs that improve the business activities related to management of goods (acquisition, delivery, transformation ...).
- *Media & Entertainment*. This sector consists of BEs related to the management and processing of media content (capture, rendering, post-production, delivering) and, more broadly, the provision of on-line entertainment services including scalable and high-performing collaborative gaming.
- *Tourism*. This sector covers the BE that is used by the tourism industry in order to optimize existing business activities or to produce new and innovative services to their customers.
- *Health*. This sector is represented by the BEs that focus on processing of medical data, compute intensive algorithms for medical science and provision of services that optimize the quality and the cost of medical treatment covering all actors contributing to the treatment.
- *Environmental Sciences* covers the BEs that focus on processing geophysical data and applying compute intensive algorithms to analysis which will help avoid damage to the environment and offer protection against natural disasters.

Different BEs use different middleware in the same sector in order to solve specific real-world challenges. The anticipated commercial and social impact and innovation dividend have been the main criteria in selecting the BE, in addition to the necessary use of Service Oriented Infrastructure technologies including Grid and Cloud Computing.

2.2.2 Business Models

The business models explored in these pilot projects have been categorized based on criteria that take into account their value propositions, their technological and economic incentives and emerging trends in the market of Grid and Cloud Computing.

The first category focuses on achieving optimized and flexible processes and lower costs by improving resource utilization. At the core of this category are innovations facilitating:

- better utilization of compute power and data storage,
- on-demand provision of additional compute power and storage in order to respond to peaks in consumption, and
- aggregation of heterogeneous data sources in virtual data-stores.

The second category focuses on collaboration and resource sharing. At the core of this category are innovations improving:

- the agility of businesses and their ability to respond to business opportunity by enabling the swift establishment of multi-enterprise collaborations,
- the execution of collaborative processes spanning across-enterprise boundaries,
- provision of, and access to, shared network-hosted ("cloud") services that facilitate collaboration, and
- seamless access to heterogeneous geographically distributed data sources.

The third family of categories is focused on new service paradigms centered on "pay-as-you-go" (PAYG) and new paradigms of ICT services (*-aaS) including Software as a Service (SaaS), Platform as a Service (PaaS) and Infrastructure as a Service (IaaS).

2.2.3 Research and Technological Innovation Themes

The technological advancements and innovations inspired or validated by the BEs have been categorized in *thematic areas*. These are areas where we witnessed either significant challenges that inhibit widespread commercialization of Grid Computing or where the anticipated impact of the innovation (i.e. the "innovation dividend") is particularly high.

- *Virtual Organization Management* capabilities help businesses establish secure, accountable and efficient collaborations sharing services, resources and information.
- *Trust & Security* capabilities address areas where a perceived or actual lack of security appears to inhabit commercial adoption of Grid Computing and SOI. These include solutions for brokering identities and entitlements across

enterprises, managing access to shared resources, analyzing and reacting to security events in a distributed infrastructure, securing multi-tenancy hosting, and securing the management of in-cloud services and platforms. These innovations underpin capabilities offered in Virtual Organization Management and other categories.

- *License Management* capabilities are essential for enabling the adoption of PAYG and other emerging business models, and had so far been lacking in the majority of Grid and Cloud computing solutions.
- Innovations to improve the management of *Service Level Agreements* cover the whole range from improvements to open standard schemes for specifying agreements, to ensuring fine-grained monitoring of usage, performance and resource utilization.
- *Data Management* capabilities enable better storage, access, translation and integration and sharing of heterogeneous data. Innovations include capabilities for aggregating heterogeneous data sources in virtual data-stores and ensuring seamless access to heterogeneous geographically distributed data sources.
- Innovations in *Grid Portals* enable scalable solutions based on emerging Web2.0 technologies that provide an intuitive and generic instrumentation layer for managing user communities, complex processes and data in SOI as Grids and Clouds.

The technological innovation results take the form of core, generic functionality or processes that can be implemented over commercial and experimental service oriented middleware and infrastructures in order to add or help realize business value that is known to be important for commercial success. These technological innovation results have been delivered by means of the following outputs of the program:

- *Common technical requirements* that identify specific challenges where technical innovation is required. These were elicited by analyzing BEs across vertical market sectors; their interdependences have been analyzed within and across thematic areas; and they have been prioritized in terms of innovation potential and anticipated business impact based on feedback from BEs in several market sectors and criticality[1] in terms of their interdependences.
- *Common capabilities* that capture the generic functionality that would need to be in place in order to address these requirements. These are necessary for enhancing current service offerings and delivery platforms in order to meet the business challenges described at the introduction of this chapter.
- *Design patterns* that describe one or more possible solutions that describe how systems may be architected in order to realize each common capability.
- *Reference implementations* that realize selected common capabilities over commercial middleware. These were subject to quality assurance processes including: *release testing* (focusing on robustness, installation and usability of

---

[1] In simple terms, criticality of a technical requirement is a function of the number and relative priority of other requirements that depend upon it.

artifacts); *conformance testing* to assure that the artifacts are adequately implementing the functionality of the capability; *documentation* and *training material* explaining how to deploy, integrate and improve the artifacts.

- *Integration scenarios* illustrating how a critical mass of interdependent common capabilities can be implemented together to maximize added value.
- *Validation scenarios* illustrating the benefits of implementing selected common capabilities to enhance business solutions in real-life case-studies.
- *Best-practice guidelines* explaining how these common capabilities can be taken advantage of in indicative business contexts.

2.3 Knowledge Repository for SOI, GRID and Cloud Computing

Research and innovation in the BEinGRID project is complemented with the development of the public knowledge and toolset repository IT-Tude.com (http://www.it-tude.com or www.it-tude.eu), previously known as Gridipedia (http://www.gridipedia.eu/), that aims to concentrate a comprehensive selection of service designs, best practices, case studies, technology implementations, and other resources that may enable the adoption of SOI technologies such as Grid and Cloud Computing. This knowledge repository also includes descriptions of the capabilities produced by the BEinGRID project, as well as information and software for their reference implementations and other auxiliary content such as technical reports, white papers, presentations, demonstration videos and training material.

Part II: Grid and Cloud Basics – Definition, Classification, Business Models

Introduction

The second part of this book provides a general view of Grids and Clouds and a thorough understanding of what Grid and Cloud Computing are. Topics that are covered in detail are definitions and classifications of Grid and Cloud Computing, underlying architectures and components, business models and value networks of Grid solutions and legal aspects that are important when moving towards Grids and Clouds. Part II is a rich body of general knowledge on the commercial application of Grid and Cloud Computing that will be complemented with practical concepts, experiences and findings from the BEinGRID project in Part III of this book.

Part II starts with a definition of terms related to Grid Computing and its commercial application, a classification of different types of Grids, a description of Grid architectures and an outline of the evolution from Grid to Cloud Computing in chapter 3. In chapter 4, an understanding of Cloud Computing is derived based on the review of many definitions provided by industry analysts, academics, and practitioners. Further, chapter 4 provides a description of different classifications of Cloud Computing and a comparison of Grid and Cloud Computing. Chapter 5 is dedicated to Grid business models and presents an overview of business models adopted by Grid application and services providers in the market based on an analysis of Grid business cases. Chapter 6 explains what a Grid solution is by drawing upon the concept of value networks. First, different types of Grid market players and flows between them are generally described. Then, concrete value networks for different ways how a Grid solution can be offered are examined. The final chapter of Part II (chapter 7) is dedicated to the most relevant legal issues that a typical customer should take into consideration when reviewing the terms for the provision of Grid/Cloud services from a technology provider.

3 Grid Basics

Katarina Stanoevska-Slabeva, Thomas Wozniak

3.1 Introduction

The term Grid or Grid Computing implies different technologies, markets and solutions to different people. The meanings associated with the terms range from cluster computing, High Performance Computing (HPC), utility computing, peer-to-peer computing to specific new types of infrastructure. In order to clarify the position, the aim of this chapter is to define and explain Grid Computing. Thereby, the following aspects will be considered:

- Definition of Grid Computing
- Explanation of Grid Computing Architectures
- Overview of basic functionalities and components of Grid Computing
- Overview of advantages and risks associated with Grid Computing
- Classification of Grids
- Overview of trends related to Grid Computing such as Service-oriented Computing (SOC), Software-as-a-Service (SaaS), and Cloud Computing.

3.2 What is Grid Computing?

Grid Computing is a complex phenomenon that has its roots in eScience and has evolved from earlier developments in parallel, distributed and HPC (see for example Weishäupl et al. 2005 and Harms et al. 2006). It emerged in the early 1990s, when high performance computers were connected by fast data communication with the aim to support calculation- and data-intensive scientific applications. At that time, this was denoted hyper computing or meta computing and the emphasis was on coordinated usage of available computing resources for high performance applications (Reinefeld and Schintke 2004).

The first most cited definition of Grid Computing reflected these origins and was suggested by Foster and Kesselman (1998):

> "A computational grid is a hardware and software infrastructure that provides dependable, consistent, pervasive, and inexpensive access to high-end computational capabilities."

Based on the hyper computing examples and the example of cluster computing, it became evident that resource sharing might be relevant for other application areas as well. Consequently, it became clear that resource sharing should be provided in a generic manner and not targeted only for specific high performance applications (Reinefeld and Schintke 2004). Given this, development of support for generic IT resource sharing started to be considered as the real "Grid problem". According to Foster et al. (2001):

K. Stanoevska-Slabeva et al. (eds.), *Grid and Cloud Computing: A Business Perspective on Technology and Applications*, DOI 10.1007/978-3-642-05193-7_3,
© Springer-Verlag Berlin Heidelberg 2010

"The real and specific problem that underlies the Grid concept is *coordinated resource sharing and problem solving in dynamic, multi-institutional virtual organizations*. The sharing that we are concerned with is not primarily file exchange but rather direct access to computers, software, data, and other resources, as is required by a range of collaborative problem-solving and resource brokering strategies emerging in industry, science, and engineering." (Foster et al. 2001)

In this descriptive definition a virtual organization (VO) is a dynamic group of individuals, groups or organizations who define the conditions and rules for sharing resources (Joseph et al. 2004). According to Foster (2002), a Grid system is therefore a system that:

- Coordinates resources that are not subject to centralized control
- Uses standard, open, general-purpose protocols and interfaces
- Delivers nontrivial qualities of service.

The main resources that can be shared in a Grid are (Lilienthal 2009):

- Computing/processing power
- Data storage/networked file systems
- Communications and bandwidth
- Application software
- Scientific instruments.

In addition, as the prevalence of embedded computing continues, the notion of a Grid resource can be extended toward simpler devices, such as home appliances, portable digital assistants, cell phones as well as active and passive Radio Frequency Identification (RFID) devices (Castro-Leon and Munter 2005).

The new and more precise definition was taken up by the scientific community. Grid Computing is now considered by the research community to be a middleware layer enabling a secure, reliable, and efficient sharing of computing and data resources among independent organizational entities (Weishäupl et al. 2005).

After being successfully applied in eScience, Grid Computing attracted attention in industry as well. The new definition and focus of Grid Computing was adopted by industry with different interpretation. IBM for example describes Grid Computing indirectly by referring to its features:

"Grid computing allows you to unite pools of servers, storage systems, and networks into a single large system so you can deliver the power of multiple-systems resources to a single user point for a specific purpose. To a user, data file, or an application, the system appears to be a single enormous virtual computing system." (Kourpas 2006)

Some analysts, as for example Quocirca (2003), defined Grid as a specific architecture:

"Grid computing is an architectural approach to creating a flexible technology infrastructure, enabling the pooling of network, hardware and software resources to meet the requirements of business processes. The components of a Grid architecture (e.g. computing units, storage, databases, functional applications and services) work together to maximise component utilisation while minimising the need for continual upgrading of individual component capacity."

In a comprehensive Grid market study, Insight Research defined Grid Computing as "a form of distributed system wherein computing resources are shared across networks" (Insight Research 2006). Other authors have interpreted the new focus of Grid in the context of specific application. For example, Resch (2006) defined Grid as "an infrastructure built from hardware and software to solve scientific and industrial simulation problems."

The Grid Expert Group coined the term Business Grids and defined and described Grid as a specific infrastructure:

> "We envision Business Grids as the adaptive service-oriented utility infrastructure for business applications. They will become the general ICT backbone in future economies, thus achieving profound economic impact." (NESSI-Grid 2006)

The first successes with national Grids in the area of eScience as well as with open initiatives such as for example Seti@Home gave rise to further scenarios towards utility computing, or provision of computing power and applications as a service (see also Rappa 2004). It became evident that Grid Computing uses Internet as a transport and communication medium and is a further generalisation of the Web as it extends the class of accessible resources with applications, data, computing resources, instruments, sensors and similar (Geiger 2006). Inspired by the electrical power grid's pervasiveness, ease of use, and reliability, computer scientists in the mid-1990s began exploring the design and development of an analogous infrastructure called the computational power Grid enabling access to computing power and application at any time or place as needed without the need to own the infrastructure necessary to produce the service (Buyya et al. 2005).

The different definitions propagated by industry, academics and analysts resulted in a big terminological confusion in the market over the meaning of the terms Grid and Grid Computing. For the purpose of this book, we will use the following definitions:

- **Grid middleware** is specific software, which provides the necessary functionality required to enable sharing of heterogeneous resources and establishing of virtual organizations. From a market perspective, Grid middleware is a specific software product that is offered on the market under certain licensing conditions and which is installed and integrated into the existing infrastructure of the involved company or companies. Grid middleware provides a special virtualization and sharing layer that is placed among the heterogeneous infrastructure and the specific user applications using it.
- **Grid Computing** is basically the deployed Grid middleware or the computing enabled by Grid middleware based on flexible, secure, coordinated resource sharing among a dynamic collection of individuals, institutions, and resources. Grid Computing means on the one hand that heterogeneous pools of servers, storage systems and networks are pooled together in a virtualized system that is exposed to the user as a single computing entity. On the other hand, it means programming that considers Grid infrastructure and applications that are adjusted to it.

- **Grid infrastructure** refers to the combination of hardware and Grid middleware that transforms single pieces of hardware and data resources into an integrated virtualized infrastructure which is exposed to the user as a single computer despite of heterogeneity of the underlying infrastructure.
- **Utility computing** is the provision of Grid Computing and applications as a service either as an open Grid utility or as a hosting solution for one organization or VO. Utility computing is based on pay-per-use business models.

Grid Computing has evolved into an important discipline within the computer industry by differentiating itself from distributed computing through an increased focus on the "Grid problem", i.e., resource sharing, coordination, manageability, and high performance (Foster et al. 2001). Thus, the following resources cannot be considered as Grids, unless they are based on sharing: clusters, network-attached storage devices, scientific instruments, networks. However, they can be important components of a Grid.

Grid Computing needs to be distinguished also from HPC. It focuses on resource sharing and can result in HPC, whereas HPC does not necessarily involve sharing of resources.

To summarize, Grid Computing is a new computing paradigm based on IT resource sharing and on provisioning of IT resources and computing in a way similar to how electricity is consumed today. It is enabled by specific Grid middleware provided on the market either as packaged or open source software, or in form of utility computing.

3.3 Grid Architectures and Functionality

A Grid architecture provides an overview of the Grid components, defines the purpose and functions of its components, and indicates how the components interact with one another (Joseph et al. 2004). The main focus of a Grid architecture is on the interoperability and protocols among providers and users of resources in order to establish the sharing relationships. According to Foster and Kesselman (2004), the required protocols are organized in layers as presented in figure 3.1:

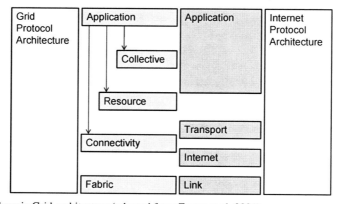

Fig. 3.1: Generic Grid architecture (adapted from Foster et al. 2001)

The main functionality of each layer can be summarized as follows (Foster and Kesselman 2004):

- The **Fabric layer** comprises the physical resources which are shared within the Grid. According to Foster and Kesselman (2004), this includes computational resources, storage systems, network resources, catalogues, software modules, sensors and other system resources.
- The **Connectivity layer** "*contains the core communication and authentication protocols required for a Grid-specific network transaction*" (Foster and Kesselman 2004). Communication protocols enable the exchange of data between the resources of the fabric layer. The most important functionalities at the connectivity layer include: transport, routing and naming as well as support for a secure communication. According to Foster and Kesselman (2004), the most important requirements for security support involve: support for single sign on, support for delegation so that a program can run and access resources to which the user has access, support for interoperability with local security solutions and rules.
- The **Resource layer** uses the communication and security protocols (defined by the connectivity layer) to control secure negotiation, initiation, monitoring, accounting, and payment for the sharing of functions of individual resources. It comprises mainly information and management protocols. Information protocols are used to obtain information about the structure and state of available resources. Management protocols are used to negotiate access to resources and serve as a "policy application point" by ensuring that the usage of the resources is consistent with the policy under which the resource is to be shared.
- The **Collective layer** is responsible for all global resource management and for interaction with collections of resources (Foster and Kesselman 2004). Collective layer protocols implement a wide variety of sharing behaviours. The most important functionalities of this layer are: directory services, coallocation, scheduling and brokering services, monitoring and diagnostics services and data replication services. The services of the collective layer are usually invoked by programming models and tools: Grid-enabled programming systems, workflow systems, software discovery services and collaboration services. This layer also addresses community authorization together with accounting and payment services.
- The **Application layer** involves the user applications that are deployed on the Grid. It is important to note that not any user application can be deployed on a Grid. Only a Grid-enabled or gridified application, i.e. an application that is designed or adjusted to run in parallel and use multiple processors of a Grid setting or that can be executed on different heterogeneous machines (Berstis 2002), can take advantage of a Grid infrastructure.

The five layers of Grid Computing are interrelated and depend on each other. Each subsequent layer uses the interfaces of the underlying layer. Together they create the Grid middleware and provide a comprehensive set of functionalities necessary for enabling secure, reliable and efficient sharing of resources (computers, data) among independent entities. This functionality includes low-level services such as security,

information, directory, resource management (resource trading, resource allocation, quality of service) and high-level services/tools for application development,
resource management and scheduling (Buyya et al. 2005). In addition, there is a
need to provide the functionality for brokerage of resources, accounting and billing
purposes. The main functionalities of a Grid middleware are (see also Meliksetian
et al. 2004):

- Virtualization and integration of heterogeneous autonomous resources (Reinefeld
  and Schintke 2004)
- Provision of information about resources and their availability (see for example
  Boden 2004)
- Flexible and dynamic resource allocation and management (see for example
  Boden 2004, Reinefeld and Schintke 2004)
- Brokerage of resources either based on company policies (Next Generation
  GRIDs Expert Group 2006) or open markets (Buyya et al. 2005)
- Security and trust (Geiger 2006, Boden 2004). Security includes authentication
  (assertion and confirmation of the identity of a user) and authorization (check of
  rights to access certain services or data) (Angelis et al. 2004) of users as well as
  accountability (see also Boden 2004).
- Management of licences (Geiger 2006)
- Billing and payment (Geiger 2006)
- Delivery of non-trivial Quality of Service (QoS) (Boden 2004)

Given the complex functionalities above, it is obvious that Grid is a complex system
and no single technology constitutes a Grid. For example, according to Smith et al.
(2006), components of the typical service-oriented Grid middleware are: Globus
Toolkit 4.0 (GT4), Tomcat 5.5 and Axis. Each of the three is a large scale software
system encompassing thousands of Java classes. In many cases the necessary functionality is assembled by several software and middleware providers. This means
that building and providing a Grid requires a functioning ecosystem of complementary services from software providers and integrators (see also chapter 6). It is not
possible to purchase a Grid off the shelf (Castro-Leon and Munter 2005).

3.4 Potential Advantages and Risks of Grid Computing

Grid Computing provides advantages and opportunities for companies on two levels:
on the IT management level, it enables a more efficient utilization of IT resources;
on the business level, it increases efficiency, agility and flexibility.

The major potential advantages of Grid Computing for an improved management of IT in companies can be summarized as follows:

- Grids harness heterogeneous systems together into a single large computer,
  and hence, can apply greater computational power to a task (Bourbonnais et
  al. 2004) and enable greater utilization of available infrastructure (McKinsey
  2004). In particular, with Grid Computing existing underutilized resources can
  be exploited better (Berstis 2002).

- Grid Computing enables cost savings in the IT departments of companies due to reduced total cost of ownership (TCO) (Insight Research 2006, Boden 2004). Instead of investing in new resources, greater demand can be met by higher utilization of existing resources or by taking advantage of utility computing.
- Grid Computing enables greater scalability of infrastructure by removing limitation inherent in the artificial IT boundaries existing between separate groups or departments (McKinsey 2004).
- Grid Computing results in improved efficiency of computing, data and storage resources (Insight Research 2006) due to parallel CPU capacity, load balancing and access to additional resources (Berstis 2002). As computing and resources can be balanced on demand, Grid Computing results also in increased robustness (McKinsey 2004) and reliability (Berstis 2002) – failing resources can be replaced easier and faster with other resources available in the Grid.
- Grid Computing furthermore enables a more efficient management of distributed IT resources of companies. With the help of virtualization, physically distributed and heterogeneous resources can be better and uniformly managed. This makes possible to centrally set priorities and assign distributed resources to tasks.
- In combination with Utility Computing, Grid Computing enables the transformation of capital expenditure for IT infrastructure into operational expenditure and provides the opportunity for increased scalability and flexibility. However, the usage of Utility Computing results in higher security and privacy risks.

Overall, Grid Computing has the potential to improve price for performance of IT in companies (McKinsey 2004). The increased flexibility and scalability of IT resources and the ability to faster adjust business processes to new business needs results in advantages on the business level. Potential quantifiable advantages on the business level are summarized below:

- Improved performance and time-to-market (Boden 2004, McKinsey 2004)
- Lower costs and increased revenues due to improved processes (Boden 2004)

Further benefits on the business level that cannot be easily quantified can be summarized as follows:

- Improved collaboration abilities (Boden 2004)
- Improved sharing (Boden 2004)
- Improved possibility to create a VO with external business partners (Insight Research 2006).

The potential benefits of Grid Computing described above have to be compared with related risks and challenges. The major challenges of Grid Computing applied within company boundaries can be summarized as follows:

- Grid Computing is a new computing paradigm that requires considerable change in processes but also in the mindset of involved people. Careful and well-organized change management should prevent phenomena as "Sever hugging" – the unwillingness of some departments to share their resources (Goyal and Lawande 2005).

- The transformation of the existing scattered IT infrastructure into a Grid alone is not sufficient. In most cases, considerable investments need to be made for adjusting existing applications, i.e. Grid-enabling existing applications so that they can run on a Grid infrastructure.
- Lack of standards for Grid Computing makes investments decisions for Grid technology difficult and risky.
- Grid Computing is a complex technology affecting the complete IT infrastructure of a company. Thus, the introduction of Grid Computing in a company is typically a long-term project and requires time until first results are visible. The introduction of Grid Computing might require standardization of physical resources. Even though Grids should inherently be able to deal with heterogeneity of available resources, higher heterogeneity of resources may require higher investments in terms of time and money and thus increase the risk of failure.

The opportunities resulting from Grids and the risks and challenges associated with it need to be carefully compared and assessed in each particular case.

It is important to consider that Grid Computing is not only changing the IT infrastructure in a company, but has the potential to provide significant business value. As mentioned in chapter 1, increased agility, i.e. an organisation's increased ability to respond and adjust quickly and efficiently to external market stimuli, is considered a key success factor for companies today. Existing IT infrastructure is considered to be a major obstacle to company agility. Prevailing IT infrastructure reflects the inflexible built-to-order structure: thousands of application silos, each with its own custom-configured hardware, and diverse and often incompatible assets that greatly limit a company's flexibility and thus reduce time to market (Kaplan et al. 2004). According to NESSI-Grid (2006) and Boden (2004), what is therefore needed is an architecture that, in a similar way as the electricity grid, decouples the means of supporting the day-to-day operations of users from the underlying functional infrastructure that underpins them. This would also allow the business to reconfigure its operational strategy without necessarily amending its underlying IT systems. With the functionality described above, Grid Computing has the potential to provide the decoupling layer in companies.

In conclusion, the biggest benefit of Grids is the increased potential for companies to achieve new levels of innovation capabilities that can differentiate their business from competitors. Grid Computing enables implementing of new business processes and applications that companies would not be able to implement by using conventional information technology. Grid provides a virtual, resilient, responsive, flexible and cost effective infrastructure that fosters innovation and collaboration.

3.5 Classification of Grids

Grid Computing can be classified according to different criteria:

- Resources focused on
- Scope of resource sharing involved

3.5.1 Classification of Grids According to the Resource Focus

Even though the ultimate goal of Grid Computing is to provide sharing of any kind of resources, historically Grid middleware emerged with focus on specific kinds of resources. According to the resources focused on, the following types of Grid middleware can be distinguished (Baker et al. 2002, Quocirca 2003):

- Compute Grids, focus on sharing of computing resources, i.e. CPU.
- Data Grids, focus on controlled storage, management and sharing of large-scale heterogeneous and distributed data
- Application Grids, "*are concerned with application management and providing access to remote software and libraries transparently*" (Baker et al. 2002)
- Service Grids, result from the convergence of Grid and Service-oriented Computing and support the efficient sharing of services.

These four different types of Grid Computing are converging into an overall generic Grid middleware with combined functionality.

3.5.2 Classification of Grids According to Scope of Resource Sharing

Depending on the scope of resource sharing involved, the following Grid Computing approaches in companies can be distinguished:

- Cluster Grids
- Enterprise Grids
- Utility Grid Services
- Partner/Community Grids

These four different types of Company or Business Grids are explained in more detail below.

3.5.2.1 Cluster Grids

Cluster Grids, or clusters, are a collection of co-located computers connected by a high-speed local area network and designed to be used as an integrated computing or data processing resource (see fig. 3.2).

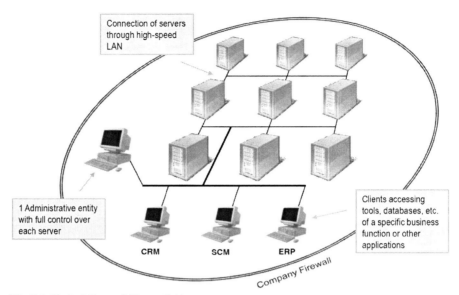

Fig. 3.2: Typical Form of Cluster Grids

A cluster is a homogeneous entity. Its components differ primarily in configuration, not basic architecture. Cluster Grids are local resources that operate inside the firewall and are controlled by a single administrative entity that has complete control over each component (Foster and Kesselman 1998). Thus, clusters do actually not involve sharing of resources and cannot be considered as Grids in the narrow sense. However, they are usually starting points for building Grids and a first step towards Grid Computing. Cluster Grids improve compute and storage capacity within a company (see also Keating 2004).

Example
Life science companies typically have high demand for HPC, e.g. for the compute-intensive gene analysis. These needs can be met by deploying a cluster. One example for the application of clusters in life sciences is the biotechnology company diaDexus (http://www.diadexus.com) that is focused on bringing genomic biomarkers to market as diagnostics. diaDexus replaced their large proprietary Symmetric MultiProcessing (SMP) machines with a Linux cluster (Keating 2004, Entrepreneur 2003). The gen analysis programs were adopted to a cluster environment and then implemented on the cluster. Compared to the previous system, the new cluster solution helped diaDexus to "speed the rate of gene analysis for the development of future diagnostic products from weeks to hours, or by more than 20x" (Entrepreneur 2003).

3.5.2.2 Enterprise Grid

The term Enterprise Grid is used to refer to application of Grid Computing for sharing resources within the bounds of a single company (Goyal and Lawande 2005). All components of an Enterprise Grid operate inside the firewall of a company, but may be heterogeneous and physically distributed across multiple company locations or sites and may belong to different administrative domains (see fig. 3.3).

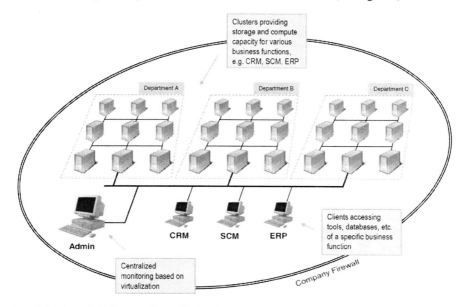

Fig. 3.3: Example Enterprise Grid infrastructure

With specific Enterprise Grid middleware, the available IT resources are virtualized and can be managed in a unified and central way. They can also be allocated to processes according to demand.

According to NESSI-Grid (2006), commercially available solutions for Enterprise Grids feature policy-based scheduling of workload management on heterogeneous infrastructures made out of desktops, servers and clusters. These systems contain basic resource control and mechanisms for fault tolerance as well as analysis tools for performance and debugging. Due to the lack of standardization in this space, these solutions typically support a variety of de facto standards and translate them into a solution specific format. Finally, these solutions often contain their own billing and user management solutions, partially integrating with common security infrastructures prevalent in enterprises.

Example

One example of Enterprise Grids is the Grid of the pharmaceutical company Novartis. Novartis started a five-year initiative for creating an Enterprise Grid in 2003 in order to support compute- and data-intensive research tasks, as for example protein structure determination, which are part of the drug development process. Back in 2003, Novartis had about 65'000 desktop PCs (Salamone 2003). It was assumed that about 90% of the computing cycles of each PC were unused. At the same time, the needs for computing power at Novartis research were constantly increasing. In general, computing power is increasingly essential to drug development. Pharmaceutical researchers rely on "in silico" experiments to explore drug actions, speed the development cycle, and reduce the need for expensive, robotic-controlled physical experiments (Intel 2003).

Novartis made Grid Computing a strategic part of its five-year plan for adding R&D computing resources. The goal was to link existing PCs into a Grid and share the unused computing cycles for compute-intensive research tasks.

The building of the Novartis PC Enterprise Grid started with a pilot involving 50 PCs in Basel, Switzerland. The 50 PCs were Grid-enabled and connected with a standard LAN in a star-like setting within a day of time. The PCs were Grid-enabled by installing a client agent on each machine that checks for idle compute cycles and donates them to the Grid while ensuring the Grid does not impact the work of the PC user (Intel 2003). The connection via simple LAN with a bandwidth of 100MBit/s was sufficient for tasks that are compute- but not data-intensive. The average size of computing tasks communicated to the Grid nodes was about 1 Mbyte (NZZ 2003). The Grid was controlled by monitoring software running on a dedicated server that managed the workflow, assigned tasks to the nodes and assembled the results. The results of the pilot exceeded expectations: within a week the Enterprise Grid of 50 PCs provided 3.18 years of additional aggregate processing time (Intel 2003). Based on this encouraging result from the pilot, the Grid was quickly extended to include 2700 PCs located in Basel, Vienna (Austria) and Cambridge (USA) (Intel 2003). The total computing power of the extended Novartis PC Grid reached up to 5 Teraflops. At that time, this equalled the computing power of the European Centre for Medium-Range Weather Forecasts in Great Britain, which was ranked no. 15 on the official list of super computers in the world (NZZ 2003).

The Novartis Enterprise Grid also illustrates how taking advantage of existing computing resources can deliver additional performance at a fraction of the cost for purchasing, deploying, and managing new systems. Instead of buying an HPC system, building another computer centre, and employing the people to support it, Novartis made an investment of roughly $400'000 in Grid software licenses and saved at least $2 million of investment that would have been necessary if new infrastructure was bought in order to gain the same computing power (Intel 2003).

The Novartis Enterprise Grid created business value by improving the innovation power and competitiveness of the company. On the one hand, with the Grid it was possible to speed up time-to-market in the competitive drug development process. On the other hand, with the Grid it was possible to extend research activities and to perform research tasks that have not been possible before. For example, research that would take computation of six years on a single computer can be run on the Grid in 12 hours. The Novartis Enterprise Grid was leveraged also by other business functions, for example for advanced data mining by business analysts (Intel 2003).

3.5.2.3 Utility Grid

A Grid that is owned and deployed by a third party service provider is called a
Utility Grid. The service being offered via a Utility Grid is utility computing, i.e.
compute capacity and/or storage in a pay-per-use manner. A Utility Grid operates
outside the firewall of the user (see fig. 3.4).

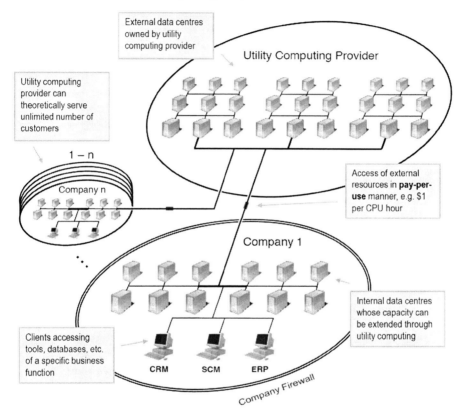

Fig. 3.4: Utility Grid architecture

The user does not own the Utility Grid and does not have control over its operation.
This means that the user company has to transmit data and computing requests to
the Utility Grid and collect results also from it. Thus, by using Utility Grids, the
security and privacy risks as well as concerns regarding reliability are increasing.
This has strong impact on the decision whether to use a Utility Grid or not, or which
data to expose to the Utility Grid and which data to keep behind the firewall. On
the positive side, Utility Computing does not require upfront investment in IT infrastructure and enables transformation of capital investment costs into variable costs.
Utility Computing furthermore provides scalability and flexibility of IT resources
on demand.

Example

The company Sun was among the first movers on the Utility Computing market. Sun launched the first version of the Sun Grid Compute Utility offering in March 2006 (Schwartz 2006). Users were able to purchase computing capability on a pay-per-use basis for $1/CPU-hr. Since then Sun has constantly evolved its Utility computing offerings. For example, besides utility computing Sun currently also offers support for developers, who are implementing applications that are supposed to run on the Utility Grid (see also section 4.4.2.1 in chapter 4).

The Sun Grid Compute Utility has been used by organizations from communications, technology and life sciences industries, e.g. chipmaker Advanced Micro Devices or genomics R&D group Applied Biosystems (Sun 2009e). Using the Sun Grid Compute Utility, Applied Biosystems (Life Sciences) was able to perform the compute-intensive data research to develop millions of new genomic assays in a matter of days rather than months. In addition, because the company only had to purchase the number of hours required, at a rate of $1 per CPU hour, it avoided an investment in infrastructure that would have cost the company hundreds of thousands of dollars.

Another example for a successful use of Utility Computing that involves not only computing services, but a combination of computing and application services is the cooperation of the film studio DreamWorks and HP. HP Labs provided a utility rendering service using a 1'000-processor data centre that was used by DreamWorks as a scalable, off-site rendering capacity for the production of high-quality film animation. The connection between HP Lab's data centre and DreamWorks' studio 20 miles away was established via a secure fibre optic link (HP Labs 2004). The data centre of HP Labs became a remote extension of DreamWorks' IT infrastructure. It provided additional compute capacity required for peak periods in the movie production process.

Organizations can benefit from utility computing offerings like the Sun Grid Compute Utility or HP Labs' utility rendering service in a twofold way. First, they can handle compute tasks that exceed the capacity of their own infrastructure, e.g. in peak times or for specific projects, or drastically reduce processing time of compute-intensive tasks, e.g. for complex simulations or analyses. Second, they do not need to make additional infrastructure investments. However, it has to be noted that these advantages come together with higher security, privacy and operational risks.

3.5.2.4 Partner/Community Grids

The idea of Partner or Community Grids originated from eScience. Many research endeavours, in particular in natural sciences (see for instance the example of CERN in chapter 1), require joint research efforts from scientists and sharing of infrastructures of research institutions from all over the world. The cooperation usually results in a Virtual Organization (VO) within which resource sharing takes place. Today, the need for cooperation is increasing in the business world too. Due to globalization, companies are more and more involved in global supply chains and the success of a company increasingly depends also on the efficient collaboration within them. Increased need for efficient collaboration is also necessary in other business processes, for example collaborative product design, collaborative online sites and similar. Ad hoc, fast and efficient collaboration is often impeded by heterogeneous and inflexible IT infrastructures that hinder efficient exchange of data and deployment of inter-company processes.

Partner or Community Grids are a specific type of Grids that can provide support for the establishment of a VO based on IT resource sharing among collaborating entities. Even though Partner and Community Grids have similar functionalities, they might support different types of VOs: Partner Grids are rather established in business context among companies or universities with common goals and defined resource sharing policies and relationships. Community Grids are rather based on donation of resources mostly from private persons. A well-known example of a Community Grid is SETI@HOME (see also the more detailed description in chapter 1).

Partner and Community Grids are enabled by specific Grid middleware, which has the following main functionalities (for a more detailed overview of functionalities necessary to support VOs see chapter 12):

- Virtualization and exposure of IT resources of each participating company to the VO.
- Support for enforcement of resource sharing policies.
- Coordination of the execution of common processes and workflows. This in particular involves allocation of shared resources to common tasks.
- Support for enforcement of individual and common security and privacy policies.
- Support for monitoring of the shared resources.
- Support for metering the usage of the common and shared resources and if required support for authentication, accounting and payment procedures.
- Optional support for access through browser over a portal interface.

In a Partner/Community Grid each participating partner provides a certain part of its infrastructure for sharing and either defines the rules under which the resources can be used by other partners or accepts the community rules for resource donation. Each participating partner provides access to its IT resources to its partners and gets access to partners' infrastructure. Common resources (for example results of common activities) are shared on one of the partners' sites or on external infrastructure.

The architecture of a Partner/Community Grid can be viewed as a collection of independent resources (for example Cluster Grids or other resources) interconnected through a global Grid middleware, and accessible, optionally, through a portal interface (see fig. 3.5).

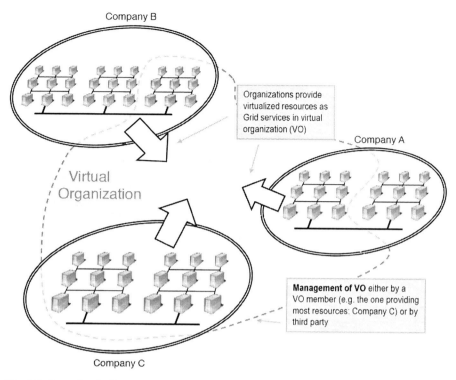

Fig. 3.5: Example of a Partner Grid

The underlying hardware and operating platforms of a Partner/Community Grid can be heterogeneous. While the Cluster Grid of one VO member may be Linux/ Intel-based, another VO member's Cluster Grid may be built from a combination of large symmetric memory Sun servers and storage/backup. This heterogeneity can be accommodated by a global Grid middleware. The infrastructure of a company shared in a VO is virtually melted together with the infrastructure shared by its partners. The own infrastructure is opened for common use and therefore security and trust are important considerations. A VO also requires a certain central control, for example for monitoring and allocation of tasks. The management of a VO is either done by a VO member, e.g. the one providing the most resources or having the business lead, or by a third party.

Examples
Currently, Partner or Community Grids are mainly used in scientific research. For example, the White Rose Grid (http://www.wrgrid.org.uk/), based in Yorkshire (UK), is a VO comprising the Universities of Leeds, York and Sheffield (WRG 2009). There are four significant compute resources (Cluster Grids) each named after a white rose. The goal of the White Rose Grid is to support collaborative efforts within eScience research at the involved universities. Two Cluster Grids are

sited at Leeds (Maxima and Snowdon) and one each at York (Pascali) and Sheffield (Titania). The connecting middleware provides support for metering the usage of the shared resources, for priority scheduling of jobs submitted to the Grid, for monitoring if agreed deadlines for job completion are respected, and other functionalities. Each participating university has allocated 25% of their node's compute resource for White Rose Grid users. The remaining 75% share can be allocated as required across the local academic groups and departments. Users across the three universities are of two types: local users who have access only to the local facility and White Rose Grid users who are allowed access to any node in the Grid. Another example for a VO in a business environment is described in chapter 11 of this book. Moreover, chapter 12 presents a generic platform for hosting and establishment of VOs.

A well-known example for a Community Grid is the already mentioned and described SETI@HOME Grid.

3.5.2.5 Towards Open Global Grids

The different types of Grids described above also illustrate the evolution of Business Grids (see fig. 3.6).

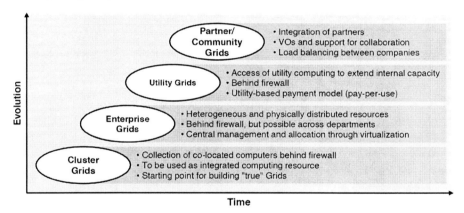

Fig. 3.6: The Evolution of Business Grids (adapted from Weisbecker et al. 2008)

The existence of one type of Grid is the prerequisite for a subsequent type. For example, Cluster Grids are usually components of an Enterprise Grid. A company can extend its IT infrastructure and obtain additional resources either from a third party (Utility Grid) or by participating and sharing resources in a VO. In general, the evolution of Business Grids is characterized by increasing openness and increasing scope of resource sharing across organizations. Requirements in terms of security, privacy, reliability, scalability and flexibility become more important as the openness of the Grid towards external resources increases. The evolutionary path of Business Grids also shows that different degrees of maturity of the company infrastructure and experiences are needed. Each higher level can only be achieved if the previous level has been experienced already. Thus, the introduction of Grid Computing in companies is a long and evolving process.

First success of Partner/Community Grids inspired further vision in the evolution of Business Grids: Open Global Grids. Open Global Grids are considered to be independent platforms, i.e. a global interconnection of multiple, heterogeneous Grids, composed of infrastructure, middleware and applications as well as based on a service-oriented infrastructure (see also Next Generation GRIDs Expert Group (2006). Such a Grid infrastructure can be used by any organization simply by connecting to it in a plug-and-play manner, i.e. no configuration is required and the Open Global Grid can be used right upon the connection is established.

3.6 New Trends in Grid Computing

Since broader awareness for Grid Computing in eScience and industry started in the mid 1990s, Grid Computing concepts have evolved, matured and have been influenced by other IT phenomena prevailing in the same time. In particular, the following three developments influenced the current concepts of Grid Computing:

- Service-oriented Computing
- Software-as-as-Service (SaaS)
- Cloud Computing

All three phenomena and their impact on Cloud Computing are described in more detail below.

3.6.1 Convergence of Grid and Service-oriented Computing

Service-oriented Computing (SOC) is a new computing paradigm that developed in parallel to Grid Computing. It was motivated and driven by developments and needs in eBusiness for easy and efficient integration of application within and across companies (Foster at al. 2002). According to Papazoglou et al. (2006), SOC is defined as follows:

> "Service-oriented Computing (SOC) is a new computing paradigm that utilizes services as the basic construct to support the development of rapid, low-cost and easy composition of distributed applications even in heterogeneous environments. The visionary promise of Service-Oriented Computing is a world of cooperating services where application components are assembled with a little effort into a network of services that can be loosely coupled to create flexible dynamic business processes and agile applications that may span organisations and computing platforms." (Papazoglou et al. 2006)

Basic building components of SOC are services, which are autonomous, platform-independent computational entities that can be "...*described, published, discovered, and loosely coupled in novel ways*" (Papazoglou et al. 2007). Up till now the most mature and also most interesting services from the perspective of Grid Computing are Web Services. Web Services use the Internet as the communication medium and are defined based on open Internet-based standards (Papazoglou et al. 2007). The relevant standards for Web Services are:

- Simple Object Access Protocol (SOAP) – the standard for transmitting data
- Web Service Description Language (WSDL) – the standard for unified description of services
- Universal Description Discovery and Integration (UDDI) – is a platform-independent, based registry for services.

All Web Services standards are Extensible Markup Language (XML)-based, which is machine readable and enables service to service communication. Based on the core standards listed above, further standards were developed that support the description of more complex constructs that are based on Web Services. One example of such a standard is the Business Process Execution Language for Web Services (BPL4WS) (Papazoglou et al. 2007).

The definitions above show that SOC has similarities with Grid Computing, i.e. what the Grid Computing vision is with regards to sharing and interoperability on the hardware level is the vision of SOC on the software and application level. Another commonality among the two concepts is the notion of services. As described in section 3.3, the Grid Computing architecture consists of protocols, i.e. services necessary to enable description and sharing of available physical resources. A convergence of the SOC and Grid Computing paradigms offers several opportunities:

- By applying the Web Service standards, Grid protocols and services can be encapsulated and described in a standardized manner (see fig. 3.7). At the same time existing technology for Web Service discovery, combination and execution might be applied.

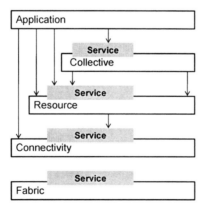

Fig. 3.7: Enhancement of the generic Grid architecture with Service-oriented Computing (adapted from Foster et al. 2008)

- Once the complementary paradigms, Grid Computing and SOC are based on the same standard, their combination becomes possible. This means that not only hardware and system resources become sharable, but also applications running on them.

In 2002, the Globus project and IBM initiated a development effort to align Grid Computing with Web Services and the SOC paradigm (Talia 2002). Out of this initiative, the Open Grid Service Architecture (OGSA) was developed. According to Foster et al. (2002), the OGSA is an extensible set of services which are provided by Grids. In more detail:

> "Building on concepts and technologies from both the Grid and Web Services communities, OGSA defines a uniform exposed service semantics (the *Grid Service*); defines standard mechanisms for creating, naming, and discovering transient Grid service instances; provides location transparency and multiple protocol bindings for service instances; and supports integration with underlying native platform facilities." (Foster et al. 2002)

The Open Grid Service Architecture is a layered architecture with clear separation of the functionalities of each layer (see fig. 3.8). Core layers are OGSI – Open Grid Service Infrastructure and OGSA platform services. The platform services establish a set of standard services including policy, logging, service level management, and other networking services. The core elements of OGSA are Grid Services, i.e. Grid-related Web Services that provide a set of well-defined interfaces and follow specific conventions (Talia 2002).

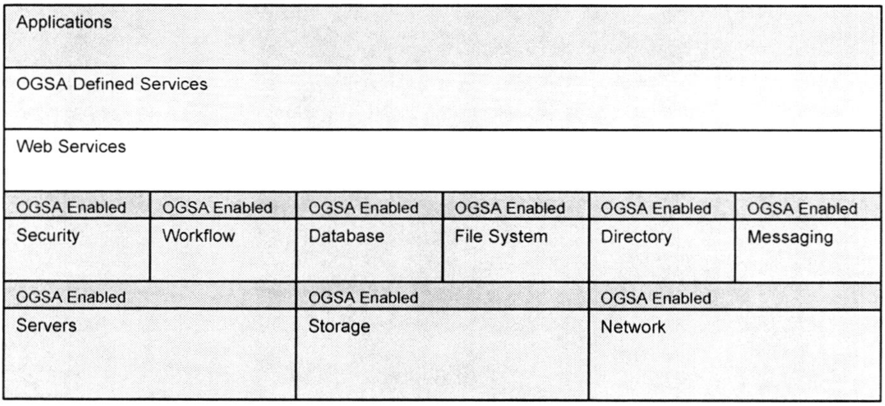

Applications					
OGSA Defined Services					
Web Services					
OGSA Enabled	OGSA Enabled	OGSA Enabled	OGSA Enabled	OGSA Enabled	OGSA Enabled
Security	Workflow	Database	File System	Directory	Messaging
OGSA Enabled		OGSA Enabled		OGSA Enabled	
Servers		Storage		Network	

Fig. 3.8: Overview of the OGSA Architecture

The convergence of Grid Computing with Service-oriented Computing means that Grid functionality is provided in form of services. The application of the service-oriented computing paradigm to Grid Computing has several advantages: First of all, it brings Grid in line with technologies currently adopted on a broad scale by companies. In addition, the service-oriented Grid paradigm offers the potential to provide a fine-grained virtualization of the available resources to significantly increase the versatility of a Grid (Smith et al. 2006). It also provides a binding element among Grid specific services on the hardware level and application services.

3.6.2 Convergence of Grid Computing and Software-as-a-Service

Another important paradigm that is gaining momentum together with Grid Computing and SOC is the Software-as-a-Service (SaaS) paradigm. The term SaaS denotes software that is owned, delivered and managed remotely by one or more independent software providers and that is offered on a pay-per-use basis (see also Mertz 2007, Wohl 2008). SaaS is consumed over communication networks (typically the Internet) and can be accessed by the user either via a Web browser or by directly accessing the application programming interfaces (APIs).

The SaaS concept means substantial changes in the way how software is developed and consumed. Traditional software or packaged software is developed to run on the end users' computers. Thus, for running packaged software, the user also has to provide the required infrastructure, which can result in additional investments. Further, qualified staff that is capable of providing maintenance and support for the software and hardware is needed. By buying a software license, a user is granted the right to use the software. Typical licenses for traditional software are: licences for usage per time (e.g. one year), licences to use the software for a certain time and number of computers (e.g. one year and maximum six computers), licences for a certain period of time and per number of users (e.g. one year and maximum six people) and similar. In addition, SaaS is provided on a pay-per-use basis. The user pays for the functionality of the software only for the time and intensity of each specific usage. The user does not own the software and does not have to bother with investing in infrastructure for running the software on and in staff required for maintaining the software. The price-per-use includes a share for the infrastructure and for licenses (see also Stanoevska-Slabeva et al. 2008).

SaaS is not a new phenomenon. The idea of sharing software, i.e. remote access to software by several users, has been a vision since the very beginning of distributed computing in companies. At that time, it was called "time sharing" of software that runs on a remote server and is used by several users over a private network (Wohl 2008). The next impulse for further evolution of providing applications as a service came with the establishment of the Internet as the main communication medium. In 1998, the term "Application Service Provisioning (ASP)" was introduced by (Heart and Pliskin 2001). ASP evolved from IT outsourcing and is based on the idea that a web-enabled application can be provided online through IP-based telecom infrastructure (Xu and Seltsikas 2002) by a central application service provider (Mittilä and Lehtinen 2005). At the beginning, the ASP model was a typical one-to-many delivery model, which means that the application is operated in a centralized manner by the ASP and is offered in the same form to many customers. The main advantages under which the ASP business model was propagated to customers are: cost savings and no need for developing and maintaining own infrastructure and skills. Even though ASP was considered as one very promising business model in the late 1990s, it did not take up on the market and its adoption has been very slow (Desai and Currie 2003). One major reason for the failure of ASP was the inability of early application service providers to offer customized services. The application was provided in the same form for any customer. There was little possibility for customization. Due to the early stage of development of Internet and Web technology, application service providers were not able to scale flexibly and to provide reliable and robust services. Further reasons for the failure of ASP have been: the centralized approach for computing, which requires the sending of input and output data, and the general lack of trust in the ASP paradigm (Xu and Seltsikas 2002, Desai and Currie 2003, Mittilä and Lehtinen 2005).

At present, Grid Computing and ASP are converging towards SaaS. The acronym SaaS is reported to have been coined in the white paper "Strategic Backgrounder: Software as a Service" published by the Software & Information Industry's (SIIA) eBusiness Division in 2001 (SIIA 2001, Wikipedia 2009c) and denotes a new evolutionary step in delivering of software as a service based on Web Services and Grid technology.

The convergence of Web Services and Grid Computing technology provides new opportunities to solve the ASP delivery problems (Xu and Seltsikas 2002, Mittilä and Lehtinen 2005). Web Services enable the modularization of applications in several services that can be combined and customized by users. Grid technology has the potential to provide the necessary flexibility and scalability on the infrastructure side of SaaS offerings. As already described in the previous sections, Grid Computing bundles heterogeneous pools of computing resources, storage systems and networks into a virtualized system that appears to applications as one single, but at the same time scalable and flexible computing entity. The applications deployed on a Grid are flexible and scalable and can be offered in modularized manner. With the help of Grid, the ASP business model is evolving from one-to many to a many-to-many model, where several service offerings are bundled and can flexibly be obtained by the user (Desai and Currie 2003).

Another converging tendency between Grid Computing and software applications is the shift towards Grid-enabled applications. The term *Grid-enabled application* is used to denote software applications, usually offered on the market as pre-packaged software, that are extended in a way that they can run in a distributed manner in a Grid environment. To Grid-enable a pre-packaged software product therefore means that a previously pre-packaged centralized application is enabled to run either on a distributed Grid infrastructure or to be offered as an online service based on the Software as a Service (SaaS) paradigm (see also Sanjeepan et al. 2005).

3.6.3 The Evolution Towards Cloud Computing

The previous two sections have sketched the current trends in computing. Grid Computing as technology is maturing. With Grid Computing the integration of heterogeneous physical resources into one virtualized and centrally accessible computing unit has become possible. Based on the convergence with SOC, Grid Computing is offered in form of Grid services that can flexibly be used by application developers that would like to deploy their application on a Grid Infrastructure. Maturing Grid technology is enabling new business models of utility computing, i.e. providing computing power on demand on a pay-per-use basis. While the developments in Grid technology are basically pushed by hardware and system software providers as Sun and IBM, at the same time there is an evolution in the software industry towards SaaS pushed by software vendors as for example Microsoft and SAP. Both developments – Utility Computing and SaaS – illustrate the increasing trend towards external deployment and sourcing of computing and applications.

What is the next step in the evolution of computing as a service (see fig. 3.9)?

The Evolution from Grid Computing to Cloud Computing

Grid Computing	Utility Computing	Software as a Service	Cloud Computing
Solving large problems with parallel computing Made mainstream by Globus Alliance Late 1980s	Offering computing resources as metered services Made mainstream by Globus Alliance Late 1990	Network-based subscriptions to applications Gained momentum in 2001	Next-generation Internet computing Next-generation data centres

Fig. 3.9: The Evolution to Cloud Computing (adapted from IBM 2009)

Utility computing and SaaS are two complementary trends: utility computing can only be successful on the market if a critical mass of applications is able to run on it. SaaS needs a flexible, scalable and easily accessible infrastructure on which it can run. Thus, in order to meet market demand, the next natural step in evolution is the integration of these two trends into a new holistic approach that offers the following functionality:

- Scalable, flexible, robust and reliably physical infrastructure
- Platform services that enable programming access to physical infrastructure through abstract interfaces
- SaaS developed, deployed and running on a flexible and scalable physical infra-structure

All this is emerging in new online platforms referred to as Clouds and Cloud Computing. Cloud Computing is resulting from the convergence of Grid Computing, Utility Computing and SaaS, and essentially represents the increasing trend towards the external deployment of IT resources, such as computational power, storage or business applications, and obtaining them as services. It has the potential to disrup-tively change the X-as-a-Service products and markets and will be explained in more detail in the next chapter.

4 Cloud Basics – An Introduction to Cloud Computing

Katarina Stanoevska-Slabeva, Thomas Wozniak

4.1 Introduction

Cloud Computing has attracted a lot of attention in recent times. The media as well as analysts are generally very positive about the opportunities Cloud Computing is offering. In May 2008, Merrill Lynch (2008) estimated the cost advantages of Cloud Computing to be three to five times for business applications and more than five times for consumer applications. According to a Gartner press release from June 2008, Cloud Computing will be "no less influential than e-business" (Gartner 2008a).

The positive attitude towards the importance and influence of Cloud Computing resulted in optimistic Cloud-related market forecasts. In October 2008, IDC (2008b) forecasted an almost threefold growth of spending on Cloud services until 2012, reaching \$42 billion. Same analyst firm reported that the cost advantage associated with the Cloud model becomes even more attractive in the economic downturn (IDC 2008b). Positive market prospects are also driven by the expectation that Cloud Computing might become the fundamental approach towards Green IT.

Despite of the broad coverage of Cloud Computing in commercial press, there is still no common agreement on what exactly Cloud Computing is and how it relates to Grid Computing. To gain an understanding of what Cloud Computing is, we first look at several existing definitions of the term. Based on those definitions, we identify key characteristics of Cloud Computing. Then we describe the common architecture and components of Clouds in detail, discuss opportunities and challenges of Cloud Computing, and provide a classification of Clouds. Finally, we make a comparison between Grid Computing and Cloud Computing.

4.2 Cloud Definitions

The term Cloud Computing has been defined in many ways by analyst firms, academics, industry practitioners, and IT companies. Table 4.1 shows how selected analyst firms define or describe Cloud Computing.

K. Stanoevska-Slabeva et al. (eds.), *Grid and Cloud Computing: A Business Perspective on Technology and Applications*, DOI 10.1007/978-3-642-05193-7_4,
© Springer-Verlag Berlin Heidelberg 2010

Table 4.1: Cloud Computing definitions by selected analyst firms

Source	Definition
Gartner	"a style of computing in which massively scalable IT-related capabilities are provided "as a service" using Internet technologies to multiple external customers" (Gartner 2008b)
IDC	"an emerging IT development, deployment and delivery model, enabling real-time delivery of products, services and solutions over the Internet (i.e., enabling cloud services)" (Gens 2008)
The 451 Group	"a service model that combines a general organizing principle for IT delivery, infrastructure components, an architectural approach and an economic model – basically, a confluence of grid computing, virtualization, utility computing, hosting and software as a service (SaaS)" (Fellows 2008)
Merrill Lynch	"the idea of delivering personal (e.g., email, word processing, presentations.) and business productivity applications (e.g., sales force automation, customer service, accounting) from centralized servers" (Merrill Lynch 2008)

All these definitions have a common characteristic: they try to describe and define Cloud Computing from the perspective of the end users and their focus is on how it might be experienced by them. According to these definitions, core feature of Cloud Computing is the provision of IT infrastructure and applications as a service in a scalable way.

The definition of Cloud Computing has been subject of debate also in the scientific community. Similar to the commercial press, there are different opinions about what Cloud Computing is and which features distinguish a Cloud. Compared to the definitions from the commercial press, the definitions in scientific literature include not only the end user perspective, but also architectural aspects. For example, Berkeley RAD Lab define Cloud Computing as follows:

"Cloud Computing refers to both the applications delivered as services over the Internet and the hardware and systems software in the datacenters that provide those services. The services themselves have long been referred to as Software as a Service (SaaS). The datacenter hardware and software is what we will call a Cloud. When a Cloud is made available in a pay-as-you-go manner to the general public, we call it a Public Cloud; the service being sold is Utility Computing. We use the term Private Cloud to refer to internal datacenters of a business or other organization, not made available to the general public. Thus, Cloud Computing is the sum of SaaS and Utility Computing, but does not include Private Clouds. People can be users or providers of SaaS, or users or providers of Utility Computing." (Armbrust et al. 2009)

This definition unites different perspectives on a Cloud: from the perspective of a provider, the major Cloud component is the data centre. The data centre contains the raw hardware resources for computing and storage, which together with software are offered in a pay-as-you-go manner. From the perspective of their purpose, Clouds are classified into private and public. Independent of the purpose of Clouds, one most important characteristic of Clouds is the integration of hardware and system software with applications, i.e. integration of utility computing and SaaS.

Also Reese (2009) notes a Cloud can be both software and infrastructure, and stresses the way how Cloud services might be consumed:

"The [Cloud] service is accessible via a web browser (nonproprietary) or web services API.; Zero capital expenditure is necessary to get started.; You pay only for what you use as you use it."

Foster et al. (2008) define Cloud Computing as

"[a] large-scale distributed computing paradigm that is driven by economies of scale, in which a pool of abstracted, virtualized, dynamically-scalable, managed computing power, storage, platforms, and services are delivered on demand to external customers over the Internet."

Two important aspects added by the definition of Foster et al. (2008) are virtualization and scalability. Cloud Computing abstracts from the underlying hardware and system software through virtualization. The virtualized resources are provided through a defined abstracting interface (an Application Programming Interface (API) or a service). Thus, at the raw hardware level, resources can be added or withdrawn according to demand posted through the interface, while the interface to the user is not changing. This architecture enables scalability and flexibility on the physical layer of a Cloud without impact on the interface to the end user.

Finally, Vaquero et al. (2008) analysed no less than 22 definitions of Cloud Computing, all proposed in 2008. Based on that analysis, Vaquero et al. (2008) propose the following definition which aims to reflect how Cloud Computing is currently conceived:

"Clouds are a large pool of easily usable and accessible virtualized resources (such as hardware, development platforms and/or services). These resources can be dynamically reconfigured to adjust to a variable load (scale), allowing also for an optimum resource utilization. This pool of resources is typically exploited by a pay-per-use model in which guarantees are offered by the Infrastructure Provider by means of customized SLAs."

Further, Vaquero et al. (2008) summarized *scalability*, *pay-per-use utility model* and *virtualization* as the feature set that would most closely resemble a minimum definition of Clouds. However, while the definition of Vaquero et al. (2008) summarizes other definitions with respect to the physical layer very well, it does not stress the integration of hardware with Software-as-a-Service in sufficient manner.

All definitions illustrate that Cloud Computing is a phenomenon that comprises a number of aspects and is related to a new paradigm of IT (hardware and applications) delivery and deployment. Generally, Cloud Computing concerns the delivery of IT capabilities to external customers, or, from the perspective of a user, obtaining IT capabilities from an external provider, as a service in a pay-per-use manner and over the Internet. Further, scalability and virtualization are very often seen as key characteristics of Cloud Computing (e.g. Foster et al. 2008, Sun 2009a, Vaquero et al. 2009). Scalability refers to a dynamic adjustment of provisioned IT resources to variable load, e.g. increasing or decreasing number of users, required storage capacity or processing power. Virtualization, which is also regarded as the cornerstone technology for all Cloud architectures (e.g. Sun 2009), is mainly used for abstraction and encapsulation (Foster et al. 2008). Abstraction allows unifying raw compute, storage, and network resources as a pool of resources and building resource overlays such as data storage services on top of them (Foster et al. 2008). Encapsulation of applications ultimately improves security, manageability, and isolation (Foster et al. 2008). Another important feature of Clouds is the integration of hardware and system software with applications. Both the hardware and systems software, or infrastructure, and the applications are offered as a service in an integrated manner.

Based on the findings of the definition analysis, a summary of the defining features of Cloud Computing, as they will be applied to guide further discussions in this book, is provided below and in figure 4.1:

- Cloud Computing is a new computing paradigm.
- Infrastructure resources (hardware, storage and system software) and applications are provided in a X-as-a-Service manner. When these services are offered by an independent provider or to external customers, Cloud Computing is based on pay-per-use business models.
- Main features of Clouds are virtualization and dynamic scalability on demand.
- Utility computing and SaaS are provided in an integrated manner, even though utility computing might be consumed separately.
- Cloud services are consumed either via Web browser or via a defined API.

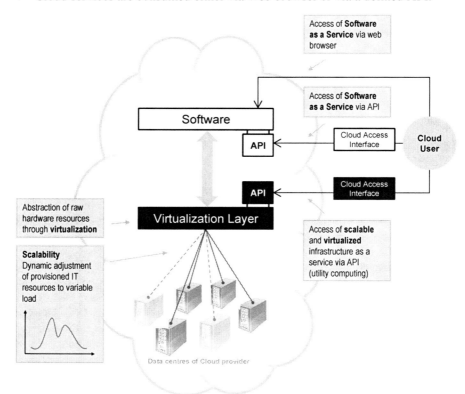

Fig. 4.1: Defining features of Cloud Computing

4.3 Architecture and Components of Clouds

In this section, we first provide an overview of concepts regarding the structure and components of Clouds. Then, we describe the most cited three-layer architectural concept for Clouds in detail.

4.3.1 Overview of Existing Concepts for Cloud Structures and Components

It is possible to find a number of concepts for Cloud structures in literature. At first sight, these classifications appear to differ from each other to varying extent. Eventually, however, they classify and describe the same phenomenon and share a common denominator.

Menken (2008) provides a very detailed concept consisting of 7 major components of Cloud Computing, namely application, client, infrastructure, platform, service, storage, and processing power. Miller (2008) looks at "different ways a company can use cloud computing to develop its own business applications", and distinguishes four types of Cloud service development, namely Software as a Service, Platform as a Service, Web Services, and On-Demand Computing. On-Demand Computing, as Miller (2008) notes, is also referred to as utility computing. Youseff et al. (2008) distinguish five layers of Cloud Computing: Cloud application, Cloud software environment, Cloud software infrastructure, software kernel, and firmware/hardware.

Forrester Research relate the components of Clouds to markets and distinguish five Cloud services markets. Two of them, Web-based services and SaaS offerings, are reported to be known markets that are delivered from the Cloud, whereas three cloud-infrastructure-as-a-service markets are new: app-components-as-a-service, software-platform-as-a-service, and virtual-infrastructure-as-a-service (Gilles et al. 2008). Finally, Reese (2009) considers SaaS as the term for "software in the cloud" and distinguishes four Cloud Infrastructure Models, namely Platform as a Service, Infrastructure as a Service, Private Clouds, and a fourth model representing all aspects of the previous Cloud infrastructure models.

All of the concepts above are very detailed and are influenced by the specific perspective on Clouds the respective authors take. Some of the concepts also involve aspects as Private Clouds and have different levels of detail for components that make up one logical entity. Given this, the concepts above do not provide a sufficiently generic description of a Cloud structure and its components. The concept most commonly used to describe a generic structure and components of Clouds is a 3-layered concept, which will be described in more detail in the next section.

4.3.2 The Three Layers of Cloud Computing

The definitions provided in section 4.2 already show that Cloud Computing comprises different IT capabilities, namely *infrastructure*, *platforms* and *software*. This may also be referred to as different 'shapes', 'segments', 'styles', 'types', 'levels' or 'layers' of Cloud Computing. Instead of speaking of different 'capabilities', thinking of it as different 'layers' makes much more sense because *infrastructure*, *platforms* and *software* build subsequently upon the forerunning level and are logically connected as different layers of a Cloud architecture. Regardless of which term used, this threefold classification of Cloud Computing has become commonplace (Eymann 2008, Merrill Lynch 2008, O'Reilly 2008, RightScale 2008, Sun 2009a, Vaquero et al. 2008).

As the delivery of IT resources or capabilities as a service is an important characteristic of Cloud Computing, the three architectural layers of Cloud Computing are (see also fig. 4.2):

1. Infrastructure as a Service (IaaS)
2. Platform as a Service (PaaS)
3. Software as a Service (SaaS)

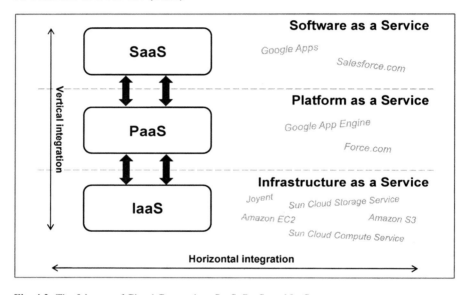

Fig. 4.2: The 3 layers of Cloud Computing: SaaS, PaaS, and IaaS

In the following subsections, we describe the three layers of Cloud Computing IaaS, PaaS and SaaS and how they are logically connected to each other.

4.3.2.1 Infrastructure as a Service (IaaS)

IaaS offerings are computing resources such as processing or storage which can be obtained as a service. Examples are Amazon Web Services with its Elastic Compute Cloud (EC2) for processing and Simple Storage Service (S3) for storage and Joyent who provide a highly scalable on-demand infrastructure for running Web sites and rich Web applications (Sun 2009a). PaaS and SaaS providers can draw upon IaaS offerings based on standardized interfaces. Instead of selling raw hardware infrastructure, IaaS providers typically offer virtualised infrastructure as a service. Foster et al. (2008) denote the level of raw hardware resources, such as compute, storage and network resources, as the fabric layer. Typically by virtualization, hardware level resources are abstracted and encapsulated and can thus be exposed to upper layer and end users through a standardized interface as unified resources (Foster et al. 2008) in the form of IaaS (see figure 4.3).

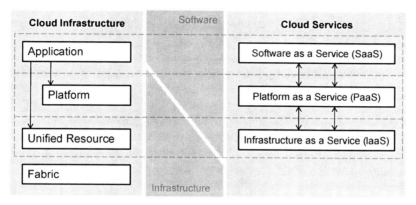

Fig. 4.3: Cloud Architecture related to Cloud services (adapted from Foster et al. 2008)

Already before the advent of Cloud Computing, infrastructure had been available as a service for quite some time. This has been referred to as utility computing, which is also used by some authors to denote the infrastructure layer of Cloud Computing (e.g. Armbrust et al. 2009, Miller 2008, O'Reilly 2008). Sun, for example, launched its Sun Grid Compute Utility in March 2006 (Schwartz 2006). The Sun Grid Compute Utility allowed users to purchase computing capability for $1/cpu-hr, i.e. on a pay-per-use basis. The Sun Grid Compute Utility could be accessed via Network.com. One year later, in March 2007, Sun announced the Network.com Application Catalog, which allowed developers and open source communities to just "click and run" their applications online (Sun 2007). Two years later, in March 2009, Sun announced its Open Cloud Platform as well as plans for its Sun Cloud, whose main services will be the Sun Cloud Storage Service and Sun Cloud Compute Service (Sun 2009b). Network.com, which once was the access point to the Sun Grid Compute Utility and the Network.com Application Catalog, was in a transition mode in early 2009 and now redirects to 'Sun Cloud Computing'(Sun 2009c, Sun 2009d).

Compared to the early utility computing offerings, IaaS denotes its evolution towards integrated support for all three layers (IaaS, PaaS, and SaaS) within a Cloud (see also Fellows 2009). From the early offerings of utility computing it became clear that for utility computing providers to be successful, they need to provide an interface that is easy to access, understand, program, and use, i.e. an API that would enable easy integration with the infrastructure of potential customers and potential developers of SaaS applications. Utility Computing providers' data centres are sufficiently utilized only if they are used by a critical mass of customers and SaaS providers.

As a consequence of the requirement for an easy and abstracted access to the physical layer of a Cloud, virtualization of the physical layer and programming platforms for developers emerged as major features of Clouds.

4.3.2.2 Platform as a Service (PaaS)

Platforms are an abstraction layer between the software applications (SaaS) and the virtualized infrastructure (IaaS). PaaS offerings are targeted at software developers. Developers can write their applications according to the specifications of a particular platform without needing to worry about the underlying hardware infrastructure (IaaS). Developers upload their application code to a platform, which then typically manages the automatic upscaling when the usage of the application grows (RightScale 2008). PaaS offerings can cover all phases of software development or may be specialized around a specific area like content management (Sun 2009a). Examples are the Google App Engine, which allows applications to be run on Google's infrastructure, and Salesforce's Force.com platform. The PaaS layer of a Cloud relies on the standardized interface of the IaaS layer that virtualizes the access to the available resources and it provides standardized interfaces and a development platform for the SaaS layer.

4.3.2.3 Software as a Service (SaaS)

As explained in section 3.6.2 in chapter 3, SaaS is software that is owned, delivered and managed remotely by one or more providers and that is offered in a pay-per-use manner (see also Mertz 2007). SaaS is the most visible layer of Cloud Computing for end-users, because it is about the actual software applications that are accessed and used.

From the perspective of the user, obtaining software as a service is mainly motivated by cost advantages due to the utility-based payment model, i.e. no up-front infrastructure investment. Well known examples for SaaS offerings are Salesforce.com and Google Apps such as Google Mail and Google Docs and Spreadsheets.

The typical user of a SaaS offering usually has neither knowledge nor control about the underlying infrastructure (Eymann 2008), be it the software platform which the SaaS offering is based on (PaaS) or the actual hardware infrastructure (IaaS). However, these layers are very relevant for the SaaS provider because they are necessary and can be outsourced. For example, a SaaS application can be developed on an existing platform and run on infrastructure of a third party. Obtaining platforms as well as infrastructure as a service is attractive for SaaS providers as it can alleviate them from heavy license or infrastructure investment costs and keeps them flexible. It also allows them to focus on their core competencies. This is similar to the benefits that motivate SaaS users to obtain software as a service.

According to market analysts, the growing openness of companies for SaaS and the high pressure to reduce IT costs are major drivers for a high demand and growth of SaaS, and by that also for Cloud Computing, in the next years. In August 2007, analyst firm Gartner forecasted an average annual growth rate of worldwide SaaS revenue for enterprise application software of 22.1% through 2011, reaching a volume of \$11.5 billion (Mertz et al. 2007). Analyst firm IDC estimates the growth rate of SaaS revenue to be 31% in 2009, which is more than four times of the total software market's growth rate (IDC 2008c). In October 2008, Gartner updated the estimates stating world wide SaaS revenue for enterprise application software is expected to more than double by 2012, reaching \$14.5 billion (Gartner 2008c).

4.4 Opportunities and Challenges of Cloud Computing

As described in previous sections, Cloud Computing concerns the delivery of IT capabilities as a service on three levels: infrastructure (IaaS), platforms (PaaS), and software (SaaS). By providing interfaces on all three levels, Clouds address different types of customers:

- End consumers, who mainly use the services of the SaaS layer over a Web browser and basic offerings of the IaaS layer as for example storage for data resulting from the usage of the SaaS layer.
- Business customers that might access all three layers: the IaaS layer in order to enhance the own infrastructure with additional resources on demand, the PaaS layer in order to be able to run own applications in a Cloud and eventually the SaaS layer in order to take advantage of available applications offered as a service.
- Developers and Independent Software Vendors (ISVs) that develop applications that are supposed to be offered over the SaaS layer of a Cloud. Typically, they directly access the PaaS layer, and through the PaaS layer indirectly access the IaaS layer, and are present on the SaaS layer with their application.

In general, for all different kinds of Cloud customers, a Cloud offers the major opportunities known for X-as-a-Service offerings. From the perspective of the user, the utility-based payment model is considered as one of the main benefits of Cloud Computing. There is no need for up-front infrastructure investment: investment in software licenses and no risk of unused but paid software licenses, and investment in hardware infrastructure and related maintenance and staff. Thus, capital expenditure is turned into operational expenditure. Users of a Cloud service only use the volume of IT resources they actually need, and only pay for the volume of IT resources they actually use. At the same time, they take advantage of the scalability and flexibility of a Cloud. Cloud Computing enables easy and fast scaling of required computing resources on demand.

However, Cloud Computing has also several disadvantages: Clouds serve many different customers. Thus, users of a Cloud service do not know who else's job is running on the same server as their own ones (Sun 2009a). A typical Cloud is outside a company's or other organization's firewall. While this may not play a major role for consumers, it can have significant impact on a company's decision to move use Cloud Services. The major risks of Cloud Computing are summarized in table 4.2.

Table 4.2: Obstacles to adoption and growth of Cloud Computing

Obstacle	Source
Availability	Armbrust et al. (2009), IDC (2008a)
Security	IDC (2008a)
Performance	Armbrust et al. (2009), IDC (2008a)
Data lock-in	Armbrust et al. (2009)
Data confidentiality and auditability	Armbrust et al. (2009)
Data transfer bottlenecks	Armbrust et al. (2009)
Hard to integrate with in-house IT	IDC (2008a)
Lack of customizability	IDC (2008a)

The user has to rely on the promise of the Cloud provider with respect to reliability, performance and Quality of the Service (QoS) of the infrastructure. The usage of Clouds is associated also with higher security and privacy risks related to data storage and management in two ways: first because of the need to transfer data back and forth to a Cloud so that it can be processed in a Cloud; second because data is stored on an external infrastructure and the data owner relies on the Cloud provider's assurance that no unauthorized access takes place. Furthermore, the usage of Clouds requires an upfront investment in the integration of the own infrastructure and applications with a Cloud. At present, there are no standards for the IaaS, PaaS, and SaaS interfaces. This makes the choice of a Cloud provider and the investment in integration with Clouds risky. This can result in a strong log-in effect that is advantageous for the Cloud provider but disadvantageous for the users.

Given the risks associated with the usage of Clouds, in each case a careful evaluation and comparison of the potential benefits and risks is necessary. Also, it needs to be considered which data and processes are suitable to be used for "Cloud sourcing" and which should better be not exposed to any organization outside the firewall.

4.5 Classification of Clouds

Clouds can generally be classified according to who the owner of the Cloud data centres is. A Cloud environment can comprise either a single Cloud or multiple Clouds. Thus, it can be distinguished between single-Cloud environments and multiple-Cloud environments. The following subsections provide a classification of single-Cloud environments according to the Cloud data centre ownership (sec. 4.5.1) and a classification of multiple-Cloud environments according to which type of Clouds are combined (sec. 4.5.2).

4.5.1 Public Clouds vs. Private Clouds

In section 4.2, based on the review of many Cloud definitions, we have characterized Cloud Computing as the delivery of IT capabilities to external customers, or, from the perspective of a user, obtaining IT capabilities from an external provider, as a service in a pay-per-use manner and over the Internet. In addition, we have identified scalability and virtualization as key characteristics of Cloud Computing. External data centres, e.g. those of Google or Amazon, are thus the foundation on the raw hardware or fabric level for delivering IT capabilities as Cloud services.

However, virtualizing raw hardware resources and offering them as abstracted IT capabilities as a service is not necessarily bound to the external delivery mode usually associated with Cloud Computing. Companies and other organizations also use virtualization and service-oriented computing to increase utilization of their existing IT resources and to increase flexibility. The utilization rate of traditional server environments is between 5 to 15% (e.g. IBM 2008). Increasing it to up to 18% is reported to be easily achievable (Lohr 2009, McKinsey 2009). Through aggressive virtualization, large companies can increase their server utilization rates to up to 35%, which is close to the level of Cloud providers such as Google with 38% (Lohr 2009, McKinsey 2009). Higher utilization makes possible to consolidate server environments, i.e. the number of physical servers can be reduced. This lowers hardware maintenance costs, required physical space for the servers, power and cooling costs as well as the carbon footprint of IT.

To distinguish between external providers of Cloud services (external Clouds) and companies' efforts to build internal Cloud infrastructures (internal Clouds) two distinct terms are commonly used: *Public* Cloud for external Clouds and *Private* Cloud for internal Clouds (see e.g. Armbrust et al. 2009, IBM 2009, Reese 2009, Sun 2009a).

A *Public Cloud* is data centre hardware and software run by third parties, e.g. Google and Amazon, which expose their services to companies and consumers via the Internet (Armbrust et al. 2009, IBM 2009, Sun 2009a). A Public Cloud is not restricted to a limited user base: it "…is made available in a pay-as-you-go manner to the general public" (Armbrust et al. 2009). Thus, Clouds can address two type of customers: either end consumers on the B2C market or companies on the B2B market.

Companies may not be willing to bear the risks associated with a move towards a Public Cloud and may therefore build internal Clouds in order to benefit from Cloud Computing. *Private Clouds* refer to such internal data centres of a company or other organization (Armbrust et al. 2009). A Private Cloud is fully owned by a single company who has total control over the applications run on the infrastructure, the place where they run, and the people or organizations using it – simply over every aspect of the infrastructure (Sun 2009a, Reese 2009). A Private Cloud relies on virtualization of an organization's existing infrastructure (Reese 2009), leading to benefits such as increased utilization as described above. The key advantage of a Private Cloud is to gain all advantages of virtualization, while retaining full control over the infrastructure (Reese 2009).

The definitions of Cloud Computing reviewed in section 4.2 clearly show that Cloud Computing concerns the delivery of IT capabilities to *external* customers, or, from the perspective of the user, obtaining IT capabilities from *external* providers. Thus, some authors do not consider Private Clouds, or *internal* Clouds, as part of or as true Cloud Computing (e.g. Armbrust et al. 2009, Reese 2009). Reese (2009), for example, notes that Private Clouds lack "the freedom from capital investment and the virtually unlimited flexibility of cloud computing."

4.5.2 Hybrid Clouds and Federations of Clouds

Single Clouds can be combined resulting in multiple-Cloud environments. Contingent on which types of Clouds (public or private) are combined, two types of multiple-Cloud environments can be distinguished:

- Hybrid Clouds and
- Federation of Clouds.

Hybrid Clouds combine Public and Private Clouds and allow an organization to both run some applications on an internal Cloud infrastructure and others in a Public Cloud (Sun 2009a). This way, companies can benefit from scalable IT resources offered by external Cloud providers while keeping specific applications or data inside the firewall. A mixed Cloud environment adds complexity regarding the distribution of applications across different environments, monitoring of the internal and external infrastructure involved, security and privacy, and may there-fore not be suited for applications requiring complex databases or synchronization (Sun 2009a).

The terms *Federated Clouds* or *Federation of Clouds* denote collaboration among mainly Public Clouds even though Private Clouds may be involved. Cloud infrastructure providers are supposed to provide massively scalable computing resources. This allows users and Cloud SaaS providers not to worry about the computational infrastructure required to run their services. The Cloud infrastructure providers, however, may face a scalability problem themselves. A single hosting company may not be able to provide seemingly infinite computing infrastructure, which is required to serve increasing numbers of applications, each with massive amounts of users and access at anytime from anywhere. Consequently, Cloud infra-structure providers may eventually partner to be able to truly serve the needs of Cloud service providers, i.e. providing seemingly infinite compute utility. Thus, *the* Cloud might become a federation of infrastructure providers or alternatively there might be a federation of clouds (RESERVOIR 2008).

Federated Clouds are a collection of single Clouds that can interoperate, i.e. exchange data and computing resources through defined interfaces. According to basic federation principles, in a Federation of Clouds each single Cloud remains independent, but can interoperate with other Clouds in the federation through standardized interfaces. At present, a Federation of Clouds seems still to be a theoretical concept as there is no common Cloud interoperability standard. One new initiative that tries to develop a common standard is the Open Cloud Computing Interface, which is developed by the Open Cloud Computing Interface Working Group (http://www.occi-wg.org/) of the Open Grid Forum (OGF). The goal is through a standardized API among Clouds to enable both interoperability among Clouds from different vendors and new business models and platforms as (according to OCCI 2009):

- Integrators, that offer advanced management services that spread over several Clouds or Hybrid Clouds
- Aggregators that offer a single common interface to multiple Cloud providers.

The integration and advances in interoperability of Clouds might be an important factor for the future success of Cloud Computing. Open standards and interoperability among Private and Public Clouds enable a higher flexibility for user companies. The user companies would be able to also partly outsource data and processes to the Cloud that are less security- and privacy-sensitive. At the same time, the possibility to build a Federation of Clouds would enable specialization of single Clouds as well as a broader choice for the users.

4.6 Grid and Cloud Computing Compared

The description of Grid Computing in Chapter 3 and Cloud Computing in this chapter show that there are many similarities among Grid and Cloud Computing. This has provoked many discussions in commercial and scientific literature around the question if Grids and Clouds are the same, if Cloud Computing is only a new marketing hype, or if there are substantial differences between Grid and Cloud Computing.

Currently, the discussion about differences among Grid and Cloud Computing mainly regards technical aspects (see also table 4.3).

Table 4.3: Grid and Cloud Computing technically compared

	Grid Computing	Cloud Computing
Means of utilisation (e.g. Harris 2008)	Allocation of multiple servers onto a single task or job	Virtualization of servers; one server to compute several tasks concurrently
Typical usage pattern (e.g. EGEE 2008)	Typically used for job execution, i.e. the execution of a programme for a limited time	More frequently used to support long-running services
Level of abstraction (e.g. Jha et al. 2008)	Expose high level of detail	Provide higher-level abstractions

Foster et al. (2008) for example identify differences among Grid and Cloud Computing in various aspects as security, programming model, compute model, data model, application and abstraction. According to Merrill Lynch (2008), what makes Cloud Computing new and differentiates it from Grid Computing is virtualization: "Cloud computing, unlike grid computing, leverages virtualization to maximize computing power. Virtualization, by separating the logical from the physical, resolves some of the challenges faced by grid computing" (Merrill Lynch 2008). While Grid Computing achieves high utilization through the allocation of multiple servers onto a single task or job, the virtualization of servers in Cloud Computing achieves high utilization by allowing one server to compute several tasks concurrently (Harris 2008). Beside these technological differences between Grid and

Cloud, there are differences in the typical usage pattern. Grid is typically used for job execution, e.g. the execution of a HPC programme for a limited time. Clouds do support a job usage pattern but are more frequently used to support long-running services (EGEE 2008).

While most authors acknowledge similarities among those two paradigms, the opinions seem to cluster around the statement that Cloud Computing has evolved from Grid Computing and that Grid Computing is the foundation for Cloud Computing. Foster et al. (2008) for example describe the relationship between Grid and Cloud Computing as follows:

> "We argue that Cloud Computing not only overlaps with Grid Computing, it is indeed evolved out of Grid Computing and relies on Grid Computing as its backbone and infrastructure support. The evolution has been a result of a shift in focus from an infrastructure that delivers storage and compute resources (such is the case in Grids) to one that is economy based aiming to deliver more abstract resources and services (such is the case in Clouds)."

Thus, Cloud and Grid computing can be considered as complementary. Grid interfaces and protocols can enable the interoperability between resources of Cloud infrastructure providers and/or a Federation of Clouds. Grid solutions for job computing can run as a service on top of a Federation of Clouds and/or a distributed virtualized infrastructure (Llorente 2008a, Llorente 2008b). In addition, the potential benefits of simplicity offered by Cloud technologies, such as higher-level of abstractions (Jha et al. 2008), may help to better serve current Grid users, "attract new user communities, accelerate grid adoption and importantly reduce operations costs" (EGEE 2008).

In the discussion about the differences among Grids and Clouds, less attention is given to explaining them from user perspective yet. Based on the described features of Grid Computing in chapter 3 and Cloud Computing in this chapter, the main changes from the user perspective can be summarized as follows:

- *Pure focus on X-as-a-Service (XaaS) by Clouds*: As mentioned in section 3.2 in chapter 3, the basis for Grid Computing is Grid middleware that is available on the market as packaged or open source software. Utility Computing is only one form of Grid Computing. Compared to that, Cloud Computing focuses purely on XaaS offered in a pay-per-use manner. There is no middleware that enables the building of Clouds yet.
- *Focus on different types of applications:* Grid Computing emerged in eScience to solve scientific problems requiring HPC. Current usage in industry also focuses mainly on HPC, for example in collaborative engineering based on simulation, in research and development in pharmaceutical companies and similar. HPC applications are usually batch-oriented and require high computing power for one task that is run once in a time. Given this, Grid Computing has the goal to assign computing resources, in many cases from different domains, to such HPC tasks. Cloud Computing is rather oriented towards applications that run permanently (e.g. the well-known CRM SaaS Salesforce.com) and have varying demand for physical resources while running. In order to be more flexible, one

major difference of Cloud Computing to Grid Computing is virtualization and adjustment of provided resources to demand. Thus, Cloud Computing extends the spectrum to which virtualization can be applied.

- *Different relationships among resource providers:* The goal of Grid Computing is creation of VOs with clear up-front commitment of the involved parties and encoding of agreements and polices in the software. Cloud Computing eliminates the need for an up-front commitment by Cloud users, thereby allowing companies to start small and increase hardware resources only when there is an increase in their needs (see also Armbrust et al. 2009).

- *Different scope of offerings:* Grid Computing clearly focuses on providing infrastructure as a service, or utility computing. Cloud Computing provides an integrated support for IaaS, PaaS and SaaS. Given this, Cloud Computing makes the development of SaaS applications easier.

- *Extended scope of interfaces to the user:* Grid Computing allocates heterogeneous resources to one task and focuses on communication among different resources on the physical layer and towards the application running on it. The Grid interfaces are rather based on protocols and APIs and by that only usable by technical experts. Cloud Computing is designed to provide interfaces for end users over Web browser or through APIs. Thereby there are different and specific APIs on each layer (IaaS, PaaS, and SaaS). Given the higher level of abstraction and the different interfaces, Cloud Computing is suitable to address end users in the B2C and C2B market at the same time.

To summarize, Grid Computing provides the means to share and unify heterogeneous computing resources. It is the starting point and basis for Cloud Computing. Cloud Computing essentially represents the increasing trend towards the external deployment of IT resources, such as computational power, storage or business applications, and obtaining them as services.

5 Grid Business Models

George Thanos, Eleni Agiatzidou, Costas Courcoubetis, George D. Stamoulis

5.1 Introduction

A business model (BM) establishes a framework for the transformation of economic inputs (e.g. resources and technological knowhow) into economic outputs (e.g. goods and services) required by customers in a market (Chesbrough and Rosenbloom 2002). In simpler terms, a business model describes the way the business expects to make money by interacting with customers and other players in the market.

Such a model can also be thought of as a mediator between technology development and value creation. The ultimate role of the business model is to ensure that the technological core delivers value to the customer. In order to achieve this, a number of factors and functions must be analysed and specified, such as the value proposition of the new product, the target market, the potential value chain for the delivery of the product or service, an estimation of the cost-structure, and profit potential (Peterovic et al. 2001, Weill and Vitale 2001).

A well articulated BM is the foundation of the company's business plan. The business plan serves as a decision-support tool and includes the additional level of detail that needs to be identified and proved (as well as can be prior to execution) in order for the business to attract money from potential investors. It specifies measurable goals, the reasons why they are believed to be attainable, and the plan for reaching those goals (Siegel et al. 1993, Wikipedia 2009a). It may also include background information about the company and a marketing plan. As it becomes apparent, both are to a great extent related and equally important; without a good business model, a business plan cannot be brought to effect and vice versa.

If you have developed a business model or plan, you already have a business case established as this is a prerequisite of the aforementioned. That means you have a business idea that once turned into a project (i.e. financed!) can lead your business to a profitable product or service or in other terms you have a value proposition for your customers. For example, when referring to the term "Grid business case" in this document we imply that a company has defined a project where the provisioning of a product or service and/or its value proposition is based on exploiting the benefits of Grid technology. The pathway from that idea to the realisation and sustainability of the actual project is described through a specific business plan.

The purpose of this chapter is to present an overview of the business models adopted by Grid application and services providers in the market based on a study and analysis of Grid business cases. The goal is to provide the reader with an overview of BMs from the perspective of a potential business adopter as well as of a user/customer of Grid technology. To achieve that, we briefly discuss how the Grid BMs evolved from traditional ones; we explain how a business case can be established

K. Stanoevska-Slabeva et al. (eds.), *Grid and Cloud Computing: A Business Perspective on Technology and Applications*, DOI 10.1007/978-3-642-05193-7_5,
© Springer-Verlag Berlin Heidelberg 2010

for Grid services; and explain the relationship to a BM and business plan. Next, we present the different business cases that can be found in the market today and link them to associated BMs. Finally, a more detailed analysis of particular cases for the market today is presented.

5.2 Setting the Scene

Grid technology promises a new way of delivering services across IP-based infrastructures. These services range from common ones, such as existing mass multimedia services, to more complex and demanding customised industrial applications. The start-up and key drivers behind the adoption of Grid by industry has been the performance advantage this technology promises to deliver, that in business and economic terms is translated into reducing costs, simplifying local infrastructure and speeding up processes. Under rapidly changing IT technologies and the pressure of highly-competitive global markets, the importance of these drivers is particularly high. Besides the aforementioned advantages, the Grid can be even considered as a "Green-IT" technology. Indeed, IT resources can be distributed over the world and be utilised dynamically and interchangeably based on climate and environmental conditions (e.g. by "chase the moon" (Berry 2007)), to minimise the energy consumption and consequently the associated costs.

The notion of Grid and its associated technological and business advantages has further evolved during recent years and the underpinning performance enabler advantage has been complemented by the collaborative benefits of this new technology. The early business models related to Grid have been based on either computing utility provisioning or on software products supported via in-house high-performance Grid facilities. The former case, i.e. the use of computing power as utility, is not a new idea; and some even argue that is actually a backwards move to the past in terms of mainframe and terminal architecture. This approach promises to satisfy (via cost-effective means) the continuously increasing need for more computing resources and scalability by industries, not previously belonging to the IT centric domain. Despite the fact that the core idea, that computing resources should be offered in the future as a utility (like the electrical power Grids), was broad enough to cover the single home user, this was later abandoned. Eventually, the market clearly showed that the target market should be the research institutions and Small and Medium Enterprises (SMEs), i.e. organisation that had intermittent need for high power computing resources

The case of software services provided to customers through in-house Grid-facilities was soon demarcated as two correlated very promising business cases. First, the *Application Service Provisioning* (ASP) one, where a provider hosts, operates and supports applications for his clients in a Grid-powered infrastructure. The aim was to relieve them from maintenance costs and offer them scalability, agility and reliability together with high performance. The second business case was based on the provision of services according to the Software-as-a-Service (SaaS) paradigm. In this scenario, the service is hosted for the provider (which can be an SME) by either an in-house Grid infrastructure or by utilizing the resources of an external resource provider such as Amazon, Sun Microsystems and IBM. The difference to the previous case is that the service is now offered through the web and charged via a monthly (rental) fee i.e. no license is needed from the customer's side. Furthermore, no specific software needs to be installed in the client machine as a standard web browser is all that is required to access the service.

As we enter a technological era where solutions based on *Service Oriented Architectures* (SOA) and *Cloud Computing* will constitute a large segment of the market for business services, it is most likely that Grid-related services will be integrated into this framework. Therefore, the business models will evolve and be adapted accordingly. For example, SaaS will become more dominate over the *Software-as-a-Product* (SaaP) model for Grid services provisioning and the added-value of these services will be focusing around the collaboration benefits, rather than just in the performance related benefits. A similar emerging B2B collaboration scenario, that could drive new models, would be the services related to Virtual Organisations (VOs). In a VO, different organizations share resources, either computational or data, to achieve all partners' goals. VOs can be easily created and administrated by utilising Grid services e.g. by taking advantage of the Globus Open Grid Services Architecture (OGSA, http://www.globus.org/ogsa/) framework.

To summarise, looking at the Grid service and application provider's perspective, the well-established business models such as the SaaS, SaaP, Open-Source, and Value-added-Services (VAS) ones still apply in the Grid environment. However, there are a number of important factors that must be taken into account by a new business when adapting these traditional scenarios to the Grid, especially in regards to licensing, pricing models and legal issues. For example questions like these should be taken into account: what is the right license and pricing model to use for Grid SaaS? How do I protect the Intellectual Property Rights in a geographically dispersed collaboration scenario? How do the relationships and flows (tangible and intangible ones) in a value network change in the case of a VO where the common benefits are spread over a number of participants?

In order to build a successful business case all the previous questions need to be answered. This can only be achieved through a process of building a business model and planning, through 1) careful analysis and evaluation of the technical requirements 2) the surrounding business environment and market conditions and the 3) target market. An example process for that purpose tailored to the Grid case is presented next.

5.3 Establishing a Business Model Based on the "Grid Benefit"

As discussed in the previous section, a business model seeks to transform economic inputs into valuable economic outputs. In order to achieve that, it needs to provide and support information and propositions on several fronts starting from the analysis of the requirements for developing the product, to explicitly defining the value proposition and the target customers. Furthermore, it needs to elaborate on the financial terms of the case and justify the revenue projections. These can be seen as building blocks in figure 5.1 (Osterwalder 2004).

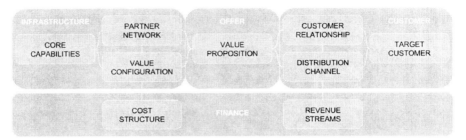

Fig. 5.1: Business model design template: Nine BM elements and their relationships

When designing a model regarding a new or emerging technology, especially when it is not yet proven in the market and thus more risky, some of these components will be found to gain more value than others. Once a good level of understanding of the new technology has been reached, the whole process should start from the value-proposition definition. This is a step that must be successfully achieved before proceeding further. This is the whole essence of a new technology: what new benefit can it deliver to the customer? Then follow the questions: what do the customers exactly want, how this can be delivered and if the required competence and resources are available. This incremental process, together with the questions to be answered at each step, is demonstrated in figure 5.2.

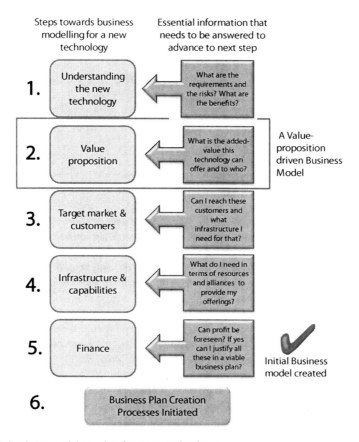

Fig. 5.2: Business model creation for a new technology

The first and most important requirement i.e. the value proposition, is a set of business enablers, in terms of Grid benefits that a successful business case could be based upon and subsequently generate economic outputs to the participants. These business enablers or "Grid benefits" are:

1. The *"Common Use of Resources and Infrastructure as a Service (IaaS)"* business enabler: economic benefits are expected to arise from offering dynamic resources using a Grid infrastructure. This enabler also accounts for those cases that Grid is used in IaaS architectures. As an example, we can think of a single organization that may require processing power that cannot be provided by means of stand-alone machines. By interconnecting multiple machines in a Grid, high processing power can be provided even for just a single application. Thus, the organization achieves both a high peak processing capacity and a high average utilization of the processing power available, since this can be flexibly allocated to multiple Grid-enabled applications. These features should also lead

to increased cost-efficiency for the infrastructure deployed. This is particularly important for a large organization with several departments scattered around the world, each possessing their own computing infrastructure. Connecting these via a Grid can generate significant enhancements, a higher exploitation of resources, cost-efficiency and economies of scale, due to the fact that the interconnection of all machines, improves the utilization of each one (Thanos et al. 2007).

2. The *"Collaborative and VO"* business enabler: economic benefits are expected by offering services or software that take advantage of the collaborative environment and functionalities that Grid can offer in a VO context. Consider a group of organizations, each of which possesses its own resources, which are complementary to each other. For example, organization A possesses a powerful database server, while B has a huge amount of data and C possesses an application running over its server that requires data such as that of B. Clearly, when collaborating in the form of Grid, all organizations can bring together a powerful outcome, while each of them exploits its own resources in a cost-efficient way, without needing to invest in the missing resources that are now contributed by others. In this case, the collaborating organizations enjoy economies of scope, since bringing all their resources together by means of Grid broadens their scope of applicability (Thanos et al. 2007).

3. The *"Software as a Service (SaaS) and advanced software architectures"* business enabler: economic benefits are expected by Grid-enabling existing services in order to offer them using the SaaS delivery paradigm or developing new Grid services, designed to be provided using the SaaS. Here, by the term "grid-enabling" we mean the redesigning of an existing application in order for it to be offered in a Grid environment. Also this category accounts for the cases that Grid services are offered (via SaaS) with the purpose of being integrated to SOA and Cloud Computing architectures. A SaaS version of an application is more affordable to infrequent users of that application, who now have a benefit compared to investing on the corresponding software license and/or computational infrastructure. Therefore, both these users and the service provider gain, because this version increases the demand for the service by making it affordable at lower costs (Thanos et al. 2007).

In the next sections we will discuss with examples how these 3 enablers can be spotted today in the market and how they can lead to building a successful business model.

5.4 Popular Business Cases in the Market Today and Associated Benefits

After defining the 3 aforementioned categories as enablers for doing business with Grid we will now examine how these can be found in the most popular business cases in the market today. These are categorised and presented in the next table.

Table 5.1: Popular business cases in the market today, their enablers and involved actor

Most popular Grid Business Cases in the market	The Grid benefit (value-proposition or added-value)	Main actors involved
1. Company utilises an internal Grid solution as a virtualisation technique to improve the utilisation of resources (also known as the "Enterprise Grid")	For the company: Performance differentiation and collaboration benefit in case of inter departments (VO-like) virtualisation of resources.	The company
		Grid s/w and application providers
		Systems integrator (can be the same with the Grid s/w provider)
2. Company rents external computing resources through the internet with Grid being the underlying infrastructure on the provider's side	For the company: Performance differentiation	The company
		Resources provider (e.g. Amazon & Sun) – See case No. 5
3. Company Grid-enables existing application or develops an application optimised to run over the Grid (BEinGRID BEs cases) and offers it to external clients	For the company: performance differentiation, new markets through SaaS provisioning For the user: new services not foreseen or affordable before	The service or application provider (the company)
		The user that either buys or rents the solution
		The Grid software provider
		Systems integrator (can be the same with the Grid s/w provider)
4. A group of organisations forming a VO in order to gain benefit from common use of resources (CERN is an example of this). Case also known as "Partner or Collaborative Grids"	– Collaboration benefit – New services from the VO partners to internal or external users, not possible before.	The users (VO participants)
		Grid s/w and application providers
		Systems integrator (can be the same with the Grid s/w provider)
		Resources provider – if external computing resources are utilised (e.g. Amazon & Sun)
5. Company acts as a computing resources provider e.g. the "Amazon", "Sun", "IBM" etc cases	For the user: Resources provided on demand. Performance differentiation – See Case No.2 For the company: revenue generation and reduced costs of offering such a service through virtualisation	The resource provider (the company)
		The users that buy resources on demand – See Case No.2
6. Company provides Cloud Computing Services with Grid as the underlying infrastructure (most popular emerging scenario). E.g. the "Amazon", "Google", "IBM", "Microsoft" etc cases	For the user: Provision of Cloud computing services (IT-as-a-Service) For the company: high utilisation of resources through virtualisation	The Cloud Computing provider
		The users that purchase Cloud Computing services

As can be seen from table 5.1, six distinct business cases are commonly found today. As illustrated in the second column, it is important not only to identify the benefits from the provider's side, but from the user's perspective as well. For example, in the third case we have a company (e.g. a SME) that Grid-enables an existing application or develops an application optimised to run over the Grid and offers it to external clients. From the perspective of the company, there are two Grid benefits: The first one is about the exploitation of common resources, category 1 as discussed in the previous section. For example, in the case that the new application offered by the company can be provided more efficiently over a Grid infrastructure i.e. it can be offered to a larger number of customers/users without compromising or needing to upgrade the existing internal infrastructure. Furthermore, in the case of a new service, this can be offered utilising the SaaS paradigm, thus opening a window of opportunity to additional economic capabilities for the company which is a category 3 enabler according to our classification.

To add to that, the user can now enjoy new web-based services (e.g. through SaaS) not possible before, that eventually might be exploited for his own purposes; for example, in the case the user that purchases the service is another company or institution he may be able to optimise his own service provisioning in his own market. In this example, as in others, there are more than one associated enablers involved according the very exact model chosen. For the purposes of presenting the whole picture we have grouped them together under each case.

In order to establish the associated business models in each case, it is important to identify the actors constituting the basic value chain of the offering. This is exactly why the third column has been included in this table. However we are not going into detail in these value chains and networks here as this is the subject of the next chapter of this book. Nevertheless we need this in order to analyse the products and outcomes of each actor in the subsequent cases in the next chapter.

5.5 Offerings and Business Models for the Involved Actors in the Business Cases

In a typical value chain, such as the ones established in the aforementioned examples, each actor contributes in a tangible (e.g., with an intermediate or supplementary product) or in an intangible way (e.g., technology expertise essential for a Grid installation) to the resulting end-product. Based on each contribution there is a linked business model established for this actor in order to earn economic benefits. For example, in the case of a technology integrator that sets up a Grid infrastructure, the resulting earnings come from offering IT services, that are one of the core competences and services portfolio of that particular company, to its customers. These are presented by case in the "Associated Products or Services" column of table 5.2.

Table 5.2: End products and associated models for the different scenarios

Most popular Grid Business Cases in the market	Main actors involved	Associated Products/ Services	Applicable BMs per actor
1. Company utilises an internal Grid solution as a virtualisation technique to improve the utilisation of resources (also known as the "Enterprise Grid")	The company	None. Solution is utilised for mini-mising costs	None directly.
	Grid s/w and applica-tion providers	Software (e.g. middle-ware)	– Software or Application provi-sioning (SaaP) – Open source
	Systems integrator (can be the same with the Grid s/w provider)	–	– IT services – VAS (e.g. consulting)
2. Company rents external computing resources through the internet with Grid being the under-lying infrastructure on the provider's side	The company	None. Can be used indirectly to support other services provi-sioning or to optimise internal processes and products	- None if used to optimise internal processes – IT/Web services/ SaaS if used as infrastructure for a solution
	Resources provider (e.g. Amazon & Sun) – See case No. 5	Services offered as SaaS – See case No. 5	SaaS/HaaS/IaaS based
3. Company Grid-enables existing application or develops an application optimised to run over the Grid (BEinGRID BEs cases) and offers it to external clients	The service or appli-cation provider (the company)	Service or Application	– SaaP if offered through a license – SaaS if offered for renting over the net
	The user that either buys or rents the solu-tion	May use the applica-tion to deliver new products/services or optimise existing	Many options such as VAS
	The Grid software provider	–	– Software or Application provi-sioning (SaaP) – Open source
	Systems integrator (can be the same with the Grid s/w provider)	–	– IT services – Value-added serv-ices (consulting)

4. A group of companies forming a VO in order to gain benefit from common use of resources (CERN is an example of this as well). Case also known as "Partner- Grids"	The users (VO participants)	– None if used for current processes and products optimisation – Services offered as SaaS	– N/A if used for optimisation – SaaS for new services
	Grid s/w and application providers	Software	– Software or Application provisioning (SaaP) – Open source
	Systems integrator (can be the same with the Grid s/w provider)	–	– IT services –Value-added services (consulting)
	Resources provider – if external computing resources are utilised (e.g. Amazon and Sun)	Services offered as SaaS	– SaaS/IaaS based
5. Company acts as a computing resources provider e.g. the "Amazon", "Sun", "IBM" etc cases	The resource provider (the company)	Services offered as SaaS	– SaaS/IaaS based – Utility computing based
	The users that buy resources on demand – See Case No.2	None. Can be used indirectly to support other services provisioning or to optimise internal processes or products	– None if used to optimise internal processes – IT/Web services/ SaaS etc if used as infrastructure for a solution
6. Company provides Cloud Computing Services with Grid as the underlying infrastructure (most popular emerging scenario). E.g. the Amazon, Google, IBM, Microsoft etc cases	The Cloud Computing provider	Cloud Computing Services provided mainly as SaaS	– SaaS based – SOA based – IT-as-a-Service – VAS (e.g. consulting)
	The users that purchase Cloud Computing services	–	– None if used to optimise internal processes – SaaS/SOA etc if used as a service component for another solution

Furthermore, there are cases like that of example 1 where the company adopts a Grid solution for internal purposes. In these cases there may not be a directly resulting product to be offered to external customers. However, this should result in optimisation of internal processes or offer more efficient and economic provisioning of other products. Depending on the particular scenario we can match existing or known business models to the different players as listed in the last column of this table.

The list of possible BMs as observed from the table includes the following:

- Already existing and utilised models in the market or minor adaptations of them like the VAS, SaaS, SaaP (mainly for Grid middleware) or the IT-Services one for offering consultancy services.
- The already used Open Source BM, where a version of the software such as Grid middleware is provided for free with benefits arising from the community further developing the product and contributing with ideas that can help evolve this into a more complete product. Also economic benefits may be expected from the reputation gained for the company and economies of scale and scope.
- Emerging models such as the IT-as-a-Service or SOA based services where the new products are designed to run in new architectural environments, such as Cloud Computing and SOA, and are expecting to derive revenue from the users of these architectures and services.
- Evolution or alternative configurations of existing models such as the Utility computing or ASP evolving into HaaS (Hardware-as-a-Service) or IaaS to match the requirements of Grid in a Cloud environment. Many of these concern the transformation of infrastructure capabilities as fixed costs into variable costs by applying the SaaS business models to infrastructure.

The next section elaborates more on the scenarios presented in the table by discussing specific examples from the market today.

5.6 Analysis of Examples of Business Cases

The previous two sections were dedicated to the most popular business cases in the market, the main actors that are involved and the added value Grid can bring to these business cases and the associated products or services. In this section several different examples are introduced in order to demonstrate and highlight such business cases. These examples are real business cases that already use Grid internally or in the offerings/products of their companies. Next, after presenting the Grid business case a correspondence of the main actors and the applicable business model by each actor is briefly presented (Gridipedia 2008).

5.6.1 The eBay (Business Case 1)

One of the most representative companies for the first presented business case in table 5.1 is eBay's auction site (http://www.ebay.com/). eBay is the Internet company that runs ebay.com, the well-known online auction and shopping website, where people and businesses buy and sell goods and services worldwide. eBay provides a safe online marketplace where anyone can go to trade products reliably. This is the main service that is offered and the customers are charged a small fee. The main characteristics of eBay's infrastructure are the massive growth, the constant change, the low latency in all processes and the capability to support a very high rate of transactions.

In 1999 eBay faced a series of service disruptions. In particular, over three days, overloaded servers shut down temporarily without warning, meaning users couldn't check auctions, place bids or complete transactions during that period. This led the company to re-design its IT infrastructure, rebuilding its data centers according to a Grid-type architecture in order to achieve a more flexible, scalable and reliable infrastructure (Gil 2009).

The eBay Grid infrastructure consists of many small servers supported by some higher-processor-count servers for a federation of back-end databases. eBay can actually run on as few as 50 servers, which can be Web servers, application servers and data-storage systems. Each of these servers runs separately, but communicates with the others, thus each of them is notified if there is a problem in the network. Growth can easily be achieved by adding servers to the Grid accordingly to demand. Despite that, an infrastructure of only fifty servers is quite adequate in order to run the site, eBay has one hundred and fifty servers more, in sets of fifty, in three different locations, which are spread all over the world. These servers store the same data, so if the main system crushes there are three other mirror systems to pick up the slack. This new architecture based on Grid allows very high fault tolerance, the elimination of the single point of failure, and easy growth together with low operating costs (Gibson 2004, MacFarland 2006).

eBay's business case is a representative example of a company that utilizes an internal Grid solution to improve the utilization of its resources. Its revenues are not originated from the Grid itself but from other sources (auctions, advertizing etc). However Grid is used to increase the performance of the operation while also reducing its expenses. Interconnecting all those servers in a Grid attains the aforementioned performance enhancements, the high exploitation of resources, cost-efficiency and economies of scale, due to the fact that interconnection of all machines improves the utilization of each one. The main actor in this business case is the company itself since it constructed its own Grid.

Table 5.3: Example of Grid business case 1: The eBay

Grid Business Case	The Grid benefit (value-proposition or added-value)	Main actors involved
1. Company utilises an internal Grid solution as a virtualisation technique to improve the utilisation of resources (also known as the "Enterprise Grid"): **eBay**	For the company: Performance differentiation, cost-efficiency, high exploitation of resources.	The company: **eBay** Grid s/w and application providers: **eBay**

5.6.2 CERN (Business Case 4)

The example of this section corresponds to the fourth category of table 5.1 and table 5.2. A representative real-life scenario of this specific business case is CERN, the European Organization for Nuclear Research, one of the world's largest and most respected centers for scientific research. Its subject is fundamental physics, namely finding out what the Universe is made of and how it works. The world's largest and most complex scientific instruments are used in CERN to study the basic constituents of matter, i.e. the fundamental particles. By studying what happens when these particles collide, physicists learn about the laws of Nature. One of the largest experiments that is currently in progress is the Large Hardon Collider project (LHC). The main purpose of LHC is to discover more about how the universe began and what it's made of. This will be achieved by colliding beams of protons and ions at a velocity approaching the speed of light. Those records generated by this experiment are predicted to occupy 15 Petabytes of memory every year, an enormous amount of data that cannot be accommodated either by a single IT infrastructure nor by a supercomputer. However, thankfully, Grid technology provides a solution to effectively store and process this huge amount of data.

CERN leads a major Grid project, the LHC Computing Grid, which is dedicated to providing the processing power and storage capacity necessary for the LHC. Grid was adopted because of the benefits Grid provides, such as the much lower cost, the flexibility and the ease of upgrades, compared to a single large and complex machine. In order for the network of computers to be able to store and analyze data for every experiment conducted at the LHC, a special middleware for Grid architecture was developed.

The structure of the system is organized into three tiers. The first is CERN's computing system, which is dedicated to process the information at the beginning and divide it into chunks for the other tiers. There are twelve second-tier sites that are located in several countries whose purpose is to accept data from CERN over dedicated computer connections. When the LCG gets up to full capacity, it will be made up of around 200,000 processors, mostly located in 11 academic computing clusters around the world, as shown in table 5.4, that will let around 7,000 scientists conduct experiments related to the collider, submitting their calculations to the LCG, which will farm them out around the network according to the supply and demand for resources (Cern 2006, Johnson 2008, Ranger 2005).

Table 5.4: CERN Grid Nodes locations

University Partners	
Forschungszentrum Karlsruhe in Germany	KFKI Research Institute for Particle and Nuclear Physics in Budapest, Hungary
Istituto Nazionale de Fisica Nucleare with its National Computer Centre in Bologna, Italy	University of Tokyo in Japan
ACC Cyfronet, Cracow, Poland	Moscow State University and the Joint Institute for Nuclear Research in Russia,
Port d‹Informació Científica in Barcelona, Spain	Academia Sinica in Taiwan
Particle Physics and Astronomy Research Council (PPARC)	CCLRC Rutherford Appleton Laboratory in the UK
The Department of Energy (DOE), US	National Science Foundation, US
University of Prague in Czech Republic	IN2P3 Computer Centre in Lyon, France

The collaboration of so many institutions around the world for the same purpose form a Virtual Organization (VO) which uses Grid in order to gain benefits from the common use of their resources. In fact, even with the VO, the operation of this project could be hard due to the enormous size of data that need to be processed. The partner institutes who are the actors of this scenario – despite their worldwide distribution – gain through the use of Grid and their collaboration benefits from a performance that the current technology could not otherwise provide.

Table 5.5: Example of business case 4: CERN

Most popular Grid Business Cases in the market	The Grid benefit (value-proposition or added-value)	Main actors involved
4. A group of companies forming a VO in order to gain benefit from common use of resources: **CERN**	– Performance benefit through the collaboration. Enables a purpose which was not possible using the current technology and a classic architecture.	The users (VO participants) as shown in Table 5.4
	–	

5.6.3 The Amazon and Sun (Business Cases 5 and 2)

In this subsection different examples of the same business case – namely 5 – are merged with examples of business case 2 and are presented together, in order to demonstrate the relationship between the two distinct business cases and to show how the same company can be a different actor in each different business case. Business case 5 of table 5.1 can be characterized as common since big IT companies that own a large infrastructure follow this business model in order to provide their under-utilised and/or specially provided computing resources to customers.

Amazon and Sun are examples of such companies that provide such computing resources.

Amazon (Amazon Web Services 2009) is an American electronic commerce company based in Seattle. Amazon owns Amazon.com that began as an online bookstore, but now sells DVDs, music CDs, computer software, video games, electronics, apparel, etc. Furthermore Amazon offers in its catalogue web services for access as well as for integration with other retailers like Target and Marks & Spencer. Amazon offers two interesting web services for developers, namely, Simple Storage Service (Amazon S3) and Elastic Compute Cloud (Amazon EC2).

Simple Storage Service (S3) allows any developer to store and retrieve almost any amount of data by accessing the same "highly scalable, reliable, fast, inexpensive data storage infrastructure that Amazon uses to run its own global network of web sites" (Amazon S3 2009). This allows developers to begin new businesses with little or no up-front investments or performance compromises. The provision of quick, always available and secure access to the company's data is inexpensive and simple. Any file type is allowed to be stored, up to 5GB and can be set as public, shared or private. The service is charged for $0.15 (USD) per GB of storage per month and $0,20 (USD) for each GB of data transferred upstream or downstream.

Elastic Compute Cloud (EC2) is a service that enables developers to use Amazon's computing power for their own needs. It is possible for the user to obtain and configure capacity with the minimum of effort and to have complete control of the computing resources. Also EC2 allows the quick scalability of the capacity of the system in both directions according to the changes in the computing requirements. The developer is charged only for the capacity that has been reserved and due to the very little time that is needed to increase or reduce server instances, it's possible to keep the actual capacity used very close to day to day requirements. EC2 provides developers the tools to build failure resilient applications and protect themselves from common failure scenarios. On the other hand, the architecture of EC2 is simple. The servers that provide the EC2 service are Linux-based virtual machines that are called instances. There are two instance families; the standard one which is well suited for most of the applications and the high-CPU one that includes instances that have proportionally more CPU resources than memory (RAM) and are better suited for compute-intensive applications. The charges for the instances that belong to the aforementioned families are shown in the table 5.6 (Arrington 2006, Garfinkel 2007, Hof 2006).

Table 5.6: Instance types and prices

Instances	Description
Family: Standard *Type:* Small Instance Price: $0.10 per instance hour	1.7 GB memory 1 EC2 Compute Unit (1 virtual core with 1 EC2 Compute Unit) 160 GB instance storage (150 GB plus 10 GB root partition) 32-bit platform I/O Performance: Moderate
Family: Standard *Type:* Large Instance Price: $0.40 per instance hour	7.5 GB memory 4 EC2 Compute Units (2 virtual cores with 2 EC2 Compute Units each) 850 GB instance storage (2×420 GB plus 10 GB root partition) 64-bit platform I/O Performance: High
Family: Standard *Type:* Extra Large Instance Price: $0.80 per instance hour	15 GB memory 8 EC2 Compute Units (4 virtual cores with 2 EC2 Compute Units each) 1,690 GB instance storage (4×420 GB plus 10 GB root partition) 64-bit platform I/O Performance: High
Family: High-CPU *Type:* High-CPU Medium Instance Price: $0.20 per instance hour	1.7 GB of memory 5 EC2 Compute Units (2 virtual cores with 2.5 EC2 Compute Units each) 350 GB of instance storage 32-bit platform I/O Performance: Moderate
Family: High-CPU *Type:* High-CPU Extra Large Instance Price: $0.80 per instance hour	7 GB of memory 20 EC2 Compute Units (8 virtual cores with 2.5 EC2 Compute Units each) 1690 GB of instance storage 64-bit platform I/O Performance: High

Amazon clearly belongs to business case 5. It offers computing resources to its clients and enjoys revenue from renting its own infrastructure. Clients of Amazon can be any individual or company that needs more storage or CPU, especially if needs may change dynamically. The business model that Amazon is following in this specific example is IaaS since it provides Infrastructure as a Service to its customers.

As we mentioned before, Amazon's customers could be any individual or company that needs to use storage or CPU without provisioning its own computing resources either because of the capital cost or because of dynamically changing demand. In the following paragraphs we will present such a customer of Amazon's web services S3 and EC2.

The New York Times (NYT) recently decided to make available to the public all the newspapers that have been published from 1852 to 1922 online. They called this collection of full-page image scans in PDF format as TimesMachine where all 11 million articles are included.

The amount of data to be processed was enormous. It was a series of large TIFF images associated with metadata and article text of the newspapers for 70 years. That meant terabytes of data that had to be processed and stored. Using Amazon S3 they managed to upload and store the 4TB of data while EC2 provided them with the necessary CPU power for the concurrent use of hundreds of machines to read the data, create the PDFs and store them into S3 again, from where the public could reach it within 36 hours (Gottfrid 2008a, Gottfrid 2008b).

By using the infrastructure provided by Amazon, the NYT was able to offer their clients a new service not previously available; the experience of a window into the past from their computers. By using S3 and EC2 from Amazon, the NYT avoided the purchase of the resources required to process and store such an enormous amount of data. In this way, the NYT succeeded in providing a new and exciting service at a set-up low cost. This company follows the second business case as indicated in table 5.1. It rents external computing resources from Amazon, with Grid being the underline infrastructure, and gains all the aforementioned benefits. Both the business cases 5 for Amazon and 2 for the NYT are shown in the table 5.7 indicating how these two companies undertake their specific roles. It is worth noting that the NYT is the user for the fifth business case, while for the second business case is the provider of a service to other users.

Table 5.7: Example of business cases 5 and 2: Amazon

Most popular Grid Business Cases in the market	The Grid benefit (value-proposition or added-value)	Main actors involved
5. Company acts as a computing resources provider: **Amazon**	For the user: Resources provided on demand. Performance differentiation, cost efficiency, service differentiation	The resource provider: **Amazon** The users that buy resources on demand: **The Times New York**
	For the company: revenue generation and reduced costs of offering such a service through virtualisation	
2. Company rents external computing resources through the internet with Grid being the underlying infrastructure on the provider's side: **The Times New York**	For the company: Performance differentiation, cost efficiency, service differentiation	The company: **The Times New York**

Given the success of companies renting external computing resources from large infrastructure providers, this section presents another example of these two business cases. Sun is an American vendor of computers, computer components, computer software, and information-technology services that now provides computing resources to its customers. The company was recently involved in Grid technology, with Sun Utility Grid (Sun 2009g, Sun 2009h) – recently re-branded and offered as a Cloud Computing service (Wikipedia 2009b). Sun Utility Grid is a large commercial Grid that consists of the first global pay-to-play resource. It allows its customers to create jobs and submit an application (Gohring 2006, Singer 2004a, Singer 2004b). Sun Utility Computing for Grid based solutions can start as low as $0.99 per dual CPU node, per hour with a click-through license and a four hour minimum usage requirement. For its all-inclusive, pay-for-use Sun Utility Computing for Midrange Sun StorEdge Systems, pricing can start at $0.80 per Sun Power Unit (SPU), per month. Designed as a Grid computing infrastructure, Sun reported that its pay-per-use offering is perfect for its high-performance computing markets shown in table 5.8.

Table 5.8: Sun Grid's target market

Industry	Applications
Finance/Banking	Risk and portfolio analysis
Energy	Reservoir simulations seismic analysis
Entertainment/Media	Digital content creation, animation, rendering, digital asset management
Manufacturing	Electronic design automation, computation fluid dynamics, crash test simulation, aerodynamic modeling
Government / Education	Weather analysis, image processing
Health Science	Medical imaging, bioinformatics, drug development simulation

Sun, our example in this business case, is the resource provider actor, that offers computing resources and achieves at the same time high utilization through the Grid virtualisation technology. On the other hand the customers that buy resources on demand are the users of this service. The business model that Sun is following in this specific example is IaaS since it provides infrastructure as a service to its customers.

Having demonstrated the provider's view, we will attempt to present a user in this business case. A user, a company named Virtual Compute Corporation (Sun 2009f), utilizes the computing resources of Sun as its infrastructure to provide its services. At the same time this company provides its services, with the help of the Grid infrastructure rented from Sun. The business case into which this company falls is the second one. Virtual Compute Corporation is a global provider of on-demand high-performance computing resources and IT infrastructure management for commercial and government entities. Its target market consists of companies in the energy industry, space sciences and life sciences with the main purpose the provision of tailored solutions that meet customers' unique needs. Virtual Compute Corporation uses the Sun Grid Compute Utility to handle work from its energy industry customers that exceeds the capacity of its own IT infrastructure. The Sun Grid gives Virtual Compute Corporation the ability to quickly and efficiently run compute-intensive jobs for its customers. Using Sun Grid the company has now the required flexibility to meet variable demands instantly through on-demand compute resources and this effective and quick response to the requirements of the customers provides the company with a competitive edge. However this was not the only benefit since the company saved up to US$3 million and two months time by avoiding build-out of additional infrastructure to handle customer's projects.

The example of this company is a demonstration of a client of Sun as the fifth business case category indicates. At the same time the same company is a provider of a service as the second business case indicates. In this last case the company rents external computing resources through the Internet with Grid being the underlying infrastructure on the provider's side here being the Sun company. The company needs Grid for performance differentiation and uses it to provide services to other companies following a SaaS business model.

Table 5.9: Example of business cases 5 and 2: Sun

Most popular Grid Business Cases in the market	The Grid benefit (value-proposition or added-value)	Main actors involved
5. Company acts as a computing resources provider: **Sun**	For the user: Resources provided on demand. Performance differentiation, cost efficiency, service differentiation For the company: revenue generation and reduced costs by offering such a service through virtualisation	The resource provider: **Sun** The users that buy resources on demand: **Virtual Compute Corporation**
2. Company rents external computing resources through the internet with Grid being the underlying infrastructure in the provider's side: **Virtual Compute Corporation**	For the company: Performance differentiation, cost efficiency, service differentiation	The company: **Virtual Compute Corporation**

5.7 Conclusion

In this chapter we have presented an overview of the main Grid Business Models, namely those that can be adopted from the Grid application and service providers in the market. In order to achieve a deep understanding of these models the process of their creation needs to be defined. The first step in this process is the understanding of the new technology but the most significant one is the correct definition of the added value (the proposition) that this technology can offer to potential customers and/or users. Furthermore, a set of business enablers, or Grid benefits are presented;

these being driven from the aforementioned most important requirement. The Grid business enablers are: "Common Use of Resources and Infrastructure as a Service (IaaS)", "Collaborative and VO" and "Software as a Service (SaaS) and advanced software architectures" Grid benefits. The actual economic benefits for each one of those categories stem from one or more of: a) the offering of dynamic resources using Grid infrastructure, b) services or software that take advantage of the collaboration environment and c) services that are designed or Grid-enabled to be provided as SaaS. These Grid benefits can be found in the most popular business cases today, which are presented in the chapter. Each business case is associated with the aforementioned Grid benefits and with the main actors involved that constitute the basic value chain. Taking into consideration the tangible and/or intangible way an actor is contributing to the resulting product, a Business Model (BM) is then established for this actor, in each business case. In particular, Grid services or products are currently offered according to existing BMs in the market or some adaptations of them like the Value-added Services, SaaS, SaaP (mainly for Grid middleware) or the IT-Services BM for offering consultancy services. Also free versions of software such as Grid middleware can be provided through a Grid BM. The benefits in this model arise from the additional development of the product from the community and the contribution of new ideas that can help this to evolve into a more richly featured product. Thus, economic benefits may be expected from the reputational gain of the company and economies of scale and scope. Another important BM is the IT-as-a-Service, where the new products are designed to run in new architectural environments such as Cloud Computing. Finally, Grid BMs based on existing models such as the utility computing or the ASP are currently evolving to or integrating HaaS or IaaS business characteristics and helping to give rise to Cloud Computing.

6 Grid Value Chains – What is a Grid Solution?

Juan Carlos Cuesta, Karita Luokkanen-Rabetino, Katarina Stanoevska-Slabeva

6.1 Introduction

As explained in chapter 3 and 5 before, a Grid solution can be provided in several ways: as a Grid-enabled application, as Utility computing or as Software as a Service. Grid-enabled applications in internal IT deployments are specific software applications that utilize in-house Grid infrastructure. Utility computing is referred to as the provision of Grid computing as service on external resources. In a Software as a Service (SaaS) based solution applications run on external servers and are used in a one-to-many model with a Pay-As-You-Go (PAYG) funding model or a subscription funding model that is based on pre-defined amounts of usage.

Thus, Grid solutions vary from simpler Software as a Product (SaaP) cases to more complex SaaS solutions. While the simplest cases might be handled by one or two providers, the more complex cases consist of many kinds of services, resources and capabilities, and the provision of such services almost always require co-operation between several market actors. In other words, a Grid solution is a sum of many interacting market actors that own distinct resources and capabilities needed to create value for the end user. Moreover, the provision of Grid-based services is different from traditional service provisioning, and it is more complex in terms of contractual agreements, licensing models, definition of SLAs, accounting and billing aspects.

This all can be quite complex for the end user: Who is providing what? What does a Grid solution consists of? Who is the end user contacting with? How many providers need to interact to deliver the service? In this section we aim to build a clear picture about the Grid market and the essential market players. In the first section we describe the main market players involved in the provision of Grid solutions, and the exchanges and interactions between them. In the second section we illustrate the value networks[1] for three different kinds of scenarios – Grid-enabled application as internal deployment, utility computing, and SaaS – and give examples of the market players active in those sections of the market at the moment.

---

[1] The value networks presented in this section are based on the analysis of 25 real world business pilots who developed Grid technology based solutions in the BEinGRID project. It is important to notice that they are used to illustrate different scenarios in a general level, and many kinds of variations can be found in the market. More examples of Grid value networks and value chains can be found in Gridipedia (2009).

K. Stanoevska-Slabeva et al. (eds.), *Grid and Cloud Computing: A Business Perspective on Technology and Applications*, DOI 10.1007/978-3-642-05193-7_6,
© Springer-Verlag Berlin Heidelberg 2010

6.2 What a Grid Solution Consists of

As mentioned before, a Grid solution is a result of collaboration between several market players whose products and services together form the solution provided to the end user. Next we will discuss what is really needed to build such solutions focusing on the most essential Grid market players and the exchange flows between them.

6.2.1 The Grid Market Players

One common concern for newcomers in the Grid market is the wide variety of terms, definitions, and names relating to different market players. Often it might be almost impossible to make sense who is providing what to whom. Moreover, when reading these names and roles in IT news and publications it becomes very evident they are often used in an inconsistent manner.

While it is not our remit here to turn this inconsistency into an organised consistency, we aim to clarify the main market players and their roles as Grid service providers. The methodology for our analysis originates from the Porter's well known value chain concept (Porter 1985) which has been widely used in the business literature to describe the value creation system among organizations. The analysis of value creation systems helps to understand how the different entities work together to produce value, and the value creation analysis is considered as an efficient tool for tracing product flows, showing the value adding stages, identifying the key actors and their working relationships.

Even as Porter's value chain defends its position as one of the most applied analysing tools, more dynamic value creation analysis methods have appeared to describe the multiple interactions found in a networked economy. Value network is one of these methods, which enables the analysis of multidirectional, complex, and dynamic value creating relationships between two or more individuals, groups or organizations (Allee 2002, Pil and Holweg 2006, Tabscott et al. 2000). We define value network as a web of relationships that generates economic value and other benefits through complex dynamic exchanges. We apply value network analysis to illustrate and explain the dynamics which prevail in Grid technology based solutions, and provide an overview of players involved and how the competences and value adding activities are divided among them (Stanoevska-Slabeva et al. 2007).

The following table lists the most important market actors involved in the provision of Grid solutions. They are grouped into four clusters based on the activities they perform and the positions they take in the Grid value networks:

- **Utility Computing core cluster** comprises all the actors that provide the basic capabilities and resources required for offering infrastructure as a service, i.e, for providing utility computing. The environment created by the utility computing core cluster is the basis for providing applications in a SaaS manner by the Application/ SaaS provision cluster.
- **Application/SaaS provision cluster** includes the market players that are needed to deliver the applications and services to the end user.

- **Telco sub-cluster** is always needed to complete the two previous clusters. The telco cluster provides the connectivity and communication services among users and utility and/or SaaS providers. It is formed by the providers of the communication equipment and communication services. This type of cluster can be led by the network operator or network service provider.
- Some actors from **Value Adding Service (VAS) and consultancy sub-cluster** almost always complete the other value networks. This sub-cluster contains a wide range of actors that provide many different services to complete the solution, such as the integration into the products of different actors, and other specialised services (e.g. backroom functions like billing and insurance).

Table 6.1: Grid market players

Cluster	Actors
Utility Computing core	**Resource/Infrastructure provider** is in charge of providing the equipment (hardware, network and system resources) on which the Grid implementations run.
	Resource/Infrastructure operator gives access to the equipment and manages its use.
	Grid middleware provider delivers libraries and executable codes that implement the Grid functionality (standards and either lower, middle or upper software).
Application/SaaS provision	**Service Provider provides** software that is usually added to platforms or targeted to special niche markets. The service provider offers services that run on the technology in question. These service providers often have strong relationships with application providers or with operators. The main driver behind this business participant is that external service providers can offer their services to operators and application providers,
	Software provider/Application provider is the first customer of a specific platform. An ISV (Individual Software Vendor) makes and sells software products that run on one or more computer hardware or operating system platforms on top of development packages to integrate software with the respective technology
	Application service provider (ASP) supplies computer-based services to customers over a network. Software offered using an ASP model is also sometimes called on-demand software.
Telco or connectivity	**Telco network (equipment) provider** delivers equipment (telco hardware and network resources) that build the telco network.
	Telco network operator implements a broadband communication network, and offers real time functionality and easy access. It's an enabler of communications.
	Telco network service provider sells bandwidth under specific business criteria. Many times the network service provider and the network operator is the same company.

Value adding and Consulting	**Systems integrator** is in charge of the integration of the different modules (software, hardware) required to complete the Grid solution and brings the players together. With a technical role, the Systems Integrator may also do consultancy work besides installation, deployment and IT support.
	Solution provider offers a package of network, middleware and applications for the end-user. It may also provide consulting or Grid expertise so that solutions to problems can be determined and implemented.
	Business consulting offers a solution to business problems, optimises processes, assists in preparing the business case, quantifies and does due diligence on business models, advises on business development and marketing.
	IT consulting provides expertise for assistance in information technology processes, computing services and training.
	Payment provider owns infrastructure and management to allow the payment transactions between actors. The financial flows among the different players may be managed by a separate player, it can be a financial entity, a business consulting company, a broker, a network service provider, etc.
	A **reseller** is a company that resells/distributes an existing solution provided by another company. It can be the whole suite, or one or more of its components.
	The **broker** is an intermediary, who can also be the trusted third party. Brokers can advise which Grid solution is the best fit for a particular requirement. It provides services based on specific quality of service levels required by the end-users.
	Trusted third party deals with contractual arrangements, financial settlements, and authentication of users (e.g. a bank or other financial entity).
	Risk management services minimize the cost of services by finding the best deal from existing offerings based on the customer's requirement and profile.
	SLA/contract development and management services provide both consultancy and software tools to monitor and manage SLAs.
	Insurance services provide financial assistance in the case of system disruptions and/or failures causing monetary losses.
	Content providers create, aggregate and distribute data, information and experience that are delivered to the end-users. The end-user can also provide the content themselves. Such content may be required to be processed and/or transformed in order to build the final "product".

It is important to note that not all the roles listed in the table are required to build a Grid solution. The composition is determined by how simple or complex the solution may be. In addition, it is quite common for one market player to perform more than one role. In these cases, the delivery of a complex solution can be simplified.

Figure 6.1 displays an example of a generic Grid value network based on the clusters and market players described above. The flows between market actors form a set of sub-clusters or mini-networks which are led by a market actor that bundles the offerings of several players together and joins them with the offerings of other players to form a complete solution.

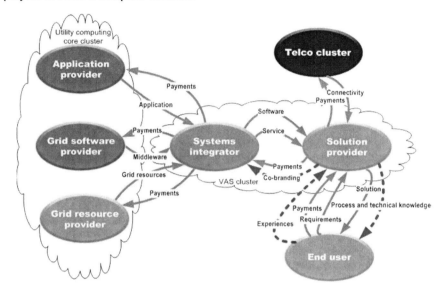

Fig. 6.1: A general Grid value network

A general Grid value network consists of the market players from utility computing, VAS, and telco clusters. In this example the system integrator and solution provider (VAS cluster) have important roles to bundle the solution and to coordinate the flows among the market players. The system integrator is in charge of integrating the application, Grid middleware and Grid resources (received from the market players of utility computing cluster) are needed to build the solution. The system integrator provides this solution (in forms of software and services) to the solution provider. The solution provider completes the solution by acquiring connectivity from the telco cluster, and provides the solution for the end user. The relationship between solution provider and end user is interactive, and the customer's requirements play an important role in the solution definition. The solution provider also provides different kinds of consultancy services for the end user. The end user makes payment only to the solution provider but it is important to note that the price it pays at the point of delivery includes shares due to all the members of the value chain.

6.2.2 The Flows

The exchange flows among the market players are multiple with variable contents. However, in practical terms the flows in Grid technology based solutions are quite similar to those in any other business and can be divided into three groups:

- the flows of intangible benefits (e.g. technical, market and strategic knowledge, branding, loyalty and confidence)
- the flows of tangible goods (e.g. software, hardware, licences)
- the financial flows[2] (e.g. revenues and payments).

The *intangible exchanges* are mostly informal, and they often have an immeasurable value in forms of tacit knowledge, confidentiality, and reputation. For example a SaaS provider who cooperates with a Grid resource and infrastructure provider with a high prestige super computing centre, can use that reputation as a marketing tool to point out and stress the reliability of his service.

The *flows of tangible goods* are mainly related to software and licences. The licenses and the content of the flows depend on the Grid solution in question. For example when considering commercial software running in an end user's premises (an internal Grid deployment) the following questions become essential: how many and what kind of licenses (e.g. node locked, floating, usage based) are needed, and what kind of payment options are available. If the end user uses an in-house application the license flows (and possible payments) are internal among the different departments of the end user organization. In the external Grid deployment the situation is different, and the service provider has to acquire the licenses from the ISVs (Individual Software Vendor), or have a special agreement with the ISV for the use of Grid-enabled application (Stanoevska-Slabeva et al. 2008).

The *financial flows* represent how the costs and revenues are shared between the different market actors, and they help to understand how the final price paid by the end user is formed. As presented in the value network picture, the payments are most commonly related to the use of computing resources, network connection, software licenses, and different kinds of value adding and consultancy services. Using the Grid value network (fig. 6.3) as an example, we can see that the only market player who receives a payment from the end user is a solution provider. This means that the price the end user pays the service provider covers multiple payments which are distributed to the different market players via normal supplier payments.

Observing the financial flows from the end user's perspective we can distinguish following payments and cost types:

- **One-time investment:** in hardware, software, installation and integration costs necessary to integrate the new solution in the existing infrastructure of the user. Depending on the level of integration of the solution, this amount may be paid to the one player providing the whole service (for example the solution provider)

---

[2] Financial flows are usually considered as tangible goods. However, we separate them for clarity in order to differentiate between different types of flows/exchanges.

or to several of them (for example one or more solution providers and system integrators).

- **Permanent payment:** payments related to run the solution including software licenses, usage of resources and network, and support services and other Value Added Services. As in the one-time investment, how many market players the end user has to pay depends of the level of solution integration.
- **Consumption based payment:** measured consumption of utility computing or SaaS. The end user makes payments to the SaaS and/or application providers on a PAYG basis.

6.3 Grid Value Networks

As seen in the previous section, Grid-based solutions can be complex. But, for the end-user, this complexity is hidden, and the end-user can think they are getting all of the solution from one provider. Normally the player that is in charge of the end-user contact bundles the different offerings into a complete solution and synchronizes different pricing and licensing models, and releases the customer from the necessity of having to deal with several providers. However, in order to evaluate the service provider's capabilities to provide the solution, the end-user should be aware of the main structure behind the solution. Next we will describe value networks for internal (Grid-enabled application) and external (utility computing and SaaS) deployments. Special attention is paid on the end-user's roles as a solution builder and receiver.

6.3.1 Grid-enabled Application (Internal Deployment)

In an internal deployment scenario, the Grid-enabled application runs in an organization's own in-house infrastructure, and the end user's motivation for Grid solution may be to maximize the use of their own existing IT infrastructure. In this scenario the end user's organization already has computing (hardware) resources available (or they will be acquired), and they deploy internal Grid solutions to make more efficient use of these resources, and/or to use additional capacity to run jobs faster. A general value network for internal Grid deployment is present in the figure 6.2. The main market players are:

- *End-user* (normally a department within the organization that uses the Grid-enabled application).
- *Grid resource provider* supplies the hardware needed to run the Grid-enabled application.
- *Grid middleware provider* develops/provides the middleware that is required to create the Grid infrastructure for Grid-enabled application.
- *Application provider* creates a new application or adapts an existing one to be executed over a Grid on top of the interfaces provided by the Grid infrastructure. The adaptation of the application to the Grid is normally done by the application provider, the Grid software provider, or the system integrator.

- *System Integrator* is responsible for integrating the different elements to complete the solution. The system integrator plays a key role in the definition of the solution, and in many cases also covers also the role of Grid software provider based on an existing middleware.

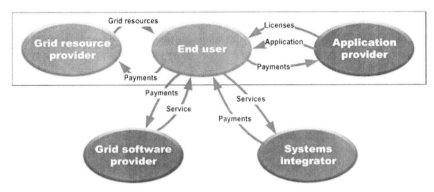

Fig. 6.2: Internal Grid deployment value network

The end-user is an essential player in this scenario, and in addition to the obvious involvement of the solution receiver and user, they may also provide the Grid resources and the application (these three roles are included in the box in the figure 6.2). End-user roles can be clarified as following:

- *End-user as a hardware provider:* The end user already owns the hardware resources where the application runs. These resources can be specialised hardware dedicated only to run the Grid application or equipment that is used for other applications, such as desktop computers whose spare computing cycles can be utilised. In this case, the cost of implementing the application is significantly reduced. In other cases, resources are rented or bought from external providers (Grid resource provider) and deployed on the end user's premises. This role is performed normally by an IT department.
- *End-user as an application provider:* The end-user provides the software application (in-house or custom software) which runs on the Grid infrastructure. The application can either be the existing application, which will be Grid-enabled or a new application what is designed to run directly on Grid infrastructure. In both cases the system integrator has an important role in the software adaptation.
- *End-user as an IT organization:* The IT department leads the Grid project internally and is a contact point for the external providers. It also ensures that the application meets the user needs and manages the provision.

Contact points for the end user: Whether the end-user has a simple or multiple role, the simplest option for it to get the solution is to contact a system integrator who has the necessary knowledge and experience to "Gridify" the current application or to build a new application which have the same functionalities as the current (but not

Grid-enabled) one. In that case the system integrator organises the whole solution. The end user pays the system integrator a one off payment for the settlement of the solution, and the permanent payments for the possible value adding services (new functionalities, tailoring the application, training, maintenance etc.). In the case that end user rents the hardware resources, he/she also makes periodic payments for the Grid hardware provider. Additionally the end user makes the periodic fixed payments for licenses (in the case that in-house software is not used) and ongoing maintenance of the software.

Other option, especially if the end user does not own the application, is to contact directly the application provider who builds and/or gridifies the existing application. In addition to application adaptation, the application provider may also supply Grid middleware and other services (e.g. training and consulting), and even integrate the whole solution. In that case the payments are similar as in the previous case.

The market regarding Grid middleware and Grid-based applications is relatively clearly segmented. There are Open Source Grid middlewares (e.g. Globus Toolkit, UNICORE, and gLite), Grid middleware providers that provide a platform to adapt applications to a Grid environment (e.g. Platform, Grid Solutions, Univa UD, and ProActive), software vendors that migrate their applications to a Grid platform, and IT consulting companies that provide custom solutions. These are all good contact points for end users interested in the internal Grid deployments.

Challenges: Building an internal Grid solution can be a complex project, and the end-user has to be prepared for time consuming migration process which may involve changes in the technical infrastructure, IT governance, and culture. Moreover, it changes the ways the resources are used and computing is performed inside the organization, it may blur the departmental borders, and it also requires changes in the existing applications. Thus, long term planning, effective change management, and real business and technical commitments are essential in order to reduce the risk that the process ends up joining the list of IT projects that went over budget and/or over time.

6.3.2 Utility Computing (External Deployment)

Utility computing is referred to the provision of Grid computing and applications as service either as an open Grid utility, or as a hosting solution for an organization or a virtual organization (VO). Utility computing providers deliver a mix of systems, storage, computing, networking and software capabilities. This capacity offering can be used to underpin many other businesses whose users may be completely unaware of the underlying infrastructure they are using.

This offering is targeted at customers from SMEs to large enterprises and Government departments. For example SMEs may elect to effectively outsource their IT infrastructure to "The Cloud" whereas large enterprises and Government departments may prefer to take care of the day to day requirements internally and handle peak requirements by accessing external services from time to time as and when required. The general value network for utility computing is present in the figure 6.3.

Fig. 6.3: Utility computing value network

The main market players are:

- The *Grid resource provider* is responsible for the provision of the resources on which the application or the virtual machines run. Super computing centres with big computing farms are examples of Grid resource providers.
- The *software/service provider* offers a range of services (computing, storage, security, etc.) for the end users to build, deploy, and run their applications or virtual machines, and one of its core competencies is the management of a massive data centre. The service provider deals with capacity planning to support elastic workloads and track consumption to determine the costs to be charged. It's also usual that these services are provided by the Grid Resources provider, although there may be a gap for third party services.
- The *Grid software provider* supplies the middleware required to run on top of the resources in the Grid. In most cases, all the big market players have built their own Grid infrastructure and developed the middleware internally.

Often these three roles are merged, and one provider takes on all the three aforementioned roles, and builds the whole solution.

Compared to the internal Grid deployment, the role of the end user changes remarkably in the utility computing scenario. While in the first scenario, the Grid adoption may require considerable internal changes, in practice, the latter one just means outsourcing certain IT activities. This outsourcing may range from long term contracts where the end-user outsources all or part of the IT activities to intermittent customers who buy capacity only as and when needed.

Most important flows between the end user and service providers are the services and payments. The end user either pays a fixed fee (e.g. a subscription) or a variable fee for a measured use of a service. A fixed fee normally includes limited computing cycles, traffic, storage and other features such as accounts, and a variable charge for additional consumption of resources. The use based payment is variable, and the amount depends on the consumption of resources.

Contact points for the end user: As mentioned before in many cases the end user can obtain the service from the one provider who also builds the whole solution. Examples of utility computing providers are the "traditional" players like IBM, HP, SUN and newer companies like Amazon, Flexiscale, GoGrid, MediaTemple and Mosso. They provide a high availability platform which is flexible and scalable, and consists of a set of services to create and manage the virtual servers or applications that run on them. Some providers also allow the creation of applications using programming languages (for example Google App Engine).

Challenges and considerations: The decision to outsource IT related activities is always critical. The most common implication of the utility computing, for the end user, is that the activities commonly performed inside the organizational boundaries are performed externally. Several issues are worth of careful consideration. First of all, what kind of activities can be performed outside the organizational boundaries? For example, national data protection laws can prohibit sending certain kind of information outside the country of origin, and/or the end-user may need to consider very carefully what kind of information it is best to keep inside its own organization (e.g. issues related to core competences). In both cases, the data confidentiality and security are of high importance. Secondly, the licensing issues may also require careful consideration. In the case that end-user wants to use commercial software in the external Grid infrastructure it needs to be clarified that the existing licensing agreements are not violated. Thirdly, end user has to evaluate carefully the provider's capacities and capabilities to provide the service (e.g. reliability, scalability, the maturity of the technology), and the service level agreements (SLAs) need to be negotiated carefully, by taking into account business needs, technical requirement, enforceability and redress.

6.3.3 Software as a Service (External Deployment)

SaaS makes software accessible according to a service/utility model. Users don't need to purchase, install and configure a software package in order to have it available on their system as and when they want to use it. They simply access, typically over a browser, the software that is pre-prepared and ready for use at some remote location. Traditional software licenses are usually replaced by the agreements between users and software providers. These agreements, besides specifying the information included in a traditional software license (eg duration, price, etc.), might also contain information about the software's efficiency, reliability, accessibility, etc. SaaS is a good solution for both large organizations and SMEs, and the reasons to choose SaaS are many, e.g. to keep the TCO[3] light, to access the software without paying the fixed licenses, or to complete on-premise licenses with SaaS in the occasional peaks. However, many of the current pricing models are designed for deployments for SMEs, and they break down, from a cost perspective, in large-scale

---

[3] The concept of TCO is used as a financial estimate to help decision makers to determine direct and indirect costs of a product or a system. In computer and software industry TCO is used to estimate the financial impact of deploying an information technology product (hardware and software) over its life cycle (Wikipedia 2009d).

deployments. While the cost benefits of solutions should become evident over time, in the short and medium terms, large-scale deployments might still be more cost-effective in an on-premise model.

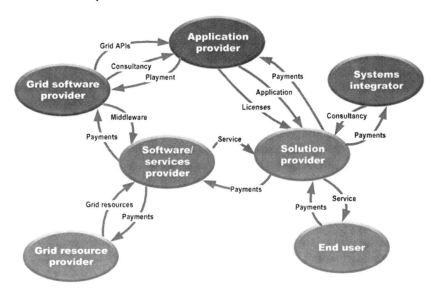

Fig. 6.4: SaaS value network

Figure 6.4 displays the value network for a Software as a Service solution, and it consist of the following market players:

- The *solution provider* is the focal actor who usually organises and provides the solution to the end-user. Its business is to offer the service to the end users, charge them based on the service consumption, and redistribute the payments between the different value network members. Usually the solution provider is active in a specific economic sector and targets the solution to this market segment.
- The *service provider* provides the software services that are used by the end-users with the quality levels specified by the service level agreements. The service provider must be able to support elastic workloads and track consumption to determine the costs to be charged. Often the roles of solution and service providers are unified, and one company provides the solution and the service.
- The *application provider* provides the software which constitutes the SaaS offer. SaaS providers are often companies that specialize in providing SaaS solutions or companies that have extended their product portfolios from SaaP to SaaS.
- The *Grid resource provider* is responsible for the hardware resources where the applications are hosted.
- The *Grid middleware provider* provides the middleware that is required to create the Grid infrastructure in which the Grid-enabled application runs.

The *System integrator* is needed to put all the parts together and bundle the solution, and often it also provides consultancy services besides coordination, installation, deployment and IT support. In addition to the actors and roles defined, other market players that form a VAS cluster (e.g. payment and consultancy providers) are involved.

For the end user, SaaS is a seemingly simple solution, and it promises a fast and easy access to the service without any (or at least any significant) changes in the end user's IT structure, because almost everything is done via the automated web marketplace, with little or no human interference. However, the pros and cons should be always analyzed carefully before making the buying decision, and depending on the SaaS in question (e.g. business critical or peripheral, and its economic value) the IT managers, application users, and legal department (SLA negotiation) should be involved.

Contact points for the end user: in a typical scenario, the solution provider is the contact with the end user, and the most important flows (from the end-user's point of view) are the services and payments with the solution provider.

Today at the market the interesting contact points for the end users are:

- Companies who already possess large infrastructures like Amazon, Google. Microsoft, Dell, Yahoo, IBM, SUN and Apple are already exploring the Grid (the Cloud) in different stadia. They have large infrastructures, have discovered ways to deliver economies of scale on storage unavailable to many other enterprises and/or they have a large position in software provisioning that needs to be defended. Google struck the first blow in February 2007 with its $50 per user, per year enterprise Gmail offer. Gartner estimates that Google's own cost of goods sold for enterprise Gmail is no more than $4 per user per year — with the biggest expenses being electricity and storage. Ultimately, the single greatest cost for e-mail operations in the next 10 years will be level-one help-desk support, bypassing both licensing and operational costs. Providers of utility computing appear to be converging with providers of SaaS to target a wider market (Cain 2008).
- Application providers who want to evolve and are evolving from SaaP to SaaS offerings, e.g. Oracle, PeopleSoft, SAP and Siebel.
- New SaaS providers like Salesnet.com and Salesforce.com.

Challenges and considerations: Despite of the apparent user-friendliness of SaaS, end user should be aware of several issues before the decision to start to use SaaS. Firstly, for the provider SaaS is quite complex and its provision involves often many market players. Moreover, SaaS is a relatively new software provision model, and the business model may not yet be fully developed. Thus, the end-user should evaluate carefully the provider's capacity and capabilities to provide the service in question. In general, the provider's reliability, the system's scalability, confidentiality and security issues are very important issues. Also the Service Level Agreements (SLAs) should be negotiated carefully by taking into account business needs and technical requirements. Secondly, the scope and scale the end-user decides to externalize and the use of certain software (e.g. business-critical vs. peripheral applications) is crucial. It should be taken into careful consideration which kind of effect disruption and/or a complete breakdown, e.g. the possible network problems (down time, latency etc.) might have on the ability of the business to function normally. Moreover, getting a SaaS implementation fully up and running, often takes more time and resources (e.g. integration to existing systems, training, configuration and data migration according) than expected (Roth 2008).

6.4 Conclusions

In this section we have provided an overview of the Grid market players and their roles in a Grid solution provision. Based on their offerings the market players can be grouped into Utility computing core, SaaS/Application, Telco, and VAS clusters which all have their specific functions in Grid value networks and Grid service provision. We have presented Grid value networks to illustrate what a Grid solution really consists of, described the specific roles of each market player and explained how they contribute to build and/or to provide the Grid solution. Also the exchange flows (tangible, intangible and financial) among different market players were described in order to clarify the content of these business relationships. Finally we paid special attention to three Grid solutions (internal Grid deployment, utility computing, and SaaS), and provided examples of possible contact points for the end users interested to deploy these solutions.

7 Legal Issues in Grid and Cloud Computing

Davide M. Parrilli

7.1 Introduction: the Lawyer's Perspective about Grid and Cloud Computing

A business scenario based on the adoption and implementation of Grid and Cloud technology presents many legal issues that have to be taken into account by companies and individuals that plan to start a Grid/Cloud-based business. In general terms, Grid/Cloud technology is not 'neutral', in the sense that it brings several particularities as regards, contractual and security profiles (Parrilli et al. 2008). In other words, a contract between a Grid/Cloud provider and a customer is likely to be slightly different from an agreement between a provider of a different technology (not based on dispersed resources) and a client.

The legal issues that affect a Grid/Cloud-based business are many, and include, just to mention a few, contract law, intellectual property rights, privacy law, taxation, etc. The aim of this chapter is that of providing the reader with some clarifications and guidelines as regards the most relevant legal issues that a typical customer should take into consideration when reviewing the terms for the provision of Grid/Cloud services from a technology provider. Two moments will be specifically analysed: (i) the contract, or contracts, signed by the customer and the Grid/Cloud provider, i.e. formation, validity and enforceability of the agreement(s); (ii) the contractual relationship following the signing of the agreement, in connection with the liabilities of and the remedies at the disposal of the parties. Special attention will be dedicated to security (and privacy) profiles, which are supposed to be the Achilles' heel in Grid and Cloud computing. A few comments will also be dedicated to the most relevant taxation issue. In other words, we guide a typical customer in the process of entering into an agreement with a technology provider and therefore we will follow the negotiations phase (if any) and the signing of the contract. Furthermore, we will identify the risks underlying the contract and explain how these risks can be reduced or avoided. When the agreement is ready for signature, our mission will end.

From a different perspective, then, the goal of the following pages is to show how legal barriers for customers can be reduced, nevertheless taking into account that these are heavily influenced by the business environment in which the Grid/Cloud provider and the client operate. In other words, in business to business (B2B) scenarios (this chapter does not address business to consumer – B2C – issues) the client does not receive special protection from the law, in recognition of the principle that businesses are normally in positions of equal strength during the nego-

K. Stanoevska-Slabeva et al. (eds.), *Grid and Cloud Computing: A Business Perspective on Technology and Applications*, DOI 10.1007/978-3-642-05193-7_7,
© Springer-Verlag Berlin Heidelberg 2010

tiations.[1] This statement is clearly unrealistic given the fact that, in most cases, the Grid/Cloud provider is a big international player and the customer might be an SME or even a micro-enterprise. The latter, of course, will have little or no power to negotiate more favourable clauses and the only option is to sign or not to sign the contract drafted by the technology provider. Nevertheless, the customer should check whether this contract is too risky, in the sense, for instance, that the provider does not take any liability and the customer does not have the right to enforce the contract, or the scope for such enforcement is very limited.

This means that the non-legal categories of trust and reputation will play a pivotal role and will guide potential investors to opt for a Grid or Cloud provider instead of its competitors. Trust and reputation, although very important, are not enough: the customer, in other terms, does not have to be impressed by the brand of the Grid/Cloud provider but should verify whether he gets enough protection under the contract offered to him. Things are different, of course, if the parties are in the position to really negotiate the content of the agreement(s), and in this situation they should balance risks and liabilities between them. It is advisable that the contract(s) is as complete and balanced as possible, in the sense that it should encompass possible situations like non-compliance, litigation, etc and should motivate both parties to respect it.

In other terms, a contract which is too unbalanced in favour of the provider, for instance, is likely to offer him reasons not to supply the services at the promised quality and to favour bigger and/or more 'important' clients. Selection and differentiation between clients is an obvious practice from the business perspective, but it should not damage or discriminate against a certain group of customers. The law and economics literature showed, in fact, that one of the purposes of contract law is "to secure optimal commitment to performing" and, in particular, that "when liability is set at the efficient level, the promisor will perform if performance is more efficient than breaching, and the promisor will breach if breaching is more efficient than performing" (Cooter and Ulen 2004).

In light of these considerations, the first issue to address regards the contracts made by a Grid or Cloud provider and a customer to regulate their business relationship. Special attention will be dedicated to the Service Level Agreement (SLA) and to its potentially related agreements.

7.2 The Contractual Relationship between Grid/Cloud Provider and Customer: the Contract

The provision of Grid or Cloud services by a technology supplier shall obviously be regulated by a contract, or a group of contracts, that will govern the specific

---

[1] The literature pointed out, as regards civil procedure (but the statement is true also as regards other legal issues), that "because the consumer is the weaker party, who often pays in advance for the transaction to take place and cannot influence the unilateral terms of contract that are offered, the balance in relation to jurisdiction leans towards the consumer." (Storskrubb 2008)

'position' of each party in the relationship, i.e. the duties, liabilities, remedies, etc. of each contractor will be stated in the agreement and each party will be bound to respect the obligations contained there. The agreement that plays a pivotal role in a Grid and Cloud scenario is the SLA, which can be defined as "a part of the contract between the service provider and its customers. It describes the provider's commitments and specifies penalties if those commitments are not met" (Leff et al. 2003). As said above, and as frequently happens in the practice, the Grid/Cloud provider and the customer can 'concentrate' all the provisions that will govern their relationship in the SLA or enter into more than one agreement. The SLA will be focused on the most relevant technical specifications linked to the provision of the service, and one of its main goals will be to define the quality of the service (QoS) promised by the supplier. QoS means, more specifically, the availability and performance levels, in other words the level of performance guaranteed (it will be showed *infra* to what extent) by the provider.

All other clauses regarding liability, warranties, confidentiality, etc may be included in another contract (that can be called, for instance, the Customer Agreement), and this is often the case in point with big international Grid/Cloud computing and storage capacity providers. Nevertheless, the reader should be aware that in practice many combinations are possible, e.g. the provision about fees can be included in the Customer Agreement, while liabilities may be regulated by the SLA. The names of the agreements are not really relevant to the ends of our analysis: what is pivotal is the content of some sensitive clauses and the fact that the agreements made by the parties must be legally valid and enforceable. We illustrate this point with an example that involves two imaginary European companies: *SuperICTResources*, a German technology provider, and *SaaSforyou*, a Dutch customer/SaaS provider. If we assume that they negotiate the content of their agreement, we see that it is probably easier for them to have a unique contract (or SLA) instead of a plurality of agreements, unless this is necessary or useful in light of the specific situations and needs of the parties. Especially if more services are involved, it may be convenient to draft a frame agreement, aimed to regulate the overall relationships, and many SLAs tailored to the specific service provisions.

From a different perspective, it is important to point out the distinction – which is relevant from the legal point of view, in relation to the negotiation of contracts and therefore the content of the contractual provisions – between (i) agreements negotiated on a case-by-case basis by the parties (like in the case of *SuperICTResources* and *SaaSforyou*) and (ii) agreements drafted unilaterally by the Grid/Cloud provider and imposed to the client (e.g. if *SaaSforyou* buys Grid or Cloud capacity from Amazon, Sun, etc). In the latter case, the customer, if he wants to buy the services of the provider, can only accept the SLA and the other agreements proposed by the supplier, with no possibility to change or amend the content of the provisions. In this regard, it is unrealistic to expect a big provider, like for instance Amazon, Sun, etc, to negotiate every agreement with its clients because of the high costs of negotiations and the risks of inefficiency linked to this.

Therefore, given the fact, that "a key goal of Grid computing is to deliver management on top of the allocated resources which include for example availability of resources (compute resources, storage, etc) and network performance (latency, throughput)" (Padgett et al. 2005), the typical minimum content of the SLA should be the following:

1. *Availability*: this clause indicates the percentage of time, usually on a monthly basis, in which the Grid/Cloud service supplied by the provider will be available. With this regard, it is very important to point out that Grid computing is expected to increase the quality of the services delivered and therefore the customer has many good reasons to require availability very close to 100 % (the same applies to Cloud computing). In our example, it is realistic to imagine that *SaaSforyou* chooses *SuperICTResources* as technology provider because the latter is able to offer an extremely high availability. In the case of a SLA specifically negotiated by the parties, the customer may be in the position to bargain and obtain a favourable and realistic level of availability. While in the case of a standard SLA drafted unilaterally by the provider the client can only accept or refuse the offer, i.e. he can enter or not enter into the agreement. The business practice shows that big international Grid and Cloud computing providers normally guarantee an availability ranging from 99,9 % to 100 %, and this demonstrates clearly that Grid and Cloud computing has a notable impact on the QoS to which the provider commits himself.

2. *Performance*: the objective of this provision is to assure the achievement of commonly accepted computing, storage, and network element performance capabilities according to the class of hardware and bandwidths installed. Legally speaking, the content of this clause will depend on the infrastructure adopted by the provider and therefore the margin for negotiations, especially if the customer is an SME or a private user (like, we assume, *SaaSforyou*), is usually quite limited.

3. *Downtime and service suspension*: this clause should not find room in an SLA (or other contract) in a Grid/Cloud environment, and in general in dispersed compute resources scenarios, provided that failures at the level of a single server or cluster (i.e. Grid/Cloud component) should be compensated by the other ones. Nevertheless, agreements unilaterally drafted by big international providers often state that access to and use of the service, or part of the service, may be suspended for the duration of (i) any unscheduled downtime or unavailability of a portion or all of the service and of (ii) scheduled downtime for maintenance or modifications to the service.

4. *Security*: this part of the SLA is of fundamental importance as it will commit the provider to a certain level of security in order to protect the information and data supplied by the customer and to prevent harmful components from being delivered to the customers' computers. The client should therefore pay great attention to this clause and, if the SLA is negotiated by the parties, should require that the security standards are set in the contract, so that the provider will be bound to respect them (see *infra* for further details). The business practice shows that the SLAs unilaterally drafted by the big Grid/Cloud players tend not to mention security requirements, so that the customer basically has to trust the supplier. Provided that trust, as pointed out above, is not a legal category, it is highly ad-

visable that the provider accepts to follow and to implement a security strategy aimed to protect customer's data at multiple levels (i.e. mainly data security, data integrity, data privacy). Furthermore, the Grid/Cloud supplier should apply security tools to his systems and should commit himself to maintain the customer's data on secured servers (e.g. located in a custom-built data centre with full physical access control). If the business carried out by the customer concerns extremely valuable data (e.g. financial, medical, etc), the SLA may and should list the names of the employees authorised to have access to the servers. From a different perspective, the customer may have reasons to require that the provider uses only his servers and that he does not outsource Grid or Cloud capacity to other providers, thus limiting the security risks. This may appear to be against the rationale behind Grid (and Cloud) computing paradigm, but it can be reasonable when losing or damaging customer's data could cause serious damage.

5. *Fees*: this clause will regulate the prices that the customer will pay to the provider for the supply of Grid/Cloud services.

6. *Support services*: these are particularly important for the client in order to minimise the damages in case of failures in the provision of the services, and it is advisable that the provider commits himself to respect a certain response time and to be available to solve problems as much and as quickly as possible (e.g. on a 24/7 basis). This also applies to disaster recovery, which should be done as soon as possible by the supplier. The lack of contractual obligations for the provider to do so may result in enormous damages for the customer without the possibility to claim compensation.

Provided this minimum necessary content is in the SLA (or other contract as applicable), the reader should be aware of some remarks as regards the validity of the agreement, more specifically the legal requirements to respect in order to have a contract which is valid and enforceable. This is a matter of national law, and therefore every jurisdiction sets specific rules in the field. Nevertheless, without entering into further details, it is possible to say that an offer made by the offeror followed by the acceptance of the offeree, together with the will to enter into an agreement, and provided that the parties have the necessary legal capacity required by the applicable law, is a valid contract (Beale et al. 2002). An additional requirement is the cause (in some civil law countries, like France, Italy, Belgium, etc) and the consideration (in common law jurisdictions, e.g. England and the United States): the former can be defined as the economic reasons behind the contract (e.g. payment of a fee in exchange for a service or good), while the latter can be described as "what the promise gives the promisor to induce the promise"[2] (Beale et al. 2002).

Special attention should be devoted to the legal capacity of the person who signs the contract, more specifically the employee or director who enters into an agreement on behalf of his company should have the power to do this. A contract signed by a person with no legal capacity can be, depending on the applicable law and on

---

[2] "The delivery of a car, the painting of a house, or a promise to deliver crops may be consideration for a promise of future payment." (Cooter and Ulen 2004)

the circumstances, void or voidable. Another aspect to take into account is whether the SLA and/or the other related contract should be made in written form (with signature of the parties). This also depends on the applicable legislation and, in general terms, the agreement for the provision of a service can be made in whatsoever form in Europe (Beale et al. 2002). With this regard, Article 9(2) of the Rome Convention[3] on contractual obligations states that "A contract concluded between persons who are in different countries is formally valid if it satisfies the formal requirements of the law which governs it under this Convention or of the law of one of those countries." This means that an agreement made, for instance, by a Dutch customer (*SaaSforyou*) and a German Grid or Cloud provider (*SuperICTResources*) is valid if it respects the formal requirements set forth by Dutch or German law.

If the parties are established in the same jurisdiction, Article 9(1), following the rationale behind the abovementioned second paragraph of Article 9 to recognise as much as possible the validity of an agreement (*favor negotii*), points out that "A contract concluded between persons who are in the same country is formally valid if it satisfies the formal requirements of the law which governs it under this Convention or of the law of the country where it is concluded."

The fact that the written form is not a validity requirement for the contract does not necessarily mean that it is not convenient for the parties to have a written and signed copy of the agreement in case it is needed or useful, especially in order to have evidence of the existence of the contract and of its content. In this regard, the Grid/Cloud provider and the customer can make an electronic contract to which the electronic signatures of the parties are attached, or, more traditionally, can make a paper-based copy of the contracts with 'real' signatures. In principle, provided the legal value conferred by the applicable legislation of the European Union (EU) to the electronic signature[4], the two versions of the agreement shall have exactly the same validity and effects.

Finally, we focus on some other important clauses that the parties should include in the SLA (or in another contract, according to the case) or that are likely to be encountered in the agreements drafted by the big international providers:

---

[3] 1980 Rome Convention on the law applicable to contractual obligations (consolidated version) [OJ C 27, 26/01/1998, p. 34-46]. For contracts concluded after 17 December 2009, Regulation (EC) 593/2008 of 17 June 2008 on the law applicable to contractual obligations (Rome I) [OJ L 177, 4/7/2008, p. 6-16] will apply. Art. 11(2) states that "A contract concluded between persons who, or whose agents, are in different countries at the time of its conclusion is formally valid if it satisfies the formal requirements of the law which governs it in substance under this Regulation, or of the law of either of the countries where either of the parties or their agent is present at the time of conclusion, or of the law of the country where either of the parties had his habitual residence at that time." With this regard, Art. 19(1) specifies that "For the purposes of this Regulation, the habitual residence of companies and other bodies, corporate or unincorporated, shall be the place of central administration."

[4] See, in particular, Directive 1999/93/EC of the European Parliament and of the Council of 13 December 1999 on a Community framework for electronic signatures [OJ L 13, 19/1/2000, p. 12-20].

1. *Description of the service*: a clear description of the service provided by the technology supplier, apart from the QoS, will avoid discussions and litigation. The listing of extra services that could be provided free of charge or under payment is equally important.
2. *Modification of the agreement*: this clause should state whether the provider can unilaterally modify the service and the agreement (and, if so, how and to what extent) or whether only modifications negotiated and agreed by the parties are acceptable.
3. *Termination of the agreement*: it is particularly important to state when the contract will end and how it can be renewed (automatically, or after new negotiations and signing of a new contract). Furthermore, the parties should state whether or not they can unilaterally terminate the agreement and, if so, which notice period applies. It is common practice that severe violations of the contractual obligations by one party give the other the right to terminate the agreement. Examples of such violations by the customer include being in default with payments, misuse of the service, attempt to break security mechanisms, bankruptcy proceedings, etc. The agreement should also regulate the effects of termination, like data preservation (the technology supplier could not erase the data provided by the client without permission) and post-termination assistance.
4. *Prohibited services*: it is advisable that the Grid or Cloud provider, in order to avoid any potential liability, requires the SLA or other agreement to include a clause prohibiting the customer to use the Grid/Cloud infrastructure to operate a site or a service that, for instance, permits gambling, facilitates child pornography or other illegal activities, engages in practices like phishing or pharming, distributes viruses, spyware or other malicious applications, violates third parties' copyright, etc.
5. *Licenses*: this provision will state that whatever software, if any, distributed by the Grid/Cloud provider to the customer will only be licensed, under specific terms, to the client (with no transfer of 'ownership'). Usually the license will be limited, non-exclusive and non-transferable.
6. *Confidentiality*: all confidential information regarding either the provider or the customer may not be disclosed without prior authorization during the contractual relationship and for a certain period of time after the termination of the agreement. Confidential information is deemed to be information designated by the disclosing party as confidential or that, given the nature of the information and the circumstances of its disclosing, should reasonably be understood to be confidential. Possible exceptions to confidentiality obligations are, *inter alia*: (i) if the information is or becomes public knowledge (without fault of the party concerned); or (ii) if and to the extent that information is required to be disclosed by a party to a regulatory or governmental authority or otherwise by law.
7. *Intellectual property rights*: the clause will state that every party keeps his intellectual property rights over the service provided, any technology or software supplied and any content or data sent or shared. In particular, the *de facto* situation of enjoyment and use of these rights does not modify the legal situation of 'ownership'.

7.3 The Contractual Relationship between Grid/Cloud Provider and Customer: the Relationship

In the previous section we addressed how the relationship between a Grid/Cloud provider and a customer can be established and we analysed the minimum content necessary for a SLA that regulates such a relation. A contractual connection can be compared to the life of a person: the signing of the agreement corresponds to his birth, the breaches of the contract and liabilities to sicknesses, the contractual and extra-contractual remedies to the medicines taken to cure the illness, the termination of the agreement to his death. The focus of this section will be on the life and on the sicknesses of this imaginary person whose name is contract.

It is pivotal to also point out that the contractual relationship between a Grid/Cloud provider and an end user undoubtedly depends on the negotiating power of the parties, and this is in particular true as regards liabilities of the technology supplier. As it will be shown *infra*, big international providers, when dealing with 'normal' customers (basically individuals and small businesses) tend to exclude as many of their liabilities as possible, so that the risk is almost entirely borne by the customer. This means that, in practice, a person or small undertaking willing to enter into Grid/Cloud-enabled business should be aware of the fact that, unless he is able to negotiate specific and more favourable clauses with a technology provider, he will basically have few if any remedies in case the technology provider does not supply the services according to the promised QoS or if he does not provide them at all because, for example, his business is wound up. This topic is extremely important and has a great impact on the operations of the customer, but firstly the reader should be acquainted with the law governing the contract, i.e. how the contractual relationship is managed from the legal point of view.

7.3.1 The Law Applicable to the Contract

As we said above, *SuperICTResources*, a German technology supplier, provides Grid or Cloud capacity to *SaaSforyou*, a small enterprise established in the Netherlands. The parties enter into an SLA which regulates their contractual relationship in its entirety, from QoS and security to liabilities and termination. The content of the agreement is quite wide and the negotiators, who do not have a legal background, do not take into account a very important question: which law will govern this SLA?

We will provide the reader with an answer (focused on the applicable European legal framework) to this question, pointing out firstly that it is extremely advisable that the contract states expressly which law is applicable to it, in order to avoid potential problems linked to the interpretation of the applicable legal sources (that may be, in some circumstances, rather obscure). The contracts unilaterally drafted by big international providers always have such a clause and, if the supplier is an American company, it is highly likely that the applicable law will be one of the States of the federation. This poses practical problems for European customers that are not familiar with American law and can be expected to increase the cost of litigation or disputes due to the need to consult a local expert.

At European level, the legal source that indicates which law will be applicable to the contract made by *SuperICTResources* and *SaaSforyou* is the abovementioned Rome Convention, which states – Art. 3(1) – the basic principle that "A contract shall be governed by the law chosen by the parties."[5] In our example the negotiators forgot to choose which law will govern the contract, and therefore Art. 4(1) is applicable, and thus "To the extent that the law applicable to the contract has not been chosen in accordance with Article 3, the contract shall be governed by the law of the country with which it is most closely connected."[6]

Two issues have to be addressed: firstly, what does it mean 'governing the contract'? Then, how is it possible to assess to which country the agreement is most closely connected? The answer to the first question can be found in Art. 10(1) of the Convention, pursuant to which "The law applicable to a contract…shall govern in particular: (a) interpretation; (b) performance; (c) within the limits of the powers conferred on the court by its procedural law, the consequence of breach, including the assessment of damages in so far as it is governed by rules of law; (d) the various ways of extinguishing obligations, and prescription and limitation of actions; (e) the consequences of nullity of the contract." This mean that, in our example, the governing law will assess how *SuperICTResources* must deliver the services, how the agreement must be interpreted, how much damages (if any) the company has to pay to the customer for breach of contract, etc.[7]

The latter issue can be solved in light of Art. 4(2), pursuant to which "It shall be presumed that the contract is most closely connected with the country where the party who is to effect the performance which is characteristic of the contract has, at the time of conclusion of the contract, his habitual residence, or, in the case of a body corporate or unincorporated, its central administration. However, if the contract is entered into in the course of that party's trade or profession, that country shall be the country in which the principal place of business is situated or, where under the terms of the contract the performance is to be effected through a place of business other than the principal place of business, the country in which that other place of business is situated." In the above example, provided that the performance

---

[5] This provision then points out that "The choice must be expressed or demonstrated with reasonable certainty by the terms of the contract or the circumstances of the case. By their choice the parties can select the law applicable to the whole or a part only of the contract." Paragraph 2 then specifies that "The parties may at any time agree to subject the contract to a law other than that which previously governed it, whether as a result of an earlier choice under this Article or of other provisions of this Convention. Any variation by the parties of the law to be applied made after the conclusion of the contract shall not prejudice its formal validity…or adversely affect the rights of third parties."

[6] Furthermore, "Nevertheless, a separable part of the contract which has a closer connection with another country may be by way of exception be governed by the law of that other country."

[7] Art. 10(2) then points out that "In relation to the manner of performance and the steps to be taken in the event of defective performance regard shall be had to the law of the country in which performance takes place."

characteristic of the contract is the provision of the service, the criterion to take into account is that of the principal place of business. In this case it is likely that *SuperICTResources* is established in Germany and the service is provided from there, therefore German law will be applicable.

The solution would not be different even if the Grid/Cloud provider has its principal place of business outside the EU. Although the Rome Convention is a source of European law (Quigley 1997), its applicability is universal, and as a consequence, pursuant to Art. 2, "Any law specified by this Convention shall be applied whether or not it is the law of a Contracting State." If *SuperICTResources* would be established, for instance, in Israel, the laws of this country would be applicable to the agreement with the Dutch company *SaaSforyou*. The same conclusion can be reached for contracts concluded after 17 December 2009, day of entry into force of the abovementioned Regulation 593/2008, provided that Art. 4(1)(b) sets forth that "a contract for the provision of services shall be governed by the law of the country where the service provider has his habitual residence."[8]

Having said that, it is advisable that the parties state in the agreement which law governs the contract and the contractual relationship between them. Which law will be applicable, i.e. the law of the country of the provider or of the customer (or hypothetically the law of a third country), is a matter of negotiation between the parties. For the technology provider it is undoubtedly more logical to insist for the adoption of 'his' law with the aim to simplify the management of his customers and of possible disputes and litigation.

The same applies as regards the individuation of the competent court or, in more general terms, of the system adopted to solve the disputes arising between the parties. These have the possibility, in fact, to decide that all future disputes between them will be solved out of court, i.e. with an Alternative Dispute Resolution (ADR) proceeding. This means that a private referee, or a group of referees, will judge the dispute and find a solution. It would go beyond the scope of this chapter to provide the reader with an in-depth analysis of ADR systems, therefore we will focus only on the jurisdictional (i.e. before a State judge) dispute resolution mechanisms. At European level the most relevant legal source is Regulation 44/2001 on jurisdiction and the recognition and enforcement of judgments in civil and commercial matter.[9] This Regulation allows assessing which court is competent to judge the disputes between the Grid/Cloud provider and the customer.

Going back to the above example, let us imagine that the negotiators of *SuperICTResources* and *SaaSforyou* forgot to include in the SLA a provision

---

[8] For the notion of 'habitual residence' pursuant to Art. 19(1) of the Regulation, please see *supra*. It is interesting to highlight here that paragraph 3 of Art. 19 states that "For the purposes of determining the habitual residence, the relevant point in time shall be the time of the conclusion of the contract."

[9] Council Regulation (EC) 44/2001 of 22 December 2000 on jurisdiction and the recognition and enforcement of judgments in civil and commercial matters [OJ L 12, 16/1/2001, p. 1-23].

about jurisdiction, so that in case of litigation they do not know which court will be competent. The basic principle, set forth by Art. 2(1) of the Regulation, is that "Subject to this Regulation, persons domiciled in a Member State shall, whatever their nationality, be sued in the courts of that Member State." The first problem to solve regards the determination of the domicile of the parties, in light of the consideration that "with contracts made over the Internet, it is difficult to determine where the party is domiciled, even though the plaintiff can identify the party and locate the transaction" (Wang 2008). Art. 60(1) gives the solution and says that "a company or other legal person or association of natural or legal persons is domiciled at the place where it has its: (a) statutory seat, or (b) central administration, or (c) principal place of business."[10] We can assume therefore that *SuperICTResources* is domiciled in Germany and *SaaSforyou* is domiciled in the Netherlands.

In order to assess whether German or Dutch courts will be competent, it is necessary to refer to Art. 5(1), which sets a so-called 'special jurisdiction'. To be more precise, a person or company, domiciled in an EU Member State, may be sued in another Member State (contrary to the principle of Art. 2) "in matters relating to a contract, in the courts for the place of performance of the obligation in question.[11]" The expression "place of performance of the obligation in question" seems rather obscure and of difficult practical implementation: point (b) of Art. 5(1) specifies with this regard that this place shall be "in the case of the provision of services, the place in a Member State where, under the contract, the services were provided or should have been provided."

Subsequent literature reasonably pointed out that this criterion is likely to encounter major difficulties when applied to e-commerce scenarios (Gillies 2001[12]; Wang 2008[13]). In our view, in case of Grid services (and the same applies to Cloud services), it is extremely difficult, if not impossible, to assess the place of provision of the services, so that the application of the relevant provision of the Regulation encounters major obstacles. The statement, proposed in the literature as regards Internet, that "businesses fear that the determination of Internet jurisdiction could be uncertain because unlike paper based contracts, online contracting is not executed in one particular place" (Wang 2008), is even truer in a Grid/Cloud scenario. The solution to this issue is left to the courts that have to implement the Regulation, when a

---

[10] Art. 60(2) sets a special rule for British and Irish companies: "For the purposes of the United Kingdom and Ireland 'statutory seat' means the registered office or, where there is no such office anywhere, the place of incorporation or, where there is no such place anywhere, the place under the law of which the formation took place."

[11] Art. 5(1)(a).

[12] "Whilst it is to be applauded that the European Union sought to distinguish between the place of performance of goods and services, what definition will be given for the place of performance of digital goods or services purchased on-line has yet to be tested."

[13] According to Article 5(1)(b) of the Brussels I Regulation, the place of performance should be deemed to be the place of delivery. Since it is very difficult to ascertain the place of performance with digitalized goods involving online delivery, in my opinion, the recipient's place of business should be considered as a connecting factor."

solution that makes sense from the technological and legal point of view needs to be found[14].

What we said so far shows the necessity for the parties to state in their SLA or in another contract which court will be competent to judge their disputes[15] (Leible 2006). This possibility is recognised by the Regulation, and art. 23(1) in fact states that "If the parties, one or more of whom is domiciled in a Member State, have agreed that a court or the courts of a Member State are to have jurisdiction to settle any disputes which have arisen or which may arise in connection with a particular legal relationship, that court or those courts shall have jurisdiction. Such jurisdiction shall be exclusive unless the parties have agreed otherwise." In the above example, *SuperICTResources* and *SaaSforyou* can decide that, for instance, the court of Amsterdam or that, more generally, Dutch courts[16] will be competent, and no other courts in principle could judge the disputes arising from the contract(s) between the parties.

The reader should be aware that this clause[17] shall be in writing or evidenced in writing, pursuant to Art. 23(1)(a)[18] and, with this regard, paragraph 2 of Art. 23 points out that "Any communication by electronic means which provides a durable record of the agreement shall be equivalent to 'writing'". This means that "a contract stored in a computer as a secured word document (i.e. a read-only document or document with entry password), or concluded by email and a click-wrap agreement falls within the scope of Article 23(2)[19]" (Wang 2008). As regards click-wrap agreements, "it seems to be preferable that the party receives the text of the choice-of-court clause (including the other provisions of the contract) separately, for instance

---

[14] It has been pointed out in the literature that "there is still a latent complexity and a necessity for citizens or small enterprises, as either claimants or defendants, to have access to intricate legal analysis if they are to be fully aware if their rights and the potential business risks and transactions costs." (Storskrubb 2008)

[15] It has been pointed out in the literature that "a well-drafted contract, which has factual links with more than one country, will contain a choice of jurisdiction or court clause. This is often referred to as an "exclusive" clause, providing that all disputes between the parties arising out of the contract must be referred to a named court or the courts of a named country." (Wang 2008).

[16] In this case the national rules of civil procedure will apply to determine which judge will be *in concreto* competent.

[17] The choice-of-court can be a clause in the SLA (or other contract) or a standalone agreement. The requisite of the written form apply to both cases.

[18] Unless the following point (c) is applicable: "in international trade and commerce, in a form which accords with a usage of which the parties are or ought to have been aware and which in such trade or commerce is widely known to, and regularly observed by, parties to contracts of the type involved in the particular trade or commerce concerned." The agreement made by clicking on an 'I agree' button in a webpage seems to be the case in point, provided that it is common practice to conclude contracts in this way on the Internet.

[19] "This provision covers the agreement on a choice-of-court clause by exchanging e-mails. E-mails provide a durable record because they are saved either in the mailbox or on the hard disk and because they can be printed out on paper. An electronic signature according to the rules of the Signature Directive is not required." (Leible 2006)

in a pop-up window that can be printed and saved as an html, doc or pdf file" (Leible 2006). In practice it is advisable that the Grid/Cloud provider adopts this technique in order to avoid any doubt as regards the validity of the contract.

Finally, we want to highlight that very often the SLA or other contract drafted unilaterally by big international technology providers state that the competent court will be an American court, for the very fact that these companies are established in the United States. These clauses are not negotiable and this means, in practice, that the customer may not be able to enforce his rights due to the high cost of overseas litigation[20], given the fact that "to decide whether to initiate a suit, a rational plaintiff compares the cost of the complaint and the expected value of the legal claim" (Cooter and Ulen 2004).

7.3.2 Liabilities of the Grid/Cloud Provider

One of the most important issues for the customer is the liability of the Grid/Cloud provider, i.e. when he will be liable and for what. The basic legal principle, if not stated otherwise in the agreement, is that the supplier will be liable if he does not deliver the promised services at all or if he does not achieve the contracted QoS. Therefore, in these cases, he shall pay damages (direct, indirect, consequential, etc according to the applicable legal framework), if any, to the customer, and the parties can state that the provider will pay a certain amount of money in case of non-compliance, even if the client did not suffer any real and measurable damage.

However, the application of the legal principle of liability (expressed, for instance, by Art. 1218 of the Italian Civil Code, Art. 1142 of the French and Belgian Civil Code, § 280(1) of the German Civil Code), can be limited by the parties in their agreement, and this is (very usually, if not always) the case in point in the contracts (SLAs, Customer Agreements, etc) unilaterally drafted by big international technology providers. The customer should read very carefully the clauses on liability and above all those regarding limitation of liability, for the very fact that in practice the supplier can be in the position to decide if and to what extent it is convenient for him not to respect his contractual obligations without the risk of having to pay damages. The importance of these clauses as regards security issues will be more specifically assessed *infra*.

Before analysing the limitation of liability frequently imposed by the big technology providers, it is important to point out that, even if no contractual limitations are set forth in the agreement, the supplier will not be liable if (i) he did not have the possibility to respect his contractual obligations or if (ii) the customer, with his positive or negative behaviour, made the delivery of the service impossible or extremely difficult. In other words, if the Grid or Cloud provider cannot supply the service due to, for instance, a power outage, Internet failures, a natural disaster like an hurricane or a violent storm, etc – in the English-speaking countries, these facts are called 'acts of God', and often the French expression *force majeure* is widely used – (Beale et al.

---

[20] "In America, each side usually pays his own legal costs. In Europe (and much of the rest of the world), the loser usually pays most of the winner's legal costs." (Cooter and Ulen 2004)

2002), he will not be liable for that. From a different perspective, if, for instance, the Grid/Cloud provider expressly states that certain system or software requirements are necessary in order to receive the service, and the customer does not update his systems or does not comply with such requirements, the provider will not be liable if the service cannot be delivered.

Having said that, the legal limitations of liability are not enough to 'protect' the Grid/Cloud providers and let them maximise the profits with little or no risks of being sued and being found liable to pay damages, especially in innovative business sectors in which it is not always clear to assess whether the contractual obligations have been respected and, if not, who is liable for that. For these reasons, non-nego-tiated (i.e. imposed) agreements that state that the provider does not warrant (i.e. guarantees) that the service will function as described in the SLA and that it will be uninterrupted or error free are common. In other words, the technology supplier will not be responsible for any service interruptions, including, but not limited to, the so-called acts of God.

In practice this means that the customer will take all the risks and that he is required to simply trust the Grid or Cloud provider, without receiving any legal guarantee that the service will be supplied as expected and promised in the SLA. Legally speaking this is a case of obligation with no sanction, and the supplier is in the position to decide if and how to deliver the service. According to the law and economics literature, this kind of agreement is not efficient, provided that "coopera-tion is efficient when the promisor invests in performing at the efficient level and the promisee relies at the efficient level" (Cooter and Ulen 2004), but it is undoubtedly very convenient for the provider.

From this consideration we can infer that an SLA (or other contract) negoti-ated by a Grid/Cloud provider and a customer should balance the risks between the parties and should 'motivate' both of them to respect their obligations (provided that the main and more or less only obligation of the customer is to pay the fees for the service). This implies that, for instance, the agreement should prevent the Grid/Cloud provider from reducing the quality of the services delivered to the customer in order to satisfy the requests of other, more demanding and/or more important, clients and, if he decides to do so, he should at least pay the damages suffered by the former customer or to compensate him in a different way.

Such a different way is usually the service credit system. It is common practice that the SLA states that, in case the availability level or, in general, the QoS has not been reached during a certain period of time, e.g. on a monthly or yearly basis, the customer will be entitled to receive a 'credit' equal, for instance, to 10 % of the bill for that period. To make an example, the SLA between *SuperICTResources* and *SaaSforyou* states that the availability of the service will be 99,95 % on a monthly basis and that, if such level has not been reached, the customer will be entitled to receive a service credit of 10 %. In a certain month *SuperICTResources* is able to provide the service only for 85 % of the time, and this means that in the next month *SaaSforyou* will pay his bill with a 'discount' of 10 %.

First of all, service credits will usually not be applicable in the case of an act of God (e.g. the availability level could not be reached due to failures at the level of

the Internet network) or in other circumstances stated in the SLA (usually, unavailability of the service that results from any actions or inactions of the customer
or any third party, that derives from the client's and/or third party's equipment,
software or other technology, etc). Secondly, and from a different perspective, it
is important to highlight the distinction between service credits and liability for
damages. The above example is useful to explain this distinction. The SLA between
SuperICTResources and *SaaSforyou* sets forth, apart from the applicability of the
service credits, that the Grid/Cloud provider will not be liable for any direct or indirect damage suffered by the customer and arising from the non compliance with the
promised QoS. *SaaSforyou* needs the provision of Grid/Cloud capacity to supply
services based on the SaaS paradigm to other companies that require a fast and efficient service with few if any failures. In some cases, like for instance the provision
of Grid/Cloud-based services to hospitals, the client of the service provider may
need a completely uninterrupted provision of the service in order to save lives and
avoid expensive medical litigation.

As said above, we can imagine that *SuperICTResources* delivers in a certain
month the service only with an availability of 85 %, and if the fee for the service is
set at € 1,000 per month, *SaaSforyou* will pay the next month only € 900. The service
credit does not take into account the damages possibly suffered by the customer, like
for instance the loss of clients or the damages (if any) he has to pay to his clients[21].
In the most dramatic scenario, contractual failures of the technology provider, especially if they are frequent, may have serious consequences on the customer's business and this explains the absolute necessity for the client to negotiate and balance
the risks with the Grid/Cloud provider in the SLA (or other contract).

7.3.3 Security Issues: Further (potential) Liability of the Grid/Cloud Provider

All the abovementioned elements of a typical SLA (or other contract) in a Grid or
Cloud scenario, like QoS, availability, performance, etc are undoubtedly of pivotal
importance. An unstable or unreliable Grid/Cloud provision can create severe
problems to the customer and ultimately can damage his business. Nevertheless,
if a customer is unsatisfied with a technology provider, he can terminate the
contract and start a new relationship with another supplier. At least in principle,
a client who is not happy with the supply of the Grid/Cloud service can move to
another provider before it is too late, i.e. before his reputation is badly affected and
his clients migrate to another service supplier. *SaaSforyou*, for example, can
terminate the contract with *SuperICTResources*, which is often in breach of its
obligations as regards availability and QoS, and enter into a new agreement with
another provider before *SaaSforyou*'s customers decide to opt for a different SaaS
supplier.

---

[21] The SLA between *SaaSforyou* and the clients, in fact, can state that the former will not be
liable for any damages suffered by the customer, at least in case the failure to provide the
service is due to Grid/Cloud outages.

When we talk about security risks, in practice this possibility, often does not exist. In other words, the customer who provided data or content to the Grid/Cloud supplier may suffer fatal consequences if such data are lost or damaged. An example will clarify the point. *SaaSforyou* provides simulation services for aerospace companies using the paradigm of SaaS and, specifically, it collects data from the clients in order to create tailored simulations. In order to make such simulations, which require huge compute capacity, *SaaSforyou* opted for the Grid or the Cloud, and therefore the clients' data are processed in the *SuperICTResources*'s infrastructure before being delivered back to the final customers. One day, for technical reasons, the data processed in the Grid/Cloud network gets corrupted or lost, so that *SaaSforyou* is not able to deliver the promised simulations to the clients. The damage for the company is huge, in terms of image, reputation and, ultimately, it affects the existence of the enterprise. *SaaSforyou* could not foresee this problem and therefore it just has to face and solve the consequences. The company will expect some sort of compensation from the technology provider and for these reasons the contractual clauses on security and limitations of liability are absolutely fundamental. From the technology provider's side, he is supposed to limit (or to try to limit, during the negotiations) as much as possible his liability for security failures, while the customer should try to allocate the risks to the supplier. If the SLA (or other agreement) is negotiated between the parties, the customer should try to avoid clauses similar to those frequently imposed by big international providers.

These provisions often state that the technology supplier will have no liability for any unauthorised access or use, corruption, deletion, destruction, loss etc of any customer's data or content, howsoever caused. In other words he does not guarantee that he will be successful at keeping such data and content secure. In the case of Grid/Cloud-based storing capacity, the provider may state that he does not warrant that the data stored by the customer will be secure or not otherwise lost or damaged. These clauses shift all security risks onto the customer, who should be aware of that. These practices by big international market providers of Grid/Cloud-capacity provision has induced many practitioners and commentators to point out the security risks of Grid and Cloud computing (Brodkin 2008) and ultimately we could even wonder whether the use of dispersed resources will prove to be a successfully business model.

What should the customer ultimately do to protect his business? It is advisable to follow a twofold strategy: firstly, the client should require the provider to list his security measures and systems in the SLA. A well drafted and complete clause commits the technology supplier to adopt some specific standards, and in this regard a provision like 'the provider will do his best to keep customer's data and content secure' is too vague. In fact, in case of litigation, it will be necessary to assess whether the provider really did his best to adopt security measures, therefore concrete criteria should be preferred. At the same time, the list of security measures shall be flexible enough to contemplate future updates, so the provider must be obliged to respect the most recent and efficient security measures even if they are not listed in the SLA. If the parties do not draft this clause, the abovementioned general legal principle of liability applies and, *in concreto*, the provider will not be liable if he can prove that he was diligent in protecting the customer's data. Nevertheless, proving this may be cumbersome. The same applies to the client if he wants to prove that the supplier did not implement in his systems the best (or at least adequate) security measures. The standard of care required to the debtor, i.e. the Grid/Cloud provider, depends on the applicable national legislation, and of course it can be difficult to assess what 'care of a reasonable person' or 'reasonable care and skills' in practice mean. The relevant legal sources are, for instance, Art. 1147 of the French civil code, Art. 1176 of the Italian civil code, § 276(1) of the German civil code.

Secondly, the security obligations of the provider shall not be without sanction. It is pointless for the customer if, the supplier who commits himself to keep the data and content secure, is not liable for not doing so. The relevant clause in the SLA (or other contract) therefore should balance the risks between the parties and should state specifically that the provider is liable for not guaranteeing the protection of the customer's data and content and he is not liable whenever security measures shall efficiently be adopted by the client himself. This means, in practice, that the customer shall be obliged to use encryption technology to protect his data and content, to routinely archive it, etc. At the same time, the provider shall not be liable for the security risks at the level of the transmission of the data, e.g. on the Internet, if such transmission (or a portion of it) is not under his control.

Similar considerations apply to the relationship between the customer (in our example, *SaaSforyou*) and his clients. The SLA (or other contract) should balance risks and liabilities between the parties and should clearly state that the processing of the client's data is made using a Grid or Cloud infrastructure that may be owned and managed by a third party or parties. Regarding security issues, keeping the end user fully informed is surely the best strategy.

7.3.4 Privacy

Together with security issues, privacy has to be assessed as part of the contractual relationship between the Grid/Cloud provider and the customer. First of all, according to the applicable European sources[22], privacy should be a concern of the parties only if some personal data are processed. Pursuant to Art. 2(a) of the Data Protection Directive, personal data "shall mean any information relating to an identified or identifiable natural person ('data subject'); an identifiable person is one who can be identified, directly or indirectly, in particular by reference to an identification number or to one or more factors specific to his physical, physiological, mental, economic, cultural or social identity". In other words, phone numbers,

---

[22] Namely Directive 95/46/EC of the European Parliament and of the Council of 24 October 1995 on the protection of individuals with regard to the processing of personal data and on the free movement of such data (Data Protection Directive) [OJ L 281, 23/11/1995, p. 31-50] and Directive 2002/58/EC of the European Parliament and of the Council of 12 July 2002 concerning the processing of personal data and the protection of privacy in the electronic communications sector (Directive on privacy and electronic communications) [OJ L 201, 31/7/2002, p. 37-47].

addresses, e-mail addresses of clients, customers (as far as they are physical persons and not companies[23]), employees etc are deemed to be personal data and should be adequately protected. Conversely, all other sorts of data, like company's information, industrial data to be processed in a simulation, etc are not personal data.

To illustrate which privacy measures should be adopted by the parties we can imagine that *SaaSforyou* offers to his clients solutions in the field of employees' management based on the SaaS paradigm. The customers/end users send data regarding their employees to *SaaSforyou* who process them and deliver back the payrolls and/or calculation of contributions to pay. All this data is processed in the Grid or Cloud of *SuperICTResources*, with which *SaaSforyou* has an agreement as specified in the previous paragraphs. What do the parties have to take into account in order to avoid any breach of legal provisions?

In our case, and the same may apply in similar situations, the companies, customers of the SaaS provider are the data controllers as they determine the purposes and means of the processing of personal data; *SaaSforyou* is the data processor, who processes data on behalf of the controller, following the instructions contractually given by the above customers; *SuperICTResources*, subcontractor of *SaaSforyou*, is also a data processor[24]. The reader should be aware that the distinction between data processor and controller should be assessed on a case-by-case basis and it depends on the level of decision making power of the parties involved. According to the concrete modalities of providing the services and to the opinions expressed by the national data protection authorities concerned, *SaaSforyou* and/or *SuperICTResources* may be deemed to be data controllers, and therefore more stringent requisites will apply (it is therefore highly advisable that the parties verify first the provisions stated in the applicable national legislation and the positions of the competent national data protection authority)[25].

From a practical perspective, then, it is pivotal to state that *SaaSforyou* and its clients shall enter into a contract regulating privacy aspects (to be notified by the

---

[23] The reader shall be aware that as soon as a company/person has or manages data of contact persons within a company, then data protection legislation becomes applicable.

[24] See Art. 2(d) and (e) of the Data Protection Directive.

[25] Therefore, the controller is the person who bears the responsibility to implement the data protection principles and to comply with the obligations they set forth. It is thus important to define clearly who is considered as controller of the data processing. The concept is not always clear and should be distinguished from the processor. Both concepts have been introduced by the 95/46/EC Directive. The controller is the natural or legal person, public authority, agency or any other body which alone or jointly with others determines the purposes and means of the processing of personal data. The processor is the natural or legal person, public authority, agency or any other body which processes personal data on behalf of the controller. Processors are usually sub-contractors who perform specific tasks on basis of the instructions given by the controller. They are compelled to follow the instruction provided and to ensure the security of the personal data they processed. The actual ability to decide upon the purpose and means of the processing will be the core criteria to distinguish controllers from processors. This analysis should be carried out on a case-by-case basis.

client[26] to his national data protection authority), preferably annexed to the SLA, aimed to regulate some specific privacy issues related to the processing of the data provided by each client. In particular, this contract shall describe the modalities of the processing of the data provided by the customer (and with this regard the fact that a Grid/Cloud-based delivery model is adopted, this should be explicitly mentioned), list the security measures applied by *SaaSforyou* and the employees that have access to the data. A fundamental point is also the proxy to subcontract the processing of the data to other companies, like *SuperICTResources*. Without this proxy, which can refer to a specific technology provider or to a list of Grid/Cloud suppliers, *SaaSforyou* cannot outsource the processing of data to another party, i.e. cannot send the customers' data to *SuperICTResources* in order to deliver back the service. This is a very important aspect to highlight, especially in the field of SaaS, provided that the SaaS paradigm relies on the involvement of a technology provider in order to deliver services[27].

Furthermore, if the Grid/Cloud supplier is established in an EU-Member State or in another non-European country that has been acknowledged by the European Commission or the competent national data protection authority as providing an adequate level of protection, there are no particular problems, given the fact that such level of protection to the processed data is supposed to be similar. Things are different if the technology provider is located in a third country (like the United States): in this case the specific regime regulating international transfers of personal data applies and, provided that this involves additional obligations for both controllers and processors, specific contracts may need to be signed based on the model contracts published by the European Commission to that effect[28]. Those contracts are expected to be 'automatically' accepted, when notified, by the national data protection authorities of the Member States. From a different perspective, it is also advisable that *SaaSforyou* communicates to its clients if the Grid/Cloud provider changes, preferably in written form submitting to the customers a proposal of addendum to/modification of the abovementioned privacy contract (please be aware that this applies also when the Grid or Cloud provider/sub-contractor is based in the EU).

Apart from that, another privacy contract shall be signed by the customer/ service provider (i.e. *SaaSforyou*) and the Grid/Cloud provider. A trilateral agreement between service provider/technology supplier/end user is also theoretically possible, although quite unrealistic. This contract, to be notified, if such notification is required by the applicable national legislation, to the data protection authority of

---

[26] Art. 4 of the Data Protection Directive states basically that the place of establishment of the data controller determines the national law applicable to the processing of the data.

[27] In other words: any transfer of personal data between parties involves the signing of a contract regulating privacy obligations of the parties. This includes onward transfers to third parties that should always be notified to counterparts. This point is pivotal in so far as the controller may be subject to an obligation of notification of such transfer to the national data protection authority.

[28] See http://ec.europa.eu/justice_home/fsj/privacy/modelcontracts/index_en.htm (retrieved 27/2/2009).

the country of establishment of the end user (the same as for the privacy contract between end user and service provider), shall basically state the modalities applied to the data processing.

Finally, another important aspect to analyse regards the location of the Grid/Cloud components, i.e. of the servers, nodes, clusters, etc that form part of the Grid or Cloud infrastructure. If such components are located in the EU, no legal problems are likely to arise. If this is not the case, the privacy contract between the end user and the service provider shall indicate in which countries the Grid/Cloud components are located and shall specify that the data will be transferred outside the EU.

7.4 Taxation: Grid/Cloud Computing and the Concept of Permanent Establishment

Taxation is one of the most relevant issues to take into account when a technology provider wants to commercialise Grid/Cloud-based solutions, as it may be a major barrier to financial success of Grid or Cloud businesses. Taxation has to be analysed from many perspectives, and in this paper we will focus on direct taxation (i.e. taxes on income). With this regard, the main issue to assess is the relation between Grid and Cloud computing and permanent establishment.

According to the principles commonly accepted at international level, and set forth primarily by the Organisation for Economic Cooperation and Development (OECD) a business presence (e.g. a branch or a factory: technically speaking, a permanent establishment) of a company in another State justifies the taxation, by the authorities of the State, of the profits generated by that permanent establishment itself.[29] This principle is likely to affect Grid and Cloud providers if they have servers, nodes, clusters etc (i.e. Grid/Cloud components) in several countries. In other words, in case of a transnational Grid and Cloud, the portions of profit generated by its components can be taxed respectively in all the countries where these components are located. This in principle means high compliance costs for technology providers, risks of litigation with the tax authorities concerned and, ultimately, a great uncertainty when calculating the portions of profit generated by each Grid/Cloud component (Parrilli 2008).

These considerations are valid, of course, if those tax authorities believe that Grid/Cloud components are permanent establishments of the technology provider. The general principle, stated by the OECD and followed by many national fiscal administrations, is that servers (and therefore Grid/Cloud components) are permanent establishments of the technology provider if they are fixed, they carry out totally or partially the business of the company and such activities are not of preparatory or auxiliary nature.[30] It must be assessed on a case-by-case basis if these conditions are met, but in principle we can say that Grid/Cloud components are deemed to be permanent establishments of the technology provider and, as a consequence,

---

[29] See OECD, Model Convention with Respect to Taxes on Income and on Capital [as they read on 28 January 2003].
[30] See OECD, Commentary to the Model Tax Convention on Income and on Capital.

the profits generated by them will be taxed in the country where the components are located. From a comparative perspective, many countries (i.e. the United States, France, Italy, Spain, etc) follow this principle, with the notable exception of the United Kingdom (where servers are not considered to be permanent establishments) (Parrilli 2008).

From the practical perspective, this risk can be mitigated through a careful tax planning policy regarding the location of Grid/Cloud components. Technology providers basically have two alternatives: (i) centralise the Grid or the Cloud in one country, so that no issues related to multiple taxation of the same profits and/or right assessment of profits among the components arise; or (ii) locate the Grid/Cloud components in countries where servers are not deemed to be permanent establishments of the technology provider.

The above described tax planning may also be linked to the tax-effective location of the headquarters of the Grid/Cloud provider. If and when the Grid/Cloud components can be remotely managed, the technology supplier can decide to be established (i.e. to locate the central place of management of the company) in a low-tax country while the Grid or the Grid components operate in countries that are attractive from the tax point of view and that have good network connections (the same applies to Cloud computing).

7.5 Conclusions

The main message coming out from the previous pages is that legal issues should not be perceived as barriers to invest in Grid and Cloud computing and to start up a successful business. The law, in a very broad sense, does not prevent Grid/Cloud computing from showing all its potential and proving to be innovative technologies able to create new business opportunities, reduce the costs and maximise the profits of the users. It is nevertheless true that in some circumstances the legal sources are not fully able to encompass all existing scenarios, included in possible Grid/Cloud-based business opportunities. For instance, in previous sections, we saw that the criteria of the provision of the service, set forth by Art. 5(1)(b) of Regulation 44/2001, cannot operate in a Grid or Cloud environment. The use of dispersed resources and the possibility to enjoy and use the services supplied by the technology provider anywhere and everywhere in the world, e.g. through a web portal, makes many legal principles and criteria simply not applicable. In a typical Grid and Cloud scenario, in particular, the volatility of the traditional concept of space is evident. The development of appropriate laws is by definition slow, definitely slower than the development of technology, but this is a natural consequence of the (more or less) democratic process that should guide their creation: discussions take time.

Maybe the future will be a world without laws, or, on the contrary, a world with a huge quantity of laws regulating every aspect of citizens' and businesses' life (and probably this will be the case: if industrial production is declining at global level, lawmakers may be prompted to produce more and more laws). In any case, technology providers and their customers should use their contractual freedom to set their own contractual 'laws' as much as possible. This advice applies also to the existing reality, characterised by many laws that are not able to encompass all business scenarios, and ultimately the reader should not rely too much on the law. It would go beyond the scope of this chapter to assess whether the legal system is complete or not. Personally, we believe that the system is incomplete and open, and the parties may fill its gaps according to their needs. The abovementioned lacuna contained in the Regulation 44/2001 could easily be filled with a contractual clause stating which court will be competent. A few minutes' discussions during the negotiation phase can prevent much longer arguments and uncertainties later – and especially if they result in litigation.

Therefore, whenever it is possible, Grid/Cloud providers and their customers should engage in negotiations aimed to produce a contract which is as complete as possible. They have to think about all major aspects of their future relationship and see how this can be made easy to manage. This means avoiding gaps and doubts in every possible case. If the law that ultimately governs and gives effects to the agreement is incomplete, the contract should strive to be complete and fair, in the sense that liabilities and risks should be balanced between the parties and not completely one-sided.

Nevertheless, potential customers planning to enter into the market of Grid/Cloud-based services should be aware of the fact that SLAs and other contracts imposed by big international technology providers are not fair, at least not according to the common sense of justice and fair play. Buying Grid or Cloud capacity from one of the big players may be cheaper and efficient – but it is not without risks. The customer is required to trust the supplier, but his contractual protection is very limited and it often consists of little more than service credits. We do not want to say that the services these companies provide are not good or that they are likely not to respect what they promise in the SLA. We just want to highlight that possibilities of failures always exist and that the price of such failures will be (more or less entirely) paid by the customer.

Negotiations carried out between more equal parties who can tailor SLAs (or other contracts) to their requirements should balance the risks of failure equally and make Grid and Cloud computing more attractive for the customers and, at the same time, should urge providers to invest in technology in order to be able to supply excellent services and respect all security standards and requirements. The success of Grid (and in general of technologies based on dispersed resources, like Cloud computing) also depends on the contractual practices that the actors in the market create and impose. Fair agreements will undoubtedly render Grid and Cloud computing very interesting for both providers and customers.

PART III: Grid Business Experiments

Introduction

The second part of this book has provided a general view of Grids and Clouds and a thorough understanding of what Grid and Cloud computing are, which the underlying architectures and business models of Grid are, which components a Grid solution is made up of and, finally, which legal aspects are important when moving towards Grids and Clouds.

This third part complements part two by concretizing the general Grid and Cloud description with practical concepts, experiences and findings from the BEinGRID project (see chapter 2). First, technical aspects and challenges of Grids and Clouds are explained in more detail. Based on the results of a broad requirements analysis across all Business Experiments (BEs) involved in the BEinGRID project, a comprehensive collection of common capabilities that exemplify required features of Grids and Cloud solutions is provided. It is furthermore explained how these can be used together to solve business problems. Second, this third part provides real-world evidence of how Grid technology can be commercially applied, and how such applications may be enhanced to benefit from new developments and current trends such as Cloud computing. Four BEs of the BEinGRID project, which represent promising cases and which concern solutions in different economic sectors, are described in detail. Finally, an overview of organizational and governance challenges experienced by BEs during the implementation of Grids and Clouds in practice is presented.

This third part of the book is divided into six chapters. The first chapter deals with technical features important for the commercial uptake and practical implementation of Grid and Cloud computing (chapter 8). Each of the remaining four chapters (chapters 9, 10, 11 and 12) covers one BE and follows the same general structure. First, each BE will be generally described, followed by a description from the perspective of the technology provider. This includes a detailed description of the Grid solution and its technical features as well as how it can be integrated into companies' existing IT infrastructures. Next, the benefits for the user of the solution are described. A concluding section summarizes the findings of each BE and provides lessons learnt. The BE's relation to Cloud computing and a potential adjustment of the technical solution to benefit from current trends as Cloud computing are discussed at the end of each chapter.

The solution covered in chapter 9 comprises a set of remote tools which use highly accurate but computationally intense methods to help in the calculation, and in the virtual verification of radiotherapy cancer treatment plans. This is offered as a service to hospitals and radiotherapists. The BE covered in chapter 10 demonstrates how Grid can be used in the crucial early design phase of a ship building process. Shipyards and their suppliers are provided with access to external computational resources from IT service providers, which are required to carry out the computationally intense ship design and simulations before a ship can go to production or before the shipyard can bid on a tender. Chapter 11 covers a solution that introduces Grid technology into the agricultural sector. The solution allows the composition and monitoring of dynamic supply chains in agriculture food industries using

Grid technology making use of trust-building commercialization support mechanisms. Finally, chapter 12 covers an advanced Information and Communication Technologies (ICT) environment where business services can be integrated with one another across organizational boundaries and domains, and which also provides the means to virtualize the environment where the business services operate. This enables new SaaS models for the business service and infrastructure providers, as well as fast service composition and business flexibility.

The application of Grid computing, be it in form of internal or external high performance or utility computing or in form of support for virtual organizations, results in substantial organizational and IT governance changes and challenges that need to be addressed by companies. The final chapter 13 of part III summarizes the organizational and governance challenges experienced by the BEs during practical implementation of Grid computing.

8 Common Capabilities for Service Oriented Infrastructures – Grid and Cloud Computing

Theo Dimitrakos

8.1 Introduction

The mission of the BEinGRID project was to generate knowledge, technological improvements, business demonstrators and reference case studies to help companies and other organizations to establish effective routes to foster the adoption of Grid and Cloud Computing, which are often summarized under the term Service Oriented Infrastructures (SOI)[1], and to stimulate research to help realize innovative business models using these technologies (for more details about the BEinGRID project see chapter 2). In terms of technology innovation, the BEinGRID team has analysed and classified the technical issues involved and the generic solutions developed by and for the Business Experiments (BE).

The technological advancements and innovations considered in the BEinGRID project have been categorized in thematic areas that were witnessed by BEs either significant challenges that inhibit widespread commercialization and adoption of the technology or where the anticipated impact of the innovation is particularly high. The technological innovation results were provided in different output formats: common technical requirements, common capabilities, design patterns, reference implementations, integration and validation scenarios as well as best practice guidelines.

This chapter presents the main common capabilities that capture the generic functionality that would need to be in place in order to address the identified technical and business requirements identified by the BEs. The required common capabilities have been categorized in the following thematic areas:

- Capabilities for *Life-cycle management of Virtual Organizations* help businesses establish secure, accountable and efficient collaborations sharing services, resources and information. These include innovations that enable the secure federation of autonomous administrative domains, and the composition of services hosted by different enterprises or in-cloud platforms.
- *Trust & Security* capabilities address areas where a perceived or actual lack of security appears to inhabit commercial adoption of SOI. These include solutions for brokering identities and entitlements across enterprises, managing access to shared resources, analyzing and reacting to security events in a distributed infrastructure, securing multi-tenancy hosting, and securing the management of

---

[1] In this chapter, the term Service Oriented Infrastructures (SOI) is used as a summarizing term for Grid and Cloud Computing.

K. Stanoevska-Slabeva et al. (eds.), *Grid and Cloud Computing: A Business Perspective on Technology and Applications*, DOI 10.1007/978-3-642-05193-7_8,
© Springer-Verlag Berlin Heidelberg 2010

in-cloud services and platforms. These innovations underpin capabilities offered in Virtual Organization Management and other categories.

- *Software License Management* capabilities are essential for enabling the adoption of Pay-As-You-Go (PAYG) and other emerging business models, and had so far been lacking in the majority of SOI technologies including Grid and Cloud computing.
- Innovations to improve the management of *Service Level Agreements* cover the whole range from improvements to open standard schemes for specifying agreements, to ensuring fine-grained monitoring of usage, performance and resource utilization.
- *Data Management* capabilities enable better storage, access, translation and integration of data. Innovations include capabilities for aggregating heterogeneous data sources in virtual data-stores and ensuring seamless access to heterogeneous geographically distributed data sources.
- Innovations in *Grid Portals* enable scalable solutions based on emerging Web2.0 technologies that provide an intuitive and generic instrumentation layer for managing user communities, complex processes and data in SOI.

In the remainder of this chapter, we provide an overview of the innovative technical capabilities identified and solutions produced, of the research challenges that were addressed, the commercial drivers that motivated the development of these solutions, and their anticipated business impact (i.e. their "innovation dividend") based on the experience generated by the Business Experiments where these results have been validated.

8.2 Life-cycle management of virtual organizations

The following are often identified as the most significant recurring issues during the B2B collaboration life-cycle (Gridipedia 2009a):

1. The identification and selection of business partners (based on their reputation and the suitability of services that they offer) among an available pool of service providers or consumers.
2. The creation and management of a Circle-of-Trust among the selected partners.

The "VO Set-up" common capability offers a standards-based foundation for business solutions to these problems. This capability facilitates the identification and selection of business partners engaging in B2B collaborations, the creation of a distinct context for each of these collaborations, the creation and lifecycle management of a distinct Circle-of-Trust amongst the business partners involved in each collaboration, and the binding of each collaboration context with the corresponding Circle-of-Trust.

It is useful in typical B2B collaborative scenarios where participants (corporate users, services or resources) have to be identified and trust has to be established between them. A demand for including new participants can appear during the collaboration lifetime, and existing participants may be dropped. The security of the collaboration also needs to be maintained: the businesses participating in B2B collaborations must be able to identify one another, identify messages as coming from other members of the same B2B collaboration, and establish the validity of security claims made by other parties in the B2B collaboration about the identity and entitlements of a user or other resource.

A difference to alternative solutions is that trust between business partners can be aligned with consumer / provider relationships. Most current solutions assume mutual and bidirectional trust relationships between all collaborating partners. This solution, however, allows the establishment of directional trust relationships between each pair of partners and coordinating these directional trust relationships so that they reflect consumer / provider relationships. It therefore supports the evolution of a Circle-of-Trust towards a trust network that reflects supply network relationships. Please refer to section 8.3 for more information about how such trust relationships are enforced between identity brokers and entitlement services.

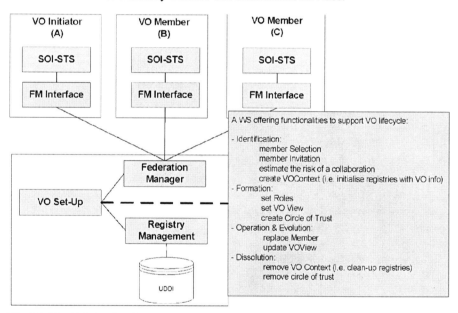

Fig. 8.1: The high-level architecture of the "VO Set-Up" Common Capability

A high level architecture diagram of this capability is shown in figure 8.1 together with a summary of its functionality for each phase of a typical VO lifecycle. To allow the lifecycle management of secure identity federations, the VO Set Up interacts (via the federation manager building block) with the Security Token Service (STS) component presented in section 8.3 of this chapter. The FM (Federation Manager) interface, shown in figure 8.1, is a component offering a programmatic interface that allows the decoupling of the VO Set Up capability from the specific STS implementation, thus enabling the VO Set-up capability to instrument heterogeneous STS implementations that agree on a basic Web-services interface specification.

Each partner of a VO needs to be associated with a Security Token Service (STS), which acts as an identity broker enabling their participation in a Circle-of-Trust. The "VO Set Up" capability and its building blocks can be offered as in-cloud services or be deployed at the site of one of the business partners[2].

This capability combines provider and service registries with identity federation management in a single loosely-coupled solution. Registries are built on top of the Universal Description, Discovery and Integration standard (UDDI 2004) and allow the publication, discovery, and update of VO members and services. The secure federation model builds on the Security Assertion Markup Language (SAML 2005) and WS-Federation (IBM 2006) models. The model is attribute and policy-based and allows the establishment of directed trust relationships that are associated with a common federation context. The following list summarizes some of the most significant improvements achieved by this architecture:

1. It can manage participation in multiple, distinct and co-evolving B2B collaborations.
2. For each B2B collaboration context, the trust relationships between the (identity brokers of) business partners reflect the structure of the value network of this collaboration.
3. It enables evaluating the risk associated with a collaboration based on trust in each participant. In its current implementation, the risk is estimated by evaluating a weighted mean of "reliability" values associated to each member.

The business benefits of this capability include offering instrumentation and coordination layers that act as 'glue' among different capabilities that are required during the life-cycle of B2B collaborations. Without the adoption of such a capability, providers willing to initiate or join in a B2B collaboration would need to deploy, manage and integrate a plethora of bespoke software components and build a bespoke implementation of a complex coordination process on top of them. Implementing different bespoke solutions that offer similar ICT functionality in different application scenarios contributes to increasing cycle-time[3] and cost and intensifying the risk of mistakes and failure due to incompatibility at the edges of bespoke solutions built to serve different objectives.

Early experimentation has indicated that the cycle-times[3] of identification of partners and the establishment of a Circle-of-Trust among selected partners are

---

[2] An analysis reported in Dimitrakos et al. (2009a) indicates that most collaborators are willing to consider an in-cloud capability for this functionality. This preference is particularly high among companies that are used to participating in eCommerce hubs or similar. However, in some situations, deployment at a business partner appears to be equally popular or preferable: these are scenarios where a main contractor is managing a B2B collaboration consisting of mainly subcontractors to the same main contractor.

[3] The term "cycle time" is used here for differentiating the total duration of a process or service delivery from its run time. It covers the sum of value-added processing time and total non-value-added time.

reduced from 60% to 90% (depending on the investment on infrastructure already in place) with analogous cost reductions. Overall, the main benefit of this capability is that it offers organizations of all sizes the flexibility and dynamism they need in order to quickly exploit new business opportunities. This capability has been trialled in Business Experiments including one on a Virtual Hosting Environment for Distributed Online Gaming, which is described in chapter 12 and one on supply chains in agriculture (AgroGrid), which is described in chapter 11.

8.3 Trust & Security Capabilities

The need for security for agile business operations is so strong that, according to Gartner (2009), despite the worldwide economic crisis – or possibly because of it – security aspects such as Identity and Access Management (IAM) remain a critical investment for enterprises of all sizes and market sectors. Through increasing business-level visibility led by data-breach headlines, security spendings continue to rise and take a growing share of overall IT spending. Indeed, IAM alone represents a growing market which accounted for almost $3 billion in revenue for 2006 (Gartner 2009). According to Forrester (2009), security initiatives will focus on: (a) protecting data, (b) streamlining costly or manually intensive tasks, (c) providing security for an evolving IT infrastructure, and (d) understanding and properly managing IT risks within a more comprehensive enterprise framework.

In order to achieve agility of the enterprise and shorten concept-to-market timescales for new products and services, IT and communication service providers and their corporate customers alike increasingly interconnect applications and exchange data in a Service Oriented Architecture (SOA). The way businesses interact is therefore evolving, to:

- A work environment that becomes pervasive with a mobile workforce
- Outsourced Data Centres and in-cloud services
- Integrated business process with customers and suppliers across value chains

The key security challenges come from this evolution of the way businesses interact, include:

- Business process integration with customers and suppliers across value chains
- Many sources of identity and policy enforced over shared IT infrastructure
- Manage access to resources in environments that are not under one's control
- Ensure accountability over a mixed control infrastructure
- Collect evidence about policy compliance for diverse regulatory frameworks
- Deperimeterisation of corporate ICT while maintaining acceptable levels of security in business operations

For security to work, the mechanisms put in place must support, not hinder, such rich and flexible scenarios. The mechanisms must be flexible and adaptive. In line with this analysis, security efficiency, with lower costs and improved service, security effectiveness, including regulatory compliance and business agility and increased productivity were the three main business drivers of innovation for security in SOI

(Dimitrakos et al. 2009b). In this section we focus only on two representative examples of the security capabilities: federated identity brokerage and distributed access management. For a full description of the security capabilities shown in figure 8.2, please refer to Dimitrakos et al. (2009a) and Gridipedia (2009b).

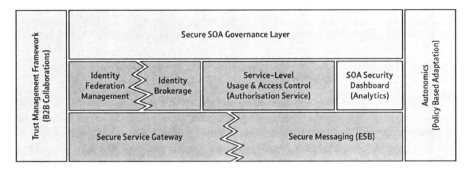

Fig. 8.2: Overview of the security capabilities required by service-oriented enterprises

These security capabilities have been validated by the Business Experiment BEinEIMRT (see chapter 9) demonstrating the secure integration of an in-cloud High Performance Computing (HPC) capability into a regional NHS network in Spain in order to facilitate the fast processing of radiotherapy analysis results while preserving patient privacy and ensuring the correct association between patients and their radiotherapy examination data. Most of these capabilities together with relevant capabilities from VO Management have also been validated in a BE demonstrating a network-centric distributed platform for scalable, collaborative online gaming (see chapter 12).

8.3.1 Federated Identity Management

8.3.1.1 Identity Brokerage and Identity Federation Context Management

This is a capability enabling identity federation and brokerage across business partners. Early developments of this capability stemmed from collaborative research between BT and the European Microsoft Innovation Centre in the TrustCoM project (Dimitrakos et al. 2004). It is a customizable platform for Identity-as-a-Service (IDaaS) provision with technological innovations that resulted in the following differentiators compared to what is currently available in the market:

- The business logic of the Identitty Broker can be optimized for each identity federation context. This innovation enables the application of different authentication procedures, different federated identity standards, attribute types and entitlements on the same user or resource depending on the purpose of a B2B interaction and the scope of the identity federation. The Identity Broker is therefore configured to compose security primitives in a behaviourally distinct instance of a Security Token Service (STS) optimized for the specific context.

- Administrators can author declarative policies to control information disclosure within the scope of each identity federation. Users can also author policies to control disclosure of user-provided data. In effect, different policies may apply on the same personal data used for different purposes in the same scope or used in different identity federations.
- The Identitty Broker has been designed with compliance in mind. An innovative policy issuance mechanism allows associating an administrator's identity with the digital signature of a policy fragment (or a user's identity with digital signatures of user-generated data). It also facilitates providing evidence that policy fulfilment and disclosure of identity data is in compliance with explicitly defined rules of use.
- This capability has been designed for use within Virtual Organizations (VO). It is easy to manage in multi-administrative environments and integrates with related VO capabilities (such as the VO-Set-Up capability described in section 8.2 of this chapter). For each identity federation context, it represents a partner-specific viewpoint of the associated Circle-of-Trust in a way that trust relationships between Identity Brokers respect supply relationships associated with the domain.
- Finally, it is designed for the in-cloud use – it is equipped with a secure web-services remote management interface that enables it to be assembled and managed remotely and provides the basis for an instrumentation layer utilized by collaboration services such as the capabilities described in section 8.2 of this chapter.

An overview of the architecture of the Identity Broker is shown in figure 8.3. In order to allow managing sets of dynamically instantiated services as pluggable modules, the management interface is split into two parts: a set of 'core' management methods and a single 'manage' action that dispatches management requests to dynamically selected modules. The signature of the 'manage' method is parametric and dynamically composed depending on the management interfaces of the modules integrated in a given STS instance of this capability. The flexibility of XML and SOA Web Services technology enables this form of dynamic composition.

Referring to figure 8.3, the core management methods include operations for creating new federation configurations from given specifications, for temporarily disabling or enabling them and for inspecting their values and meta-data. A proxy function forwards aspect-specific management requests to the management module of the respective provider – i.e. the bundle of process and module implementations fulfilling an aspect of the STS operation in a given context.

Each federation context has an associated federation selector – a mechanism that maps a virtual identity (e.g. security token) issuance request or validation message or a management operation to an STS instance configuration. This can be, for example, a WS-Trust request for issuing an XML security token, such as a SAML assertion, in the scope of a given collaboration (OASIS 2007). In a simple case, the federation selector could contain a unique identifier or a collection of WS-Federation meta-data (IBM 2006). When clients request an STS to issue tokens or to validate tokens (e.g. tokens issued by another STS), the STS will try to determine the context of the request, the associated Circle-of-Trust, and whether this can be done based on the security primitives available and the configuration information it holds in its database. A fault message will be returned to the requestor if no suitable collaboration context is identified or there is no matching configuration that can be fulfilled.

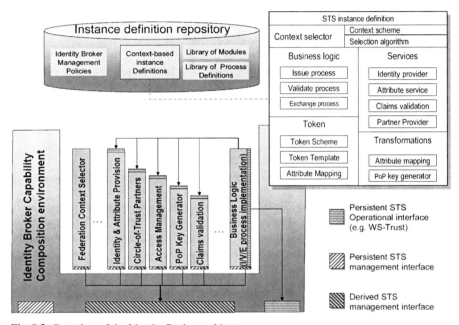

Fig. 8.3: Overview of the Identity Broker architecture

After selecting the matching federation configuration, the Identity Broker instantiates the corresponding STS business logic capability and binds it with the applicable process description. It also instantiates the primitive security functions to be composed by the business logic of the STS, such as the corresponding federation partner provider, the claims provider and the claims validity provider and binds them to the STS business logic process. Each of these internal capabilities of the STS may also have a federation-context-specific configuration, which is loaded upon their instantiation. An innovative execution mechanism by which instance execution takes the form of separate bundles of parallel threads that are allocated distinct memory spaces ensures high-performance during operation.

8.3.1.2 Managing Trust Relationships Among Federated Identity Brokers

Relationships between federated identity brokers form a trust network can reflect the service-consumer relationships for a particular value network and a particular context. Brokers can share the same federation context identifier (i.e., a shared state reference) and associate it with their internal view of the circle-of-trust that reflects their own trust relationships (i.e., local state). The latter may include assertions recognising the authority of those identity brokers they trust in this federation context[4]. Directed binary trust relationships can be defined between an identity broker and each of the trusted identity brokers with which it is associated in a federation context by having the corresponding identity brokers accept these recognition-of-authority assertions.

Depending on the distribution of recognition-of-authority statements, trust relationships in such trust networks may be adjusted to reflect the value chain of the corresponding business-to-business collaboration. The "VO Set-Up" capability presented in section 8.2 utilizes this functionality when coordinating a process that distributes the corresponding recognition-of-authority assertions to the corresponding Identity Brokers that require federating and configures their association with a shared federation context through the Federation Manager interface shown in figure 8.1. For example if (Identity Broker) IB_1 is a prime contractor recognising the authority of subcontractors IB_2 and IB_3 in federation context F_1 and each of IB_2 and IB_3 recognise only the authority of prime contract IB_1 in F_1 then IB_1 will be able to process the validity of tokens issued by any of IB_1, IB_2, IB_3, while either of IB_2 and IB_3 will be able to process the validity of tokens issued by IB_1 and itself only.

This model can be further extended by including a representation of trust metrics such as those proposed in Dimitrakos et al. (2003) and Jøsang et al. (2005).

8.3.2 Distributed Access Management

Distributed access control and authorization services allow groups of service-level access policies to be enforced in a multi-administrative environment while ensuring regulatory compliance, accountability and auditing.

Until recently most of the research into access control for networks, services, applications and databases was focused on single administrative domains and the hierarchical domain structures typical of traditional enterprises. However, the dynamic nature and level of distribution of the business models that are created from a SOI – especially when this incorporates Cloud services – often mean that one cannot rely on a set of known users (or fixed organizational structures) with access to only a set of known systems. Furthermore, access control policies need to take account of the operational context such as transactions and threat levels. The complexity and dynamic and multi-administrative nature of such IT infrastructures necessitate a rethink of traditional models for access control and the development of new models that cater for these characteristics.

The access management capability provides a means for specifying policies that control service-level access and usage in such environments and for automating the necessary decision-making while facilitating accountability and security auditing. It can recognize multiple administrative authorities, admit and combine policies issued

---

[4] One example of such recognition-of-authority assertions include the "business card" assertions proposed by Dimitrakos et al. (2004) and Geuer-Pollmann (2005) – which built on the "information card" concept (InfoCard 2009). Another example includes statements such as the administrative delegation constraints proposed in Rissanen and Firozabadi (2004).

by these authorities, establish their authenticity and integrity and ensure account-ability of policy authoring, including the non-repudiation of policy issuance. The validity of the access policies authored by different administrators is established by means of digital signatures from the policy issuing authority (e.g. the administrator authoring a policy or a recognized authority vetting the administrator) and may be time-limited and must be historically attested.

This access management capability also caters for policies addressing comple-mentary concerns (operational and management) in a multi-administrative environ-ment (see fig. 8.4). It supports policies about the following:

- Subjects access resources in a context, i.e. who can do what on which resource and in which context. These policies are issued (and signed) by administrators authorized to manage resources.
- Constraints on who can author policies access policies, such as the above, or on who can delegate which access rights about which resources in what context.
- Obligations that instruct associated policy enforcement points.

Constrained administrative delegation (Rissanen and Firozabadi 2004) is a feature that allows some administrative authorities to author (delegation constraint) policies that constrain the applicability of (access) policies authored by other administra-tive authorities. Constraints may take the form of rules that apply to a subset of the available attribute types and policy evaluation algorithms. This allows, for example, for safely delegating policy management rights empowering customers to manage the rights of their users directly accessing in-cloud resources in the case of multi-tenancy hosting scenarios, common in Data Centres and Cloud computing.

In all cases, there may not be any prior knowledge of the specific characteris-tics of subjects, actions, resources and so on. Hence, there are no inherent implicit assumptions about pre-existing organizational structures or resource or attribute assignments. This is in contrast to access control lists and traditional role-based access control frameworks in several ways:

- Attribute schemes and attribute assignment processes may evolve independently of the access policies; different authorities can be in charge of attribute defini-tion, attribute assignment, access policy authoring, and access control.
- During access policy evaluation, access decisions may consider environmental attributes and other contextual information in addition to attributes of the subject, resource and action. Contextual information evolves during the policy life-cycle.
- Policy administration and decision making may also be contextualised. Different administration and/or command structures may manage independent life-cycle models and policy groups associated with different contexts. Access policies may also need to be executed within the scope of a particular context that influ-ences the way in which their evaluation algorithms are being applied.

In some cases, it may also be necessary to ensure segregation of policy execution – that is, that ensure no interference between the policies being executed in different contexts. This capability can create new policy stores and policy engine instances on-demand for use in distinct contexts. This is particularly useful where in-depth process and policy separation needs to be achieved including remote Application Hosting and some Cloud Computing platforms.

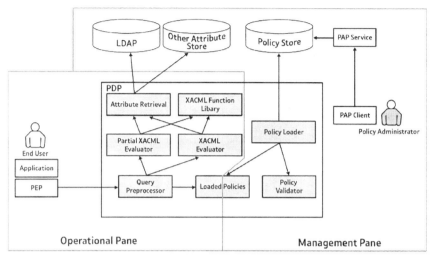

Fig. 8.4: Overview of the architecture of the Distributed Access Management capability

The policy decision point (PDP) at the core of the access management capability may be exposed as a hosted service, be deployed as a component of a policy decision making capability with a larger scope (such as a federated identity and access management capability) or be an integral part of the policy enforcement (PEP) function. It is also possible to deploy the overall access management capability as a managed service, if needed.

8.4 Common Capabilities for Managing Software Licences

Technological innovation on how software licenses are provisioned and managed throughout the service life-cycle is necessary for enabling commercial applications from independent software vendors (ISVs) on SOI and Cloud Computing environments. As explained in Dimitrakos (2009a) small and medium sized enterprises (SME) – especially from the engineering community – stand to profit from this. For example, very few enterprises maintain their own simulation applications. Instead – in contrast to academic institutions – commercial applications from ISVs are commonly used with associated client-server based licensing. The authorization of these client-server based license mechanisms relies on an IP-centric scheme: a client within a specific range of IP-addresses is allowed to access the licence server. Due to this IP-centric authorization, arbitrary users of any shared IT resource may access an exposed licence server, irrespective of whether or not they are authorised to do so. In the absence of controlled access to a local or remote licence server that is suitable for HPC utility and in-cloud hosting, it is often not possible to use commercial ISV applications in these environments. Consequently, a large number of commercial users are not able to use ISV applications in such environments.

The LMA, Licence Management Architecture, capability described in Dimitrakos (2009a) is to our knowledge the first complete solution for HPC utility or Cloud platforms solving this problem. LMA is architected as a bundle of capabilities, shown in figure 8.5, which combined enable managing software licences for shared resource use. One notable innovation has been the ability to transparently reroute the socket-based communication via a SOCKS proxy-chain that is scalable and suitable for supporting legacy and proprietary client-server protocols that are currently used in commercial environments. Another innovation has been a mechanism to authorise access based on one-time credentials (in close analogy to PIN/TAN solutions) that is suitable for use over open infrastructures with varying levels of trust and enable run-time authorisation and context-based accounting.

The LMA capability is generic, independent of specific middleware choice, and features cost-unit based accounting. It enables using licensed ISV applications in HPC utility or Cloud platforms in a wide range of provisioning scenarios. In combination with secure access to the licence server, LMA facilitates the non-interruptive business transition to pay-per-use models while supporting the current legacy technology that used to manage software licences. It therefore enables increasing of the market size in the area of SOI and on-demand Cloud Computing.

Aspects of LMA have been validated in various HPC utility contexts including a BE that demonstrated the use of a large scale multidisciplinary compute Grid to generate cost-effective and optimised solutions for water management (see BE06 2009), and a Business Experiment that demonstrated a solution to reduce the technical and economical risks that are implicit in large and complex ship building projects (see chapter 10).

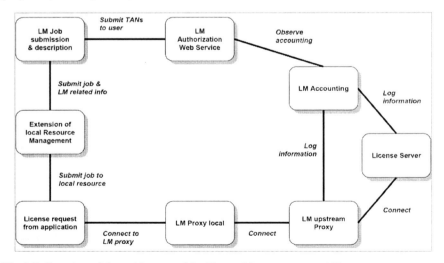

Fig. 8.5: Overview of the architecture of the License Management capability

8.5 Common Capabilities for managing Service Level Agreements

Quality of Service (QoS) is in essence about a set of quality metrics that have to be achieved during the service provision. These metrics must be measurable and constitute (part of) a description of what a service can offer. The QoS of IT services is often expressed in terms of capacity, latency, bandwidth, number of served requests, number of incidences, etc. The QoS of services offered to the customer is sometimes expressed as a package (for example bronze, silver, gold) and in relation to key performance indicators (KPI). In this case, a match between the elements of the scale and measurable metrics relative to the service is provided.

A Service Level Agreement (SLA) defines the QoS of the services offered. Typically SLA is a formal written agreement made between two parties: the service provider and the service user, defining the delivery of the service itself. The document can be quite complex, and sometimes underpins a formal contract. The contents will vary according to the nature of the service itself, but usually includes a number of core elements, or clauses. These define a specific level of service, support options, incentive awards for service levels exceeded and/or penalty provisions for services not provided, etc. Some organizations, attempting to avoid negative connotations, prefer to use the terms SLE (service-level expectation) or SLG (service-level goal) for the definition of the QoS of the services they offer.

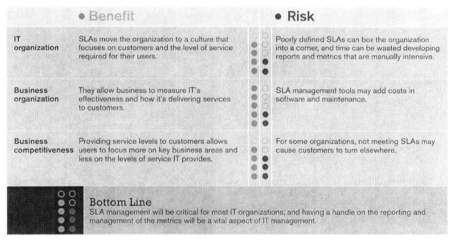

Fig. 8.6: Summary of an impact assessment of SLA use for IT services (Biddick 2008)

Functional service-level agreements attracted high interest from telecommunication service providers in the late 1990s. More recently enterprise, government, and academic environments have been moving towards SLA-driven services as more of the commonly used services are now being delivered online. However, as was the case with the telecommunications industry in the '90s, the right elements to generate and manage a successful SLA are rarely in place. Many organizations that depend on IT lack the governance structures, service catalogues, defined processes, management and monitoring services that are necessary for managing SLAs successfully.

A successful SLA strategy must include the ability to collect configuration information on network and server assets, access customer information for business impact analysis, and provide data on all internal or external SLAs[5]. Ensuring that users have visibility of what services IT makes available, what level of service is provided, and that they have the ability to verify the level of service offered can help increase customer satisfaction and improve the overall relationship between IT and the users. A service-centric approach to SLA management is the cornerstone of a user-centric approach to the IT offered. Figure 8.6 summarises an impact assessment of SLA use for IT services.

In this section we present a bundle of capabilities for managing SLAs (summarised in fig. 8.7) that can enhance common Grid computing platforms with a comprehensive environment covering the full-life cycle of SLAs for the use of ICT resources and services. One such example includes the first implementation of a comprehensive SLA framework (Rosenberg and Juan 2009) on top of the Globus Toolkit – an Open Source Grid Computing middleware commonly used in large-scale science projects and some commercial applications (GT4 2009).

Fig. 8.7: Common capabilities for SLA management against the life-cycle of managing SLAs

---

[5] The term "internal SLA" refers to agreements governing the relationship between a service provider and the ICT infrastructure services and resources used in order to deliver a service to the customer. The term "external SLA" refers to the agreement for the relationship between the service provider and the customer.

Capabilities for SLA *specification* include support for standards-based specification of SLAs and templates, such as the standard WS-Agreement (WS-Agreement 2007). Service delivery is described through the {service, SLA} pair, defining exactly what the client is expecting from the provider. The complete lifecycle of the service is mirrored by the life-cycle of the corresponding SLA specification. As such, the SLA has a lifespan that is at least as long as the period of service usage by the service consumer.

The main challenge of SLA *discovery and negotiation* resides in providing a comprehensive environment for discovering the SLA under which a service may be offered and negotiating the parameters of the SLA clauses in order to obtain a contract which is best fit for its use, minimising over- and under-provision. Service discovery based on SLA is well understood and is gaining acceptance in business. SLA negotiation however is not widely accepted at present and its business justification is being debated. In March 2009 WS-Agreement (WS-Agreement 2007) has been in its last steps to become a full standard. It offers the only standard in this area that has met some acceptance. Several implementations of this specification have been developed since 2007, including some available as Open Source software from the Grid Resource Allocation Agreement Protocol (GRAAP) Working Group (http://forge.gridforum.org/sf/projects/graap-wg). However, the technical means to perform negotiation are not yet there; the WS-AgreementNegotiation protocol, for example, is still at early stages of maturity.

Extensive experimentation across many vertical market sectors has indicated that the business justification for SLA negotiation is not widely accepted and whenever it is considered to be applicable, this is merely in relation to SLA discovery (Dimitrakos 2009a). This finding is consistent with findings of several European research projects such as TrustCoM, NextGRID, Akogrimo and BEinGRID (Parkin et al. 2008). More importantly, the business reasoning for providing a capability to re-negotiate SLAs remains unclear (as opposed to cancelling an SLA and replacing it with a new one). Extensive experimental analysis in various business sectors by the BEinGRID consortium (Dimitrakos 2009a) has also confirmed acceptance of either simple short-term SLAs for use of IT resources or of complex legal contracts. The latter are perceived as a means of treating higher value or higher risk offerings by the parties involved, their definition typically involve qualified lawyers and would not be automatically renegotiated. Furthermore national law in some European regions obligates that renegotiation is treated as a negotiation of a new contract. Nevertheless, it appears as if in some cases companies are willing to enter a fixed long-term contract, and allow for short-term contracts (typically referencing the over-arching long-term legal contract) that can be negotiated automatically, within a limited scope.

The SLA *optimization* capability matches the information offered in SLAs to the available resources. This improves the provider's scheduling strategy, allowing the provider to improve the utilisation of its resources. It also allows implementation of the business rules which govern the allocation of resources based on KPIs such as the return value of the incoming SLA requests. Most schedulers are designed to optimise the resource usage based on the incoming resource requests, but very few take into account KPIs such as the business value of the request.

The SLA *evaluation* capability compares information collected from sensors and other monitoring tools to the SLA objectives, and raises alarms when thresholds are passed or constraints are violated. The provider, having detailed information of its resource status, can act proactively to address failures, thus managing the risk associated with the penalties incurred. Depending on the SLA, the consumer may also receive such notifications, and can reallocate tasks, enhancing its ability to react to the likelihood of failures. This capability builds on a modular architecture that exploits a topics-oriented publish-subscribe model and can instrument native or "off-the-self" ICT resource monitoring tools. Intelligent event correlation and non-repudiation combined with SLA-based accounting and annotation of violations make information clearer and reliable enough for enabling evidence gathering and evidence-based decision making regarding claims for compensation.

The *SLA-based accounting* capability supports the selection and adoption of the suitable charging scheme for each service execution environment based on the metrics included in the SLA specification. Such metrics may deal with a variety of heterogeneous resources. This capability enables charging for service use based on its real execution cost. The analysis reports produced by this capability also helps clarifying resource usage and causality of retribution and penalties.

Figure 8.7 shows an overview of these capabilities against the typical life-cycle of managing SLAs. The business benefits of such a comprehensive environment for SLA management over Grid middleware include optimising resource allocation and use in response to market requirements, reducing Total Cost of Ownership (TCO) by improving efficiency of resource utilisation and faster and better targeted response to failures, increasing customer confidence by allowing transparency of operation (subject to the SLA), and enabling customisable billing by providing finer granularity of accounting and reporting. These results have been validated in various Business Experiments in different vertical market sectors including the Business Experiments in the area of online collaborative gaming (see chapter 12) and remote computation for radiotherapy cancer treatment planning (see chapter 9).

8.6 Common Capabilities for Data Management

Companies in most vertical market sectors that are considering the use of Cloud computing or Data-Grids for federating data share common concerns about storage, access, translation and integration. These can be simplified in the following key points – further analyses are included in Dimitrakos et al. (2009a) and Thomson (2009):

- Where should data be placed and how should it be retained?
- How should data be accessed?
- How should data be presented by one provider so that others will understand it?
- How can one combine data from many distributed and heterogeneous sources?

All of these questions are important to modern businesses. In many industries, collaboration and the efficient flow of information between organizations is critical. For example, Just-In-Time techniques (Toyota MMK 2006) aim to improve the efficiency of a supply chain and to do this effectively they need access to up to date information from multiple organizations.

The capabilities mentioned in this section focus on addressing the challenges of accessing, integrating and utilising existing data that may be heterogeneous and originate from multiple business partners in a value network. They enable solutions for facilitating access to remote data sources, for homogenizing the treatment of data sources, and for synchronising multiple data sources. Reference implementations of these have been developed over OGSA-DAI platform. The latter is contributed by the Open Grid Services Architecture – Data Access and Integration (OGSA-DAI) project (http://www.ogsadai.org.uk), a part of the Open Middleware Infrastructure Institute UK (OMII-UK, http://www.omii.ac.uk/).

More specifically the following common capabilities have been identified and developed over OGSA-DAI:

- *Data Source Publisher*: This capability simplifies the set-up of existing grid middleware by allowing a source of data to be published over web services. It also reduces the ease of use OGSA-DAI, hence lowering the overall entry cost.
- *OGSA-DAI Trigger*: This capability enhances OGSA-DAI with new data integration features and allows for automated data integration using OGSA-DAI. Underpinning this capability is innovation that allows executing an event-driven OGSA-DAI workflow when a database changes.
- *JDBC Driver*: This capability offers a new interface for OGSA-DAI that allows enhanced data integration in existing applications and makes integrated data resources appear as a simple database.
- *OGSA-DAI SQL views*: This capability allows adapting an existing data source for use in a Data-Grid; it enables a view that is independent of the data source and appropriate for use in a Data-Grid without affecting the original data-source.

The results in the Data Management area offer new opportunities for collaboration between business partners by enabling access to sources of information, reducing costs due to better integration of data across sites and enabling the development of simpler data-oriented applications. They also improve the OGSA-DAI framework with a more comprehensive data integration capability and reduce the barriers to adopting OGSA-DAI in business environments.

The results in the Data Management have been validated in a BE demonstrating the use of Data-Grid technologies for affordable data synchronization and SME integration within B2B networks summarized in BE24 (2009). Some aspects were also validated in a BE demonstrating improvements to the competitiveness of textile industry gained by implementing a SOI between textile firms and technology provider that focused on offering high end services such as production scheduling, global resource scheduling and virtual retailing. Other aspects were validated in a BE focusing on supporting post-production workflow enactment in the film industry, summarized in BE02 (2009).

8.7 Common Capabilities for Data and Service Portals

Portals are commonly used as a means of obtaining a unifying view of SOI and Cloud platforms and of introducing transparencies that hide the complexity of the underlying IT infrastructure. They include portals for managing user communities, portals for accessing distributed data sources and portals for managing the life-cycle of computational tasks (i.e. submitting, monitoring in real-time and controlling a job). Many businesses considering investing in Grid or Cloud computing have business needs relating to the use of such portals. Based on the analysis of their requirements (Dimitrakos et al. 2009a), the strongest business needs for technological innovation in this area were organized in three sub-categories:

1. Security, user provisioning and user management
2. Efficiency and security of file and data sharing
3. Visibility and manageability of submitting, monitoring and controlling transactions, jobs and other computational tasks

Typically, such business needs become even more critical in the case of cross-organisational portals – i.e. portals shared among a community of business partners (Virtual Organization), portals that offer access to shared resources, or portals that offer access to federated services or resources offered by a Virtual Organisation. Unfortunately, this is where most current solutions appear to be weaker.

The main research and development results in this area have taken the form of extensions to a Plug & Play portals development framework (Dimitrakos et al 2009a) built on top of the Open Source Vine toolkit (Gridipedia 2009c). The key innovations underpinning this result are a configurable abstraction layer that uses Web2.0 mash-up technology to hide complexity of Grid computing tasks, and an innovative user and account provisioning mechanism. This framework helps in reducing integration costs and preserve existing investment by facilitating integration with existing solutions through a flexible plug-in adaptor mechanism. Ease of integration with existing content management tools and legacy applications also results in reducing the cycle time of Grid portal development projects. Finally the user provisioning and administration mechanisms help reduce human error, coordinate application-specific accounts and authentication mechanisms and results in an easier to manage uniform administration layer. The high-level architecture of the main capabilities developed for this framework is shown in figure 8.8.

Further studies (Brossard and Karanastasis 2009, Raekow et al. 2009) have analyzed how this framework can be further enhanced through its integration with other capabilities mentioned in this chapter. Brossard and Karanastasis (2009) explore the added value of integrating this framework with the federated identity and access management capabilities mentioned in previous sections. Raekow et al. (2009) explore the added value of integration with the License Management capabilities mentioned in previous sections of this chapter.

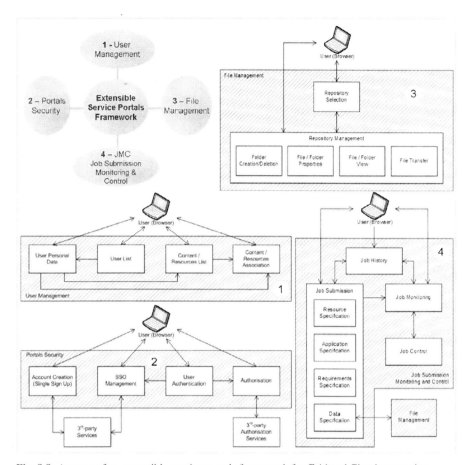

Fig. 8.8: Aspects of an extensible service portals framework for Grid and Cloud computing

Results in the area of Grid Portals have been validated in various vertical market sectors including a Business Experiment focusing on production scheduling and virtual retailing in the Textile Industry, described in BE13 (2009), and a Business Experiment demonstrating the enactment of Web2.0 workflows for Service Oriented Infrastructures in complex enterprises, described in BE23 (2009).

8.8 An example that brings it all together

The European IT Infrastructure Management Services market was worth almost 50 billion Euros in 2006 according to a report from IDC (IDC 2005) and has been increasing by almost 10% a year until 2009. It appears that a similar trend is now emerging in the Cloud computing area. Merrill Lynch (2008) derives the spending on Cloud computing from total software spending. For 2011, it is expected that

20% of spending on enterprise applications and infrastructure software and 8% of spending on custom software will be spent on Cloud computing. The worldwide Cloud Computing market is expected to reach $95 billion by 2011. This represents 12% of the total worldwide software market.

One of the recurrent challenges for businesses in this area is how to manage the deployment, distribution and configuration of the capabilities and resources required for offering a service that is distributed over multiple hosts that may not be under the control of the same enterprise. According to the analysis at (Dimitrakos et al 2009a), the top four concerns in this area have to do with:

- How to define and enforce security policy
- How to measure and optimize resource usage
- How to monitor and evaluate the quality-of-service offered against an SLA
- How to manage configuration over a federation of hosting platforms

In response to this challenge we show how many of the common capabilities mentioned in previous chapters can be integrated into, or enable, a capability that we call "*(Enhanced) Application Virtualisation*". This enables managing the deployment, distribution, coordination and configuration of the capabilities and resources required for offering as a service applications distributed over a group of network hosts. The latter can be nodes of a Grid or an aggregation of Cloud platforms offered by a single or multiple platform providers. On such environments, this capability can add an instrumentation layer configuring and coordinating different service execution environments for enabling the secure and manageable exposure to consumers of remotely hosted (and potentially distributed) applications. Even if, in the shorter term, an enterprise is not considering managing services that are distributed among different Cloud environments, this collection of capabilities offers a means for providing a unifying layer for managing security (i.e. identity, access management, secure service integration, etc.), SLA fulfilment and performance monitoring across multiple service delivery platforms.

An evolution of this bundle of capabilities could also be exploited to coordinate the integration of, and manage, Software-as-a-Service (SaaS) offered on Cloud platforms of different providers (e.g. Amazon, Microsoft Azure, etc.). It is reasonable, in fact, to suppose that different Cloud providers could differentiate their offers hence generating a market where different Cloud platforms are best fit for hosting different kinds of services. Consequently offering a capability enabling the selection of most suitable providers for hosting a SaaS solution as well as coordinating application deployment and exposure on Cloud platforms offered by different providers can be attractive and produce high return on investment. According to a 2009 survey of European SMEs by ENISA (ENISA 2009) the majority of responders (32%) consider a federation of Cloud platforms offered by various providers to be most suitable Cloud for an SME. A close second (28%) is a Cloud platform offered by a trusted partner for use by a business community.

A typical usage scenario of this capability is shown in the following figure 8.9, where an Application Service Provider (ASP) provides an in-cloud SaaS to a client on the basis of an agreed contract (SLA). In order to optimise capital expenditure

and to match use of IT resources to business demand the ASP has joined a community of Cloud platform providers that can offer the resources, platform and infrastructure services that the ASP needs in order to provide this in-cloud application
as SaaS to its own user community. In order to monitor service usage and optimise
resource utilisation the ASP creates an instance of the application for each customer
it serves based on Quality of Service parameters that reflect the corresponding
customer agreement (SLA). A separate reference to a service endpoint is produced
for each instance of the application. The creation of the application instance is initiated via the ASP via Cloud service management interfaces that are offered by the
Cloud platform federation (represented by a Broker).

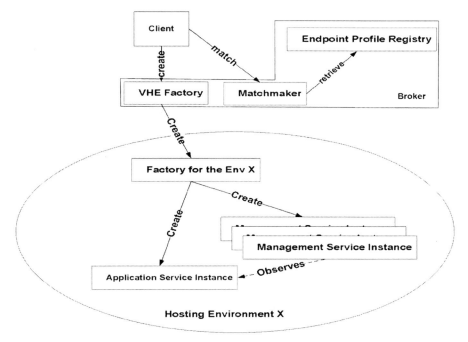

Fig. 8.9: Creation of in-cloud SaaS application instances on an in-cloud Hosting Environment

The ASP is assured by the Broker (representing the Cloud platform federation),
based on its visibility of the SLAs provided by the Cloud operators, that the created
instance can meet the SLA it has agreed with its customer and is provided with the
necessary capabilities for managing the life-cycle of the application instance and the
policies governing the (virtual) service delivery platform through which the application is offered to the ASP's customers. The ASP is not exposed to the complexity
and heterogeneity of the capabilities that have been combined in order to allow the
application service delivery. Unless described in the SLA, the ASP avoids exposure
to the specifics of where specific application resources have been deployed. The
ASP has delegated to the community of Cloud platform providers (represented by

a Broker) the selection of suitable hosting environments and the execution of processes that implement the deployment and configuration of application instances and their exposure as a service. It has been provided with specialized management services that the ASP uses for coordinating these processes and managing the operation of the in-cloud application services it offers to its customers throughout their lifetime.

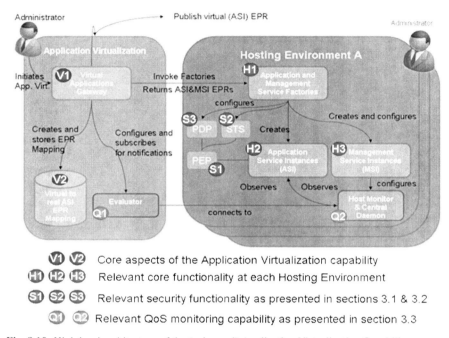

V1 V2	Core aspects of the Application Virtualization capability
H1 H2 H3	Relevant core functionality at each Hosting Environment
S1 S2 S3	Relevant security functionality as presented in sections 3.1 & 3.2
Q1 Q2	Relevant QoS monitoring capability as presented in section 3.3

Fig. 8.10: High level architecture of the (enhanced) Application Virtualization Capability

The virtualized application is exposed via an in-cloud service Gateway and the integration of any other value adding services (VAS) – potentially provided by third parties – catering for the non-functional aspects of the application is transparent to the application consumer (see fig. 8.10). The capability enables the ASP to use standardised management services in order to govern the configuration of the virtualised application, the underlying virtual service delivery platform and any third party value adding services (VAS) such as SLA and security capabilities that have been selected by the ASP to enrich the customer experience. The adoption of the Gateway offers the necessary location and platform transparency while acting as an integration point (i.e. a virtual service bus) to external value adding services.

In terms of business impact, this bundle of capabilities allows an ASP to offer their applications as a service in a simple and manageable way without being exposed to the detail of managing the enabling infrastructure. This increases flexibility and allows a separation of concerns between application provisioning and management, and facilitates their transition towards a SaaS model.

8.9 Conclusions

In this chapter we presented a selection of common capabilities (i.e. services capturing reusable functionality of IT solutions) for Grid and Cloud Computing that can be used to address business and technical challengies identified by the Business Experiments.

In our analysis, we highlighted the likely *impact of innovation* produced by each common capability, and referred to concrete examples of publicly available descriptions of Business Experiments and real-life business scenarios where the current state-of-the-art can be improved by exploiting implementations of these common capabilities. In each case, our analysis included a reflection of the inter-action between the technical experts innovating, the business analysts supporting them and a relevant pool of business stakeholders. Such analysis and validation of technological innovation is of an unprecedented size and diversity not only in the history of European research and innovation but also globally.

In this chapter we also presented a futuristic, indicative *integration* scenario that illustrates how several reusable capabilities that originate in diverse thematic areas, and meet diverse business requirements can be brought together in order to solve a challenging and complex problem that may appear as the market evolves.

The capabilities mentioned in this chapter have been developed as part of the technological research and innovation activities of BEinGRID project. They embody technological innovations in areas that are considered to be critical for the way that business will be done in the future, based on the collective experience of 25 Business Experiments that cover many sectors of the European economy. Many of these offered real-life business scenarios and a platform for validating these capabilities and for identifying best practices in close liaison with stakeholders in value chains that represent each vertical market sector and the European economy as a whole.

This chapter only covers at a high level a small subset of the common capability definitions, the associated design and implementation patterns and the validation scenarios that constitute the main body of knowledge and recommendations produced by the technology innovation stream of BEinGRID. A book edited by the author (Dimitrakos et al 2009a) includes a more extensive analysis of these results. It targets a general audience of strategists, technical consultants, researchers and practitioners in SOI technologies with emphasis on Grid and Cloud Computing. More information is also being made available at the on-line knowledge repository IT-tude.com (http://www.it-tude.com) – formerly known as Gridipedia (http://www.gridipedia.eu/) – that was developed with support of the BEinGRID project.

9 Remote Computational Tools for Radiotherapy Cancer Treatment Planning

Andrés Gómez on behalf of the members of the Business Experiment

9.1 Introduction – The Need for and Potential of Grid Computing for Radiotherapy Cancer Treatment Planning

The health sector is an important user of information technologies, both for the management and administration of the hospitals and other services as well as for the clinical usage. For example, currently, there is an important activity to install Patient Record Information Systems, including the interchange of this information among hospitals. For several years now, these information systems have included the image and other data for diagnosis in electronic form. Additionally, there are other information technologies solutions to help doctors and technicians in the diagnostic and treatment of serious illness. One of these clinical tools is the system to calculate the radiotherapy treatments for cancer patients that usually are often called TPS, the acronym for Treatment Planning System.

Cancer represents the second largest cause of death in Europe (Coleman et al. 2008, Ferlay et al. 2007). Radiotherapy is frequently used to treat it, on its own or combined with other methods. Radiation therapy exposes the cancerous growth to electron beams, X-rays or gamma rays that can kill the cells. It is effective because of heightened sensitivity of the tumour cells to the radiation, relative to healthy cells. In addition, the harmful effects of the radiation can be minimized by focusing only on the particular area to be treated and shielding the remainder of the body. There are two main types of radiotherapy: Brachytherapy, where the radiation is generated inside the body of the patient by radioactive sources inserted inside or around the tumour, and external radiotherapy, where the radiation comes from an external source, commonly an electron accelerator or Linac. In this case, the tumour is radiated from several angles so adding their individual contributions to the final prescribed dose that can be delivered.

The external beam radiotherapy (also known as teletherapy) has two main techniques: Conformal Radiotherapy (or CRT) where the X-ray beam takes the shape of the tumour seen from the Linac, and Intensity Modulated Radiation Therapy (or IMRT) where the strength and the form of the beam changes during the delivery, to allow a better control of the dose. Because of the affectivity of the external radiotherapy, other techniques have been recently released as Image Guide Radiotherapy (IGRT) or hadrontherapy. Probably others will appear in the near future because of the intense research activity in the field.

For every used technology, the treatment must be determined uniquely for each patient. The doctor initially prescribes the dose (this means, the amount of radiation)

K. Stanoevska-Slabeva et al. (eds.), *Grid and Cloud Computing: A Business Perspective on Technology and Applications*, DOI 10.1007/978-3-642-05193-7_9,
© Springer-Verlag Berlin Heidelberg 2010

which the tumour must receive. To deliver it, the medical physicists (the technicians who calculate the final treatment) follow a strict planning protocol which includes a simulation to determine the final doses in order to ensure its quality and effectiveness, using the in-house installed TPS. The plan must be available quickly to allow treatment to commence as soon as possible and frequently requires a second calculation for quality control or, in complex cases, the experimental verification, which is costly in time and money. Reducing the full time required to perform, and to check the calculations or improving its accuracy will improve quality, efficiency and satisfaction in the hospital procedure.

The Business Experiment BEinEIMRT includes a new set of remote tools to help the medical physicists to define these plans: an optimizer, and a virtual verifier. These tools were developed in the framework of a previous national Spanish research project named e-IMRT (http://eimrt.cesga.es), funded by the regional government of Galicia (Xunta de Galicia). The optimization tool provides them with a set of suitable plans which fulfil the prescriptions. The plans can be compared between them and analyzed by the technicians. In the case that one of the plans is considered valid, the medical physicist can download the plan in DICOM-RTPLAN format to be recalculated with their internal TPS. The advantage of this tool, additional to the usage of updated and accurate algorithms and its extensibility to several optimization models, is that it examines several treatment modalities simultaneously. It produces results for CRT, IMRT and few-levels radiotherapy techniques. So, the technician can compare among them and selects the most effective or that which may not be the most effective but the less invasive to deliver (and in some cases, cheaper than another plan).

The verification tool allows the medical physicists to virtually check the treatment. Usually, the internal protocols of the hospitals include a cross-checking of the treatment plan with a simpler dose calculation method. This cross-check tries to avoid errors in the treatment planning which can be dangerous for the patient. Frequently, it could be done experimentally. To do it, a phantom which emulates the patient is instrumented to record the doses in certain control points and the planned treatment is fully delivered. The recorded doses are analyzed and compared with those calculated by the TPS. Only when both of them are in agreement, the treatment plan is considered valid. However, this experimental verification is costly in time and money, and, what is worse, the Linac cannot be used to deliver treatments to the real patients during the data acquisition time. So, the medical physicists have demanded new software tools for accurate verification of the plans, and Monte Carlo simulation methods are considered the best solution. But, additionally to the complex technical details of such simulations, these methods need a large amount of CPU cycles which make them unpractical, and almost impossible with the current computing infrastructure of the hospitals.

The e-IMRT (Mouriño Gallego et al. 2007) solution has been designed to provide these services following a Software-as-a-Service (SaaS) paradigm. The application provider must first solve the problem of the computing resources that they require. It can use its own local resources, but this solution limits the scalability of the service and increases enormously the initial investments. To solve those constraints, the usage of Grid infrastructures is one of the best available options. Grid can provide the computing resources needed by the services, with a strong security that provides the trustworthiness of the platform.

Within the framework of this short BEinEIMRT experiment, the e-IMRT platform has been upgraded with several BEinGRID common capabilities. Using BEinGRID SLA Negotiation component, which has been plugged into GridWay metascheduler (Huedo et al. 2004, Llorente et al. 2005), the platform has acquired the capacity of negotiating CPU capacity on demand among a set of pre-selected providers. Additionally, the security of the exposed web services interface has been improved with the integration of two new components which verify the content of the received requests and check the authorization of the user to perform such operations. Also, the Business Experiment has started the validation of the methods and the platform within the hospital, and analyzed the viability from a commercial point of view. The experiment has involved the participation of several partners with different roles:

- Centro de Supercomputación de Galicia (CESGA) in Spain. It acted as Grid application provider and as the front-end for the final user. It had adapted the services to the usage of Grid infrastructure. In the future, it could sell the solution, both as a service and as a product and will grant licenses for third parties. Also, it could be a Grid provider for third parties that commercialize the service or for hospitals that want to have the product installed in-house.
- Radiophysics Research Group of the University of Santiago de Compostela in Spain. It acted as technology and knowledge provider. It provided the expertise in Medical Physics, and developed the backend solutions for verification and optimization of treatment plants. In the future, this group will generate new solutions as well as support the Grid application provider in the extension (including more models of Linacs from other manufacturers) and other improvements to the platform.
- Information Technology Group of the University of Vigo in Spain. It acted also as a technology provider. It had developed the web front-end, the web services and deployed the security solutions. In the future, this partner will adapt the interface to the technological evolution and to the new solutions.
- Distributed Systems Architecture Group of the Universidad Complutense de Madrid, Spain. This third technological provider has collaborated in the integration of GridWay into the platform. It has designed the SLA integration with this metascheduler.
- Fundación IDCHUS. It is the Research Foundation of the Complexo Hospitalario de la Universidad de Santiago (CHUS), Spain. It acted as the final user (as it is), defining requirements, and validating the generated solution from the platform. Hospitals like CHUS are the only ones that can test the new solutions for clinical usage, which is a must for commercial success of solutions in the health sector. So, a stable agreement with one or, better, several hospitals is necessary for the future. They help to identify new requirements and validate them before commercialization.

The experiment started in March 2008 and finished one year later. During this short time, the platform was upgraded with the new functionalities, the back-end software was improved and several tests were performed to validate both the BEinGRID inserted components as well as the solutions provided by the platform using common radiotherapy software validation tests. Although some of these radiotherapy valida-tion tests are still under execution at the moment of writing, the benefits of using Grid has been demonstrated, as will be shown later.

9.2 Description of the Technological Solution

The architecture of e-IMRT after the enhancements were added is illustrated in figure 9.1 below.

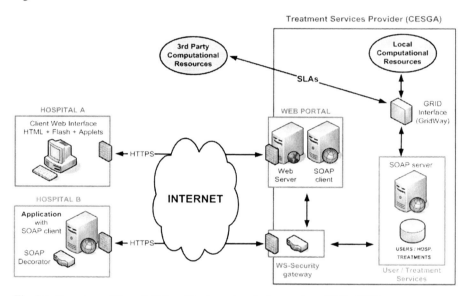

Fig. 9.1: Overview of the e-IMRT architecture after the integration of BEinGRID components

The end users can use both the web based client provided by the project or connect through their own application calling directly to the services. The computational back-end infrastructure is completely hidden to them. The expensive computational work is executed on the local or external Grid resources and managed by GridWay.

The e-IMRT platform is designed following a three layer model (see fig. 9.1). The first layer can be a thin client based on a web interface, which makes intensive use of Java and Flash applets. This user interface is used by the medical physicists to define the parameters of the service request as the maximum or minimum doses for the optimization, or the reference values for the comparison between dose maps in the verification. Specific Java applets are used to manage the upload of the needed treatment and patient's information based on DICOM files. Before leaving the client, the patient's personal data is removed from these files. This anonymization decreases the level of security measures to be implemented by the service provider both in the server and in the host building, to comply with the European regulations on health data protection, because the patient's identity is never known outside the hospital premises. The web client communicates with a web portal which translates the request in a suitable message to call the second layer: a set of web services. These services expose the main functionality of the platform. There are specific services for the different supported operations such as user data management, file management, or process request. These are the unique ways to access the stored information and to control the status of the requests. In the last layer, the back-end stores the information about each user, the treatment plan and manages the execution of the different processes. Alternatively to the web client, the hospital can call directly to the web services (but in this case it will be responsible for removing the patient's personal data from the files) from its own application, although this method has not been used yet.

There are three kinds of users in the platform: the main administrator who works for the service provider and manages the platform; the hospital leader, who administers the information needed about the hospital facilities, as the model and parameters of the Linacs or the tomographs; and the final users, mainly medical physicists, who demand the main services. No other user type is provided by the platform, so the patients and doctors are not expected to use it.

To leverage the security of the platform, two components were added, integrated, and validated during the Business Experiment (represented as WS-Security gateway in fig. 9.1). The first one is a Policy Enforcement Point (PEP). It is an XML security gateway which securely exposes services by checking and validating service requests. All requests are checked against a security policy to ensure they are legitimate. To do so, the PEP may require additional security services such as an identity broker or an authorization service. In particular, in this scenario, the PEP delegates access control requests to an authorization service: the Policy Decision Point. The PEP can also perform other tasks, such as checking them for XML threats and validating them against the service interface definition. In particular, it has the ability to encrypt/decrypt and sign/check the signature of the communication thus ensuring privacy, integrity and confidentiality. The PEP used is a commercial product: Vordel's XML Gateway. The second component is the Policy Decision Point or PDP. It is an authorization service based on the XACML standard for representing and evaluating access control policies and requests, returning its decision to the requestor. The response can be either PERMIT, DENY, NOT APPLICABLE, or INDETERMINATE. Access control policies can be more or less fine-grained, are defined by the administrator and can deal about who is permitted to do what and when. E-IMRT used Axiomatics's Policy Server to implement PDP.

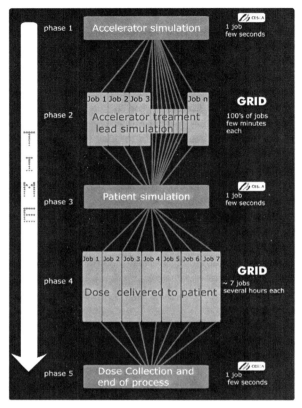

Fig. 9.2: Schematic view of the treatment plan verification workflow

The second main addition to the platform was GridWay. The main aforementioned services, optimization and verification, use remote computing capacity quite intensively. For example, in figure 9.2 the workflow of the verification process is shown (Gómez et al. 2007, Pena et al. 2009). It comprises several phases. Three of them (1, 3, and 5) are executed locally because they need limited computing capacity. However, steps 2 and 4 demand a large amount of CPU time but, fortunately, can be split in many jobs and distributed to remote computing farms using Grid interfaces. The amount of jobs and their duration depends on the type and definition of the treatment plan and is calculated on-the-fly within the workflow. The optimization process has a similar workflow, where part of the work can be done locally, but there are compute intensive calculations that have to be done remotely to accomplish the expectations of fast return of the end users. The Grid jobs are managed by GridWay, a metascheduler that can submit the jobs to several Grids using different middleware as Globus or gLite, and permits their usage simultaneously. GridWay has been enhanced with a plugin (Broker GW-SLA) which uses the SLA Negotiation BEinGRID component to add computing resources dynamically (Bugeiro et al. 2009) (for more details on this component see section 8.5 in chapter 8). This plugin monitors the status of the resources known by GridWay. When it detects that there are not enough resources to fulfil the demand, an automatic negotiation with previously registered Grid providers starts. The component only negotiates the final number of CPUs and the price within the limits previously agreed and stored in the server. These limits, which we call pre-SLAs, must be negotiated off-line by the parties in advance and a contract must be signed. Currently, SLA Negotiation does not provide electronic signature of the agreements.

Another important technical feature is that the workflows submit the jobs using the Distributed Resource Management Application API or DRMAA (Rajic et al. 2008). It adds flexibility to the platform because it makes it independent of the final scheduler. So, GridWay can be substituted by another scheduler which supports such a standard. It facilitates the migration to another computing allocation and submission paradigm such as Clouds or an installation inside a hospital in a cluster with a usual local scheduler such as Grid Engine or Portable Batch System (PBS). So, the platform can be easily adapted to the technical evolution and different work environments, improving its adaptability.

9.3 Added Value for the User

The aim of the e-IMRT platform is to provide remote tools for radiotherapy based on the use of vast computing power to improve the accuracy and quality of the solutions. From this point of view, the provision of these services clearly benefits from the usage of Grid technologies. Grid started in the data and computing domains to permit the collaboration among partners, sharing their resources to tackle the problem of storing and analyzing large amounts of data or to make complex simulations. Now, the platform uses the developed technology to provide real added value services to medical physicists to help cancer treatment planning. The usage of Grid infrastructure opens this possibility because:

- It permits the execution of complex workflows that need a large CPU capacity that is not usually available within the hospitals. By using Grid, medical physicists can have access to this capacity remotely and, what is most important, reduce the time-to-solution to a level that can be acceptable for their daily work. The time for executing it with only 1 CPU makes unpractical to use this Monte Carlo simulation technique for daily work. Only when more than 40 CPUs are available, the execution time becomes acceptable for inclusion of this process in the internal treatment planning protocols. This is a big infrastructure for a radiotherapy department and it is out of scope of its business objectives. For example, the execution time of a treatment verification can be reduced from 193 hours to only 4 hours. This means, from more than one week to an acceptable time for a day of work (see fig. 9.3). A further reduction of this time is still possible and work is continuing to improve the scheduling of jobs.

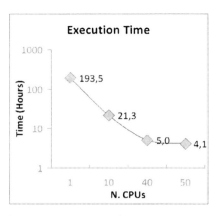

Fig. 9.3: Execution time of one treatment plan verification versus the number of available CPUs

- It decreases the market entry cost. The service provider does not need its own computing farm. In fact, only two front-end servers (for redundancy) are needed to start the provision. The computing power can be leased from Grid providers on demand. Even in the case of having its own infrastructure, the Grid application provider can adapt to peaks in the demand renting CPU capacity or sharing resources of other providers. Also, those hospitals which install the solution in their premises can adapt to their internal demand, renting CPU capacity to other Grid providers.
- It increases the trustworthiness of the platform. In the health sector, the security of the personal medical information is a must. Any external health service must include secure measures which guarantee the confidentiality of patient's data. Grid includes them from scratch and can be extended with new ones, as in the case of BEinEIMRT experiment.

Of course, Grid is not the unique solution for these requirements. For example, the emerging Cloud paradigm seems to adapt well to it, as it is discussed later. Additionally, the usage of the platform inside the hospitals' daily work adds other benefits. First of all, it helps to improve the quality and effectiveness of the cancer treatments. The hospitals are continuously looking for new techniques for doing this at an affordable cost. E-IMRT provides new tools that allow the hospitals to verify treatment plans virtually, avoiding costly experimental verifications. Also, it includes one tool which helps them to look for a valid treatment in very complex cases, a task that must currently be done manually. Finally, because the platform works for the medical physicists off-line, they can do other duties in the hospital, increasing their productivity. So, it contributes to palliate the scarcity of these specialized technicians in the market.

The managers of the hospitals have another advantage: the cost model. E-IMRT services can be provisioned following a pay-per-use model. This means that the costs of using the services can be directly assigned to the treatment. The hospital only pays when the service is needed for the treatment definition and delivery.

However, there are also barriers to overcome. There are hospitals that have limited internet access from the internal network. Due to security reasons, they protect their internal networks, by limiting the open ports or directly disconnecting production equipments from Internet. E-IMRT solution uses standard web ports to avoid this barrier when there is limited connectivity and implements secure methods to facilitate the acceptation from the internal network managers. In the case of zero connectivity, the solution can be sold as a product, but this reduces its functionality (for example, the hospital cannot rent CPUs dynamically and has to adapt to its internal capacity).

Secondly, e-IMRT is introducing a new way to use computing technology into the hospitals. Remote services are not a new concept. However, they are new in the sector which uses mainly local workstations (TPS) to plan the treatments. Usually, they are very conservative in the introduction of new methods and appliances, and they have to demonstrate clear benefits before deploying them. So, it is necessary to convince the hospital managers about their benefits and the availability of the solution when it is needed. A schema of 7x24 provision must be taken into account in the business model and in the basic infrastructure. To overcome this initial barrier, e-IMRT services have been designed as complementary tools to the existing TPS and do not substitute it. This decreases the risk of initial rejection by the users. At the beginning, the services can be used only in complex cases to advise the medical physicists and maybe later, when they trust in the platform results and have enough experience using it, it can be included in the internal protocols.

A third barrier is the legal regulation. Currently it is not clear if an external service like the e-IMRT must be approved by the health authorities before being used in production. There is a new European Directive (2007/47/EC, which modifies 93/42/EEC), which includes software as a medical device in specific cases: "medical device means any instrument, apparatus, appliance, software, material or other article, whether used alone or in combination, together with any accessories, including the software intended by its manufacturer to be used specifically for diagnostic and/or therapeutic purposes and necessary for its proper application, intended by the manufacturer to be used for human beings" (Directive 2007/47/EC). Being conservative, it is better to apply for the FDA clearance and the CE Mark and try to follow the strictest regulation. It includes the need of software quality assurance processes, for example, implementing ISO standards. When this has been done, the service will be better accepted by the final users. However, the regulation adds another issue against the usual methods in remote service provisioning: it limits the continuous evolution and improvement of the platform. New methods and services must wait for the approval by the authorities and, additionally, the platform must be prepared to have several versions running simultaneously: the hospitals cannot migrate automatically and transparently from one version to another, because they must validate the new software stack. E-IMRT has implemented this possibility, and the user can select the version of the software or the type of algorithm to be used for each treatment plan, from among those that have been validated by the hospital leader.

9.4 Summary and Lessons Learnt

This Business Experiment has demonstrated the proof-of-concept of using on-demand remote computing capacity to bring innovative services to hospitals with radiotherapy facilities via the Internet, keeping a high level of safety, reliability, security and trustworthiness, which are crucial for any health solution. Although the developed services are focused on radiotherapy, the model can be applied in the future to other clinical services, such as the surgical simulation. It has already shown that the benefits for the hospitals of outsourcing such applications are higher than the risks: They do not have to worry about the hardware infrastructure (which must be updated continuously), can gain access to actualized software easily, and can concentrate on their main activity – caring for their patients.

This experiment has also left many useful results, both from the technical and business perspectives which should be taken into account in the future. From the technical perspective, looking at the aforementioned results in the execution time, the use of Grid technologies is feasible for solving the demand for extra CPUs via such a platform to allow the provision of such services. The execution time of the optimizer can also decrease to half an hour, but this still needs one or two improvements. The major concern about the response time is that the time-to-solution is observed to increase when there are several treatments running simultaneously, because they use the same hardware. Thanks to the dynamic negotiation of new resources using Service Level Agreements, it is possible to acquire more resources, and this problem may already be solved. However, the limited resources of the experiment did not permit a full check of this hypothesis, but there will always be a threshold where this problem will appear again. As a consequence, the platform needs another mechanism to isolate the simultaneous execution of two treatment plan operations. This will help enormously to guarantee the response times, avoiding unwanted oscillations in service delivery which might decrease the trust in the services and its usability.

Having a safety platform is a must in the health sector. The inclusion of specific software to improve the service security together with the usage of Grid, helps to fulfil this request. Also, to avoid the movement of patient's data around the world, we have used the anonymization of the image files, removing their data from headers. This common technique does not guarantee totally the anonymity, because, for example, the image of the head can be used to reconstruct the patient's face. Although the probability of such security break is low, the inclusion of additional tools to prevent it would be beneficial. For example, the Medical Data Manager (Montagnat et al. 2008) adds layers to connect to DICOM repositories directly and safely.

From the business point of view, the experiment has validated that such a service is perfectly possible and very viable. Possible, because the main actors (the hospitals) have not rejected it. In fact, during the execution of the experiment, the contact with hospitals has shown that some of them are very interested in using the platform. The market model based on pay-per-use and the cost per treatment (initially 100 Euros per treatment for verification) seems to be acceptable, taken into account the final cost and price of such treatments. For those that do not want to use the pay-per-use model or cannot access the Internet, it is possible to install the software (and hardware) internally, although losing the flexibility of the external provision. Viable because although there are strong competitors, there is room for new ones and, even having a modest market penetration, the business could be profitable. In fact, one small company can generate benefits executing only few thousands of simulations per year. This is a small fraction of the total cancer cases, which are measured in several million per year. However, the new company must surpass some important barriers, as explained before.

9.5 Outlook

We strongly believe that the future of radiotherapy treatment planning must be based on open solutions which will be provided via the Internet and that will require high computing capacity. Both services and computing could be provisioned on-demand with quality of service and improved security. The proposed model has shown that these services demand a high number of CPUs for returning results in a reasonable time. According the Directory of Radiotherapy Centres (DIRAC) of the International Atomic Energy Agency (IAEA) (IAEA 2009), there are 6214 radiotherapy centres in the world, with 7168 Linacs and more than 6000 TPS. Just in the European Union, there are 980 radiotherapy institutions with a mean of 1.9 Linacs per centre. The country with more Linacs is United States of America (USA) with more than 2100 (2114 in 1870 institutions) followed by People's Republic of China (981) and Japan (842). The ideal objective is having 4 linacs per million inhabitants, so we can expect that the number of centres will continue to increase.

Because the high number of dedicated CPUs needed for provisioning the service, to meet the demand from a fraction of these radiotherapy centres, implies access to big dedicated server farms to guarantee the quality of service. However, the proposed architecture can clearly benefit from the utility computing model as Cloud. Using similar methods for CPU renting as the proposed in this Business Experiment, it would be possible to add elasticity to the service and avoid the unwanted overload which will decrease the confidence in the platform. For example, a full set of virtual machines can be deployed dynamically and integrated in a local scheduler, using for example the OpenNebula framework (Sotomayor et al. 2008).

Other important upgrades of the platform in the future are the control of the Service Level Agreements. Currently we have implemented a model where the contracts with the providers will indicate the limits of the CPU provision, leaving for the on-line negotiation the selection of the real values (because, for example, the number of guaranteed CPUs can change with time. Having a high number of guaranteed resources will increase the price substantially). The platform must include mechanisms to control the agreements. We are studying the integration of other SLA components such as the SLA Evaluation and Monitoring that allows the platform to enforce agreements. Also, there is room for improvement in the security, adding capabilities to keep encrypted patient's images (or the data extracted from them) even when they are used by the software while it is running the simulations. These techniques will avoid the risk of patient's data interception and/or identification.

In summary, the e-IMRT platform is a good case for developing and checking the provision of external services following a utility model in the health sector. Its architecture permits the integration on the Cloud or some other utility model and its clear requirements allow the developers to check the feasibility of such models.

10 Business Experiment Ship Building

Ottmar Kraemer-Fuhrmann, Yona Raekow

10.1 Introduction

10.1.1 The Need of Grid Computing in the Ship Building Industry

Shipyards in Europe cannot compete on price alone against overseas competitors, especially those who have the benefit of lower labour costs. Therefore, European ship builders need to concentrate on high-quality construction projects that need a highly skilled workforce and are specially tailored to the requirements of their customers. Consequently each ship is a unique product, produced only once or in a very small type series.

To improve their competitive position, it is essential for modern shipyards to be able to harness the most advanced simulation and design tools to produce complex structures cost effectively. The objective is to recognize and reduce the technical and economical risks that are implicit in large and complex ship building projects. The vision is the complete virtual design and build of a ship.

Modern ship building is furthermore distributed over several industry sectors. The direct turnover of the shipyards themselves is only 10-30% of the added value. The predominant part of the added value is made by suppliers. Thus, a ship is the result of an intensive collaboration among shipyards and their suppliers, which starts during the early design phase and continues during the production of a ship. This Business Experiment applies to all industry sectors that are involved in ship building. A close collaboration between the suppliers and the shipyard was enabled by the Ship Design and Integration system (SESIS, http://www.sesis.de) that was developed in collaboration of Fraunhofer SCAI, the German Aerospace Center (DLR), the shipyards Flensburger Schiffbau-Gesellschaft (FSG) and Lindenau, the Center of Maritime Technologies (CMT), the supplier SAM Electronics and the Hamburg University of Technology (TUHH). Part of the work of the Business Experiment presented here was to extend SESIS by a Grid interface, in order to enhance the available collaboration support with easy access to computational power for the shipyard and its suppliers.

Figure 10.1 shows the time line of the ship building process. Building a ship takes about 18 months. 85% of the costs are already fixed after 2 months, long before the actual ship building has started. This implies that the initial design phase needs to be very accurate, so that miscalculations are impossible. Every mistake in the initial design phase can become a major problem for the shipyard later on.

The ship building Business Experiment focused on the early design phase of a ship and illustrated how the ship building industry can benefit from using computing resources, like Grid or Cloud resources, in order to maximize their revenue while

K. Stanoevska-Slabeva et al. (eds.), *Grid and Cloud Computing: A Business Perspective on Technology and Applications*, DOI 10.1007/978-3-642-05193-7_10,
© Springer-Verlag Berlin Heidelberg 2010

minimizing their risk in this crucial phase of a ship building process. A central tool in achieving this goal is computer simulation in order to identify which components represent the most cost effective design elements for the ship under construction.

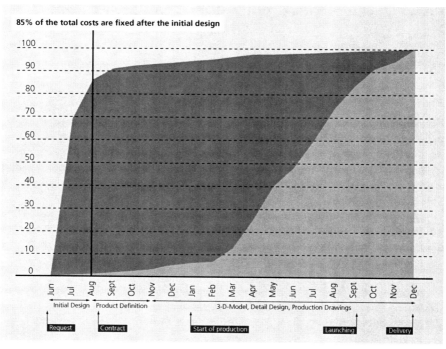

Fig. 10.1: Design cost versus building cost (Schrödter and Gosch 2008)

Before a ship goes from design to production many requirements have to be met: On the one hand, the customer sets parameters, like capacity, manoeuvrability, speed, fuel consumption, etc. On the other hand a predefined set of rules regarding national and international safety and usability standards have to be fulfilled, e.g. stiffness, vibration, fatigue, noise, fire and sea safety. It is a difficult task to comply with all these requirements and still produce a ship quickly and cost efficiently.

The Business Experiment described here demonstrated its success by showing how Grid technology can help in the design and simulation of fire safety of a new component technology. The so-called sandwich technology is a composite material consisting of two metal plates with a foam kernel. Depending on the materials used on each layer the behaviour of the composite material varies. The sandwich technology used at the shipyard was developed by supplier industries such that a close co-operation between the engineers at the shipyard and the supplier had to be supported.

Simulation of fire security and heat transfer of this new composite material required computational power, which was not directly available at the engineer's sites, either at the shipyard or at the supplier engineering company. The Business Experiment therefore integrated the utility computing services of an IT service provider into the ship design and simulation process.

The simulation of fire safety of the new component technology is an example of how the shipyards can benefit from simulation in general. There are many more simulations that need to be run before a ship can go to production or before the shipyard can make a successful bid on a tender.

10.1.2 The Business and Technical Goals of the Business Experiment

From a business point of view this Business Experiment had three objectives. First the shipyard and its suppliers were equipped with a technology that allowed them to make use of computational power that is not available at their sites. Access to computational power helps the ship building industry to minimize risks that are introduced in the early design phase and to better calculate and estimate costs. This is particularly important when the shipyard is bidding on fixed price tenders, since the proposals they make need to be sound and later on implementable within the proposed budget.

Second the Business Experiment deployed the collaboration platform SESIS and hence enabled the close collaboration between the suppliers and the shipyard.

Last but not least, the Business Experiment allows IT service providers to enter a new market segment. It is expected that the result of the experiment will not only be of interest to the ship building industry, but also to other sectors, e.g. the automobile industry and the aircraft industry. IT service providers will win new customers from the engineering community. In particular, engineering companies that require high computational power only during a short period of time might be interested in using the kind of on-demand services provided by an IT service provider.

In terms of potential, the market is huge, especially due to the imposed time constraints of the early design phase. As an example we note that the achievable cost savings with respect to fuel efficiency (due to better design) could exceed 1 billion dollar per year for European based shipping companies. We estimate that with large scale numerical simulations of the interaction of hull, ship propeller and rudder it is feasible to increase fuel efficiency by 2-4%. If we assume a ship life-time of 25 years, 200 days of operations per year, 100 tons of fuel consumption per day, a fuel price of ca. 400 dollars per ton (ship diesel) and a construction of 200 ships per year in Europe. In total this sums up to cost savings of 1.6–3.2 billion dollars per year – calculated with current fuel prices. Since fuel efficiency only addresses one aspect of the required simulations in the early design phase, we estimate the sum of the potential benefits to be much higher. If so, the market must be bigger too.

From a technical point of view the goal of this Business Experiment was to provide a technical solution that facilitates and accelerates the early design process in ship building. The solution enables shipyards and suppliers to exchange results and data in an easy and efficient manner. The collaboration platform that was deployed at the shipyards and the suppliers allows close cooperation and provides an easy workflow when combining specialized software available at different sites without obtaining new licenses. Before this Business Experiment the communication between shipyard and the suppliers were in person, via phone or fax. With SESIS it is possible to securely share data and collaborate online.

The collaboration platform was extended by a Grid interface that allows easy access to the required computational power via a Grid middleware. A focus was on cases with a high demand for computational power (fire security and heat transfer of the new sandwich components), which are typically not available at the shipyard or supplier. The experiment showed that reliable and significant results can be delivered within acceptable response times and costs. The technical objectives were realized as an extension to the interactive ship design and simulation environment SESIS. Due to the modular structure of SESIS, different Grid middlewares can be accessed, e.g. UNICORE (http://www.unicore.eu) or GTK4 (http://www.globus.org), and it is very easy to configure the system to provide access to other high performance computing resources, like Cloud systems. Before this Business Experiment, Grid technology had not played a role in the sector of ship building and there was no Grid interface for compute intense applications.

10.1.3 The Expected Benefits of Grid-enabled Collaborative Simulation

Some years ago, the engineers at the shipyard faced the problem that they had a huge software suite that had been built over three decades and that had grown to a point such that it was hard to manage and/or to extend. They decided to invest in new technologies, from a software technology point of view, such that their software becomes manageable, modular and extendable. At the same time they investigated options on how to improve on computation time. When a new ship is designed there are a lot of issues that need to be considered. Often the engineers rely on their many years of experience, but when new materials and technologies are used this experience often needs support from simulation results.

The more efficient simulations can be done in the shipyard, the more the engineers can investigate which technologies are best suited for their new ship, e.g. which materials for the hull, which engine, which control systems, etc. are the best fit. It is easy to exchange components in simulation and see if better results can be obtained if different components are used. So when bidding on a tender, the shipyard can have higher confidence that their offer has the best cost-performance ratio.

Unfortunately the shipyards do not tend to have a lot of computational power available on their sites, since it is expensive to always have the latest technology and the corresponding skilled personnel to manage those resources. Also, it may not be profitable for the shipyard to invest in technology, if they only build about two ships per year. Heavy calculation for simulation is done in the early design phase of a ship, i.e. for each ship in the first 4-8 weeks. This means that if the shipyard constructs 2 vessels per year their resources may only be fully utilized for about 16 weeks per annum and have much less demand the rest of the time.

Therefore the engineers at the shipyard are interested in a solution where they can have access to hardware resources for the time they need it, and during the rest of the time focus on the core business. This is exactly what Grid and Cloud computing offer: Computing on demand.

Before SESIS, and the corresponding Grid interface at the shipyard, it was necessary to mail detailed information about technologies and materials that were to be used for constructing the ship or to provide information over the phone. Several iterations were necessary before the suppliers and the shipyard had all the data that they needed in the same version. Sometimes phone and mail were not sufficient and the engineers had to travel to meetings. Travelling of highly skilled personnel is a cost factor that should not be underestimated. Every time modifications to the data were made (either at the supplier or the shipyard) the process of exchanging data started again. With SESIS and the Grid it is easy to share and work on the same data. Everyone can have immediate access and works on the same version, at the same time, without introducing high travelling costs.

To sum up for the end users (i.e. shipyards and suppliers) the expected benefit of the proposed Grid-enabled collaborative simulation technology that was demonstrated within the Business Experiment were:

- Easier and cheaper co-operation and joint development between shipyard and supplier.
- Cost reduction by avoiding travel expenses of highly qualified personnel, by having results faster and hence more time to react or to find a more optimal solution.
- Access to resources which are not available locally or which are only needed temporarily on a PAYG (Pay-As-You-Go) charging model (i.e. reduced cost-of ownership).
- Acceleration of the ship design processes.
- Reduction of technical and financial risks in the ship design.
- Co-operation with the IT service provider and technology integrators helping to concentrate on core tasks and competences rather than IT business.

For an IT-Service provider the advantage of this Business Experiment is that it opens the door to an entirely new business sector. If the engineers at the shipyard make use of Grid technology and benefit from it, other engineering companies might become interested in this technology as well.

Since SESIS and its Grid interface are very flexible (due to the modular design), it is also possible that other engineering sectors, like the automobile industry will become interested in running jobs at the service provider site via SESIS and its Grid interface.

10.1.4 Partners involved in the Business Experiment

The Business Experiment was carried out by the following five partners:

The Flensburger Schiffbau Gesellschaft m.b.H & Co. KG (FSG) is a shipyard, which focuses on construction of so-called RoRo-ferries, container ships and other highly specialized vessels. In recent years the main focus has been on RoRo ferries (see for example fig. 10.2).

Fig. 10.2: Ship constructed by the FSG, the Flensburger Schiffbau Gesellschaft

The CMT – Center of Maritime Technologies e.V. – is a non-profit organisation. The goal of the organization is the growth of research, development and innovation in the maritime area through promoting co-operation between several maritime organisations, between industry and science and within the European research framework. Grid technology will be an important tool to achieve this goal.

The Fraunhofer-Institute for Algorithms and Scientific Computing SCAI engages in computer simulations in product and process development and is a strong industry partner. SCAI designs and optimizes industrial applications and performs numerical calculations on high-performance computers. The goal is to reduce development times, make experiments less expensive and optimize technical products.

DLR-SISTEC: The Simulation and Software Technology division (SISTEC) is the central facility for Software Engineering of the German Aerospace Centre (DLR). Current activities focus on Grid computing, data management, component-based software development for distributed systems, software technologies for embedded systems and software quality assurance.

T-Systems-SfR: T-Systems focuses on services for industrial and public research and development. It integrates the IT applications of its customers and provides them with networks connecting all their global business locations. The Grid and Cloud activities of T-Systems-SfR have the long-term target of a customer-service Grid in which all services are integrated into a Web Service environment and in which the primary task of the service-provider is the mapping of business-processes to clusters of such components.

10.2 The Architecture of the Grid-enabled SESIS

Before the system could be deployed at the shipyard the following steps were necessary: First, it was necessary to select the middleware to which the system connects and to install it on the service provider site; i.e. the core of the middleware and some basic services were installed. After that, specific services for the successful execution of the experiment were developed. These services included load balancing for parallel execution and a graphical user interface for easy handling. The simulator is able to compute the fire security and heat transfer of the new sandwich technology. The implementations of these services conform to the de-facto web service standard (WSRF), guaranteeing a high degree of interoperability. The service that was installed was an open source code for fire simulation called FDS (Fire Dynamics Simulator, http://www.fire.nist.gov), which is a computation fluid dynamics (CFD) model of fire driven fluid flow.

The Business Experiment was based on SESIS, which resulted from a national research project dedicated to developing a design and simulation system for the early stages of ship development. The goal of SESIS is to facilitate the development of new ships at the shipyards. This is achieved by performing collaborative simulations between the shipyards and the suppliers in a virtual organization (VO). Within the VO, the partners co-operate in a heterogeneous environment. SESIS is built upon state-of-the-art software technologies, such as Grid Services, extendable GUI-Frameworks, and wrappers for the integration of legacy code and simulation applications (see fig. 10.3).

SESIS is a system with clearly defined interfaces that allow the addition of new functionalities via software plug-ins. Thus it is possible to combine existing software components with other commercial solutions. The software enabling the development of the SESIS system is the Reconfigurable Computing Environment (RCE), which has been developed by DLR and Fraunhofer SCAI.

The concept of the SESIS system architecture is that every computer in the system contains an installation of the basic software. Depending on the purpose of the system (client, server) or individual requirements of the engineer using it, this installation might have another configuration via one or more additional plug-ins.

SESIS has a component architecture based on "OSGi™ – The Dynamic Module System for Java™". All SESIS installations have a predefined set of plug-ins guaranteeing secure distributed data access and communication.

The Grid integration into SESIS is done by additional plug-ins, which handle all the communication between the SESIS system and the Grid middleware (see fig. 10.3). This concept is not bound to a particular Grid middleware. In the Business Experiment presented here SESIS was extended to be able to use Grid resources from SESIS application methods to start external applications on remote hosts. The methods in this case are Grid clients.

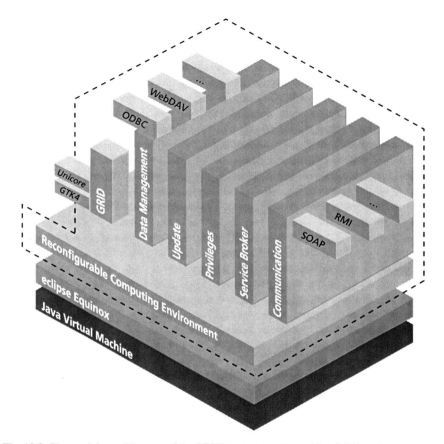

Fig. 10.3: The modular architecture of the SESIS system together with a Grid interface

This Business Experiment added support for the middlewares UNICORE and GTK4 to SESIS. For the Grid integration, a client side support implementation for the following areas were developed:

- System related: Authentication and Resource Discovery
- Job related: Submission
- Data management related: File Input/Output and Transfer

A graphical user interface enables the engineer to configure FDS (Fire Dynamics Simulator) jobs before submitting them to a remote server, owned and operated by T-Systems. The Grid protocols are based on the middlewares Globus GTK4 and UNICORE.

A Service Level Agreement regulates the allocation of hardware and software resources to guarantee reliable Quality of Service and also determines the prices for these services. After job execution, the simulation results are transmitted back to the engineer's desktop for analysis and evaluation.

The workflow for structural analysis during the Business Experiment was the following: The CMT designed the funnel structure for the FSG. These designs were simulated and optimized with ANSYS (http://www.ansys.com) at the CMT. Higher detailed non linear calculations are not done yet. The reason is that the computing power is not yet available neither at FSG or at CMT. In special cases FSG does a fire calculation, but this calculation takes too much time for including it in a standard construction procedure. The usage of computing power provided by T-Systems is new and will offer a faster analysis of structures and their vibration, fatigue and fire behaviour. This raises the quality of the structures, lowers the amount of time needed to design them and makes ships safer.

10.3 Case Study – Collaborative Design with Grid-enabled Simulation

The solution that was provided by this Business Experiment was tested in a distributed environment, where many partners collaborated. The following diagram shows how such a collaboration can be achieved using SESIS (see fig. 10.4).

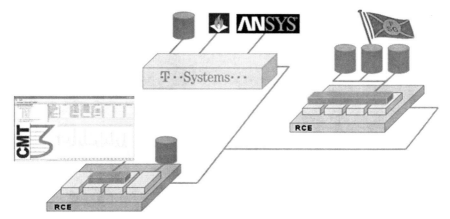

Fig. 10.4: SESIS at work

The players in this case study are the shipyard Flensburger Schiffbau Gesellschaft (FSG) depicted on the right. The players on the left hand side are a resource provider, (here T-Systems), and an engineering company (here CMT), that is providing consultancy services to the shipyard.

The use case is as follows: The Flensburger Schiffbau-Gesellschaft developed a new funnel in sandwich technology, whose non-linear fire analysis is done by the consultant CMT using fire simulation software like FDS or ANSYS. In order to present a satisfactory fire analysis it is required to simulate one hour of fire in a funnel and demonstrate with this simulation that the temperature will not exceed a given maximum temperature at any time.

Since such a fire simulation is very complex, the computation time on standard hardware would take too long. Hence the calculation is performed on the resources of T-Systems. In case licenses for commercial software are required, it might become necessary to define additional agreements between the service provider, the ISV and the engineering office.

The SESIS environment allows its users to collaborate with each other and to provide access to shared data. For example the CMT is able to present a sketch of the funnel to the shipyard before starting the computation. The shipyard can retrieve results immediately from the system provider once the calculation has finished.

SESIS has a very fine grained data management system that allows it to share files between several instances in such a way that only authorized users are able to access files they are permitted to access.

10.4 Added Value for the User

The co-operation between CMT and FSG is currently based on the travelling of skilled personal, by phone, fax or by email. At the moment no Grid technologies are used for an easier and faster way of working together. The travelling of highly skilled personal is expensive in terms of time and money. The work process via phone or mail is inefficient and unsatisfactory compared to a work process within a Grid-enabled organization. The additional usage of Grid technology offers new and fast ways for organizations to communicate and increases the speed of the work process.

The reduction of time needed to finish the construction of a part of a ship (here a funnel) with all design and calculation steps required, directly reduces the cost of this part of the design. The saving of time also enables the shipyard to design ships faster and enhance the quality and safety of their products.

The Business Experiment provides a Grid-service solution and a corresponding infrastructure allowing the end users (i.e. shipyards and their suppliers) to co-operate, to share data and results, and to use remote resources and services delivered by an IT-service provider on demand. The workplace of the engineer is connected to the computing resources of an independent application service provider who offers hardware and software services.

To enable the design engineers to generate precise results within the very limited time available in early design, IT support for their work is highly beneficial. The range of tools used goes from "simple" engineering formulas for single technical problems to complex 3D models.

As the performance of the computers and tools available is constantly increasing, more and more complex problems can be solved during the early design phase. Thus, today, engineers are enabled to design an optimized ship for the owner's needs within shorter time scales.

The engineers at the CMT act as consultants, who design special components of a new ship according to the request of the customers. Data is shared between the shipyard and the consultant via the Ship Design and Simulation System SESIS. In this way, the designers can ensure that the components will fit perfectly into the actual ship during construction. The structural analysis of the components is carried out by computer based simulation and computer analysis. Therefore a large amount of computing resources i.e. high performance CPU power and software licenses are needed, which are not available at the engineering company. The interface allows the submission of compute intensive jobs to the resources provided by the service provider.

The service provider T-Systems supplies IT infrastructures of any size, starting from single node servers up to high performance mainframes. Simulation jobs can be executed on demand, and make use of commercial simulation software. If necessary, software licenses are ordered from a remote license server.

The SESIS environment allows the shipyards to retain their tried and tested ship development skills proved over many years, which is in the ship building market the main source of innovation, and differentiation from overseas competitors which is the major asset for surviving in a niche market. But SESIS also equips the shipyard with new innovative technology that helps them to make more out of this well-proven software.

10.5 Summary and Lessons Learnt

The Grid solution of this Business Experiment is embedded in the value network of a ship design as depicted in figure 10.5

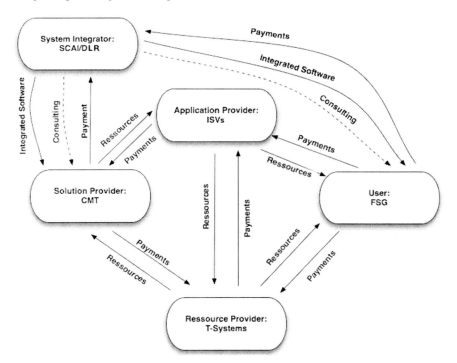

Fig. 10.5: Value network of the Ship Building Business Experiment

The engineers at the shipyard develop a new ship using the Ship Design and Simulation System SESIS. This ship design contains sandwich components for the funnel which are designed by consultants from supplier companies.

The use case shows the required simulation of a 60 minute real time fire which was specified by the future ship owner because the funnel has to meet an A-60 fire rating, which means the temperature must never exceed $180°$ C on the unexposed side of the wall during a 60 minute fire exposure. Such a simulation needs approximately one month of computing time on a single PC. This can be reduced to around one day on a 32-node cluster system available at a Service Provider. This Grid scenario can become typical for future ship design.

The shipyard is using the fire simulation currently at the shipyard during the design phase. The jobs are currently distributed on the computing resources that are available at the shipyard. However the users at the shipyard noticed that the trend is going towards using more computational power and they predict that it is only a matter of time until they will hire external utility computing providers. In particular for CFD and explicit FEM Codes hiring external resources seems to be unavoidable.

However the Business Experiment clearly illustrated that the following operational and performance requirements need to be fulfilled from the shipyard point of view before Grid-enabled simulation can be a standard part of their production workflow.

10.5.1 Operational Requirements

Before a contract with a service provider can be signed there needs to be a pay scale model for the outsourced services, i.e. how much does it cost to use a CPU of a certain type for one hour. If commercial software is used it is also necessary to define how much it will cost to use this software for an hour. Another important aspect is the quality of service, i.e. how reliable are the resources, once the job is submitted to the service provider, how long will it take (on average) to finish.

Software licenses must be available, either at the target systems of the service provider or they must be remotely accessible from there via a license server. Since this has been an unsolved problem in Grid environments, a new solution has been developed in the BEinGRID project (for a more detailed description of the solution see section 8.4 in chapter 8).

Since the data that is exchanged and the calculations that are performed externally are highly confidential, security is a major issue. The shipyard requires that the system should interact only with authenticated and authorized users. When sharing data only the consultant or supplier that needs to work with this data may get access to the ship data. This requirement is solved by the SESIS system.

The system should provide generic interfaces, i.e. it should be possible to access resources from different service providers, so that the shipyard can choose the provider that makes the best offer. This implies that the system should support open standards to guarantee interoperability with other service providers using different middlewares and access mechanisms.

10.5.2 Performance Requirements

Certain performance requirements need to be met in order to make the system usable for the users and generate sufficient revenue for the suppliers. First the amount of time that it takes for uploading a file to the service provider should not be too long, and also the time it takes to download the result files should be reasonable. A recommended benchmark is that the amount of time required to upload a 10 MB file to the service provider should not exceed one minute. In order for the system to be cost effective the increase in speed needs to be significant. The shipyard required that calculations on the servers of the application service provider should be 5 times faster than running them on in-house computers. This time includes waiting times in batch queues, where the jobs have to wait for free resources.

   A fast network connection is required between the internal systems of the engineer, consultant and service provider.

10.6 Conclusion

The challenges European shipyard faces are competitors, in particular those based in the Far East, who produce ships in large series, comparatively cheap. Shipyards in Europe are very specialized and focus in general on niche markets and/or provide customized vessels. The problem is that the same ship is rarely built twice and every time a shipyard starts a new project they have to produce a new design or adapt an existing design and invest in new technologies, research which solution provides the best price / value ratio and satisfies the demands of the customers. Grid computing can help in improving the early design phase and stabilize the position in the niche markets but the pricing pressure from cheaper competitors remains a cause for concern.

   Another challenge is to introduce the new workflow in the design phase at the shipyard and their suppliers. Since Grid computing is a fairly new technology compared to technologies already in place in shipyards, it will take time to be accepted and deployed as widely as foreseen in this Business Experiment. The same holds true for the SESIS environment that eases collaboration. Although shipyards and suppliers participated in the development, it will take some time before they come to fully rely on the new technology to replace ways of working that have been established over many decades.

   The shipyard and its suppliers are often using commercial software that is very specialized. This software is usually very expensive and the usage is limited by strict terms of use. In general software licenses cannot be bought on a pay-per-use-basis; instead they are normally valid for one year at a time. Some independent software vendors sell their licenses under the condition that they run only on a certain machine, or within a radius of a few kilometres of the company that bought them. Such restrictions prevent the shipyards from making use of the Grid, since in Grid computing it may not be clear where the hardware resources used are located. Parallel to the Business Experiment, a license management architecture was developed that allows secure connection to a remote license server and that might help solve this problem at least from a technical perspective (Raekow et al. 2009). From a business point of view the independent software vendors need to be convinced that Grid can be an additional source of revenue. However, some independent software vendors have already noticed the potential of Grid and Cloud computing and are currently working on adjusting their license models accordingly.

11 AgroGrid – Grid Technologies in Agro Food Business

Ulrich Heindl, Ansger Jacob, Marcus Mueller, Peter Racz, Burkhard Stiller, Eugen Volk, Martin Waldburger

11.1 General Description of the Business Experiment

Today's global food industry represents a huge market of US$ 3,500 billion pa (Wijnands et al. 2006). Nevertheless, food supply chains are characterized by fixed trade relations with long term contracts established between heterogeneous supply chain companies. In addition, consumer demands have undergone a dramatic change during the last four decades. Quality, food safety and uniqueness are the leading factors for buying decisions. Altogether, this causes three main problems companies in the food sector need to be prepared for. First, new ways to coordinate companies in to a supply chain must be installed in order to reach an efficient exploitation of globally distributed capacities. Second, cost-effective mechanisms for collaboration are needed. And third, an integrated tracking and tracing solution is essential to ensure food quality and safety on a global scale.

AgroGrid is a Business Experiment addressing above mentioned challenges by providing a Grid-based solution for supply chains in the agricultural industry. AgroGrid implements a Grid-enabled market place that allows companies operating in agriculture food markets to offer and source capacities, to negotiate quality of food to be delivered, to establish contracts, and to create customised dynamic supply chains (Volk et al. 2009b). Thereby, capacities in AgroGrid include any products and services offered by a participant, e.g., food products, transport and/ or storage capacities. AgroGrid also provides facilities to monitor the quality and safety of food products delivered across supply chains.

In this section, the AgroGrid Business Experiment is introduced, in particular, by providing the essential background information about the relevant market environment. Furthermore, the key set of challenges that AgroGrid addresses is outlined, and all partners involved in this experiment are presented.

11.1.1 Background of the Business Experiment

The global food industry spans farming, processing, transport, export cargo handling, airlines and shipping, importers, retailers and food-service organisations. In addition to reviewing current market size, IGD (2009) forecasts that the global food retail market will grow at an annual rate of 4.8% worth US$ 6,353 billion in 2020. The future picture IGD (2009) draw is that Asia Pacific and Central Asia will comprise 41% of the global food retail market in 2020, up from 33% in 2003. Europe will comprise 30% and Nafta 21% in 2020.

K. Stanoevska-Slabeva et al. (eds.), *Grid and Cloud Computing: A Business Perspective on Technology and Applications*, DOI 10.1007/978-3-642-05193-7_11,
© Springer-Verlag Berlin Heidelberg 2010

To complicate matters, the agricultural food industry is dominated by compliance requirements and regulations, including Good Agricultural Practices (GAP), minimum chemical residue level control, hazard analysis and critical control point, food safety laws, supermarket industry regulations, article numbering, air cargo handling regulations, environmental requirements, packaging restrictions, phytosanitary inspections and food safety issues, traceability requirements, controls on genetic engineering, cold chain handling and consumer laws (IGD 2009).

Emerging trends and credence factors influencing the costs of major food supply chains are animal welfare, poverty alleviation, contractual fairness, sustainability and corporate social responsibility. With globalisation, the industry is now dominated by major supermarket and food-service organisations that make many of the decisions regarding how to optimize and synchronize the end to end supply chain process. This in turn results in supermarkets taking greater responsibility for establishing contract farming and operational synergies to control costs and maintain a regular supply of products.

In addition to that, consumers nowadays force structural changes in food production and delivering processes. Due to the trend of individualised and ubiquitous food, retailers are asked to offer special food in very small quantities (see table 11.1). Consumers increasingly demand food, which respects their way of life or their state of health. Examples are competitive athletes, brain workers, vegetarians, allergic persons or the rising number of so called LOHAS (Lifestyle On Health And Sustainability, Schommer at al. 2007) consumers – a very promising customer segment for the next years.

Table 11.1: Changing consumer demands (Wijnands et al. 2006)

Year	Consumer demand	Management concern	Management technique	Performance agri-business	Organisational focus
1960s	price	efficiency	just in time	efficiency	firm
1970s	quality	quality	material requirements planning	quality	firm
1980s	variety	quality	supply chain management	flexibility	bi-lateral
1990s	delivery time	flexibility	efficient consumer response	velocity	chain
2000s	uniqueness	innovation	–	innovation power	chain network

As a result of these characteristics and trends in the food retail industry, the highly competitive environment in the retail markets drives innovation and creates a favourable business environment for optimized food chain management solutions supported by ICT (Information and Communication Technology). But contemporary solutions in this area are facing a lot of problems traditional software cannot solve. Thus, new computing concepts – like Grid computing – are needed to deal with upcoming and existing challenges.

11.1.2 Problems of Current Solutions

In order to achieve the economic potential in terms of cost savings and increasing earnings by using modern ICT, some gaps need to be bridged. Food supply chains usually consist of companies very heterogeneous in nature – many small or medium-sized farmers located around the world, local consolidators, logistics providers and some very large food retailers like Carrefour or WalMart. Figure 11.1 shows the distribution of European agricultural holdings by economic size, where 1 ESU (European Size Units) is roughly corresponding to either 1.3 hectares of cereals or 1 dairy cow or 25 ewes. All farmers with less than 16 ESU are categorized as small principal or part-time farmers, which are more than 78% of all farmers in the European Union (Benoist and Martins 2008).

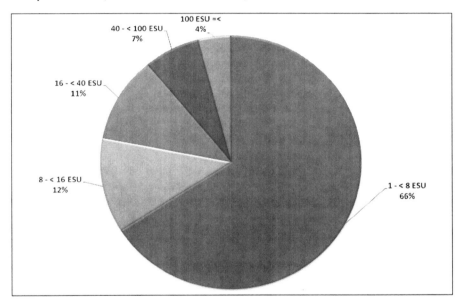

Fig. 11.1: Distribution of European agricultural holdings (Benoist and Martins 2008)

Most of the companies are running different Enterprise Resource Planning (ERP) software or even paper-based solutions to manage their production or transport capacities. Due to this heterogeneity, supply chain partners are not able to coordinate their capacities towards new dynamic production networks by using advantages of modern ICT to lower transaction costs. Also, trust-building and commercialisation support mechanisms are not available today or at least not in an integrated solution.

On the one hand this leads to dead capital; on the other hand, tremendous amounts of food are wasted because overcapacities cannot be sold. Kantor et al.

(1997) calculated that 27% of all edibles available in the USA are thrown away instead of being eaten. Latest studies of the University of Arizona show, that 50% of all produced perishables in the US were never consumed (Ilic at al. 2009). The combination of the previously mentioned huge market size and the possibility to reduce waste of perishable goods show the enormous economic impact.

Another problem in the food industry is the lack of quality and food safety ensuring mechanisms. A customer receiving food products from another supply chain partner can't be sure that he has received fresh and safe food, not affected by dangerous substances like dioxin contaminated chickens, hormone injected cattle etc. Therefore an integrated tracking and tracing solution is essential. Most existing solutions are based on a centralized architecture and therefore they can't ensure data ownership – an essential issue for protecting company's data from industrial spying. Additionally, today's tracking and tracing is used mainly for documentation purposes, in order to find out *manually* where the failure in the supply chain has occurred in the *past*. The better way would be an integrated solution for continuous automated real-time monitoring and evaluation of tracking and tracing data.

To solve the problems of coordinating companies alongside the supply chain and providing a cost effective, trust building, quality assurance building mechanism for collaboration in order to exploit capacities in an economically efficient manner, AgroGrid blueprints and implements a full life-cycle solution for dynamic capacity markets integrated with distributed tracking and tracing, VO (Virtual Organisation) management and automated monitoring and evaluation mechanisms. AgroGrid's dynamic capacity markets mainly address supply chain companies from the European food and agriculture industry. Supply chain companies are enabled to offer, negotiate, book, monitor and evaluate (over) capacities, such as production or logistics capacities. And AgroGrid is fully integrated with TraceTracker's GTNet® – Global Traceability Network, the world's leading solution for distributed tracking, tracing, and collaboration in food markets (TraceTracker 2009). This represents a unique win-win situation because of the close cooperation between AgroGrid and GTNet®.

11.1.3 The Business Experiment – Partners and Work Performed

The Business Experiment AgroGrid started in April 2008 and ended in June 2009. During the project phase, the software engineering process was completed, and all the preparations to start up a business from the scratch were done. In particular, this means that a detailed design specification based on an accurate requirements analysis was worked out. The design phase was followed by the implementation of the AgroGrid system and finally, the implemented AgroGrid solution was tested against the previously defined use case.

TraceTracker AG, the industrial partner within the Business Experiment provides a sophisticated state-of-the-art tracking and tracing solution (GTNet®). This solution is based on a decentralized data storage architecture where all the relevant tracking and tracing information can be accessed via a browser or via other web service interfaces. By using GTNet®, companies are able to track and trace back products and product related information in order to ensure quality and safety. Beside GTNet®, TraceTracker AG also offers deep market knowledge in the field of ICT solutions for food supply chains.

The High Performance Computing Centre (HLRS) is a research and service institution affiliated to the University of Stuttgart. It has been the first national supercomputing centre in Germany and is offering services to academic users and industry. HLRS is participating actively in the Software as a Service (SaaS) / Service Oriented Architecture (SOA) movement and has been doing so since the advent of the Grid. The current research focus continues along this line to include aspects related to Cloud computing, distributed data management, future models for distributed execution, quality of service maintenance, virtual collaboration and organization etc. HLRS is and has been involved in several large initiatives in this domain for quite some time now, involving amongst others Akogrimo, TrustCoM, NextGRID, BREIN and BEinGRID.

The Communication Systems Group (CSG) at the Department of Informatics (IFI) at the University of Zürich (UZH) is the business models and exploitation task leader within the Business Experiment. Related activities in AgroGrid – found primarily in the area of business planning and Grid technology support – benefit from this research group's established scientific footprint, which puts a major focus on addressing economic management of networking resources, Point to Point (P2P) and overlay networks, and security considerations. Furthermore, accounting and auditing in distributed and heterogeneous systems, charging of Internet Protocol (IP) services as well as Virtual Organisations outline the research focus of those experts.

Finally, the project partner Universitaet Hohenheim hosts one of the leading German research groups in the area of enterprise application systems for service and logistic industries: the chair Information Systems 2. In addition, Universitaet Hohenheim has a very long tradition and an international well established reputation in agricultural research. The chair Information Systems 2 contributes agricultural domain and logistics knowledge, Grid experience and expertise in Virtual Organisation Management. Information Systems 2 was the specialist for Virtual Organisations in Grid and expert in supply chain tracking and tracing.

11.2 Description of the Technological Solution

In order to solve identified problems described in the previous section, AgroGrid introduces Grid technology in the agricultural sector by offering a full lifecycle solution for dynamic capacity markets which integrates VO and SLA (Service Level Agreement) management with the market leading solution in global distributed tracking and tracing, GTNet® (Volk et al. 2009b). Additionally, AgroGrid provides a means to monitor and evaluate quality and safety of food trade units delivered across the supply chains.

To address the challenges of quality, food safety and data ownership, and, in contrast to centralized tracking and tracing solutions, AgroGrid's solution is based on a decentralized architecture for distributed tracking and tracing data. This allows companies participating in supply chains to share only that product information which is relevant for other supply chain members the company is trading with.

The SLA concept in Grid is used to express the contract, to define, negotiate and monitor guaranteed service level – Quality of Services (QoS) – between the service provider and service consumer, in electronically form. The SLAs as used in Grid refer typically to computer related resources, as bandwidth, CPU usage, data storage etc. The most important aspect of SLAs in Grid is the automated monitoring and evaluation of guaranteed service level to ensure immediately detection of any violation occurrence, which results in immediately notification of affected parties.

In order to address the challenges of supply chain building and continuous monitoring of quality and food safety, AgroGrid uses SLAs to negotiate, contract, monitor and evaluate capacities traded between the capacity provider and consumer. In contrast to computer related capacities, the capacities in AgroGrid include any products and services offered by a participant, e.g., food products, transport and storage capacities.

In order to take care of the challenges of *dynamic* supply chain building, AgroGrid uses the VO management concept to operate the lifecycle of a VO including setting up a circle of trust. Thereby a VO in Grid corresponds to a supply chain in AgroGrid. The supply chain in AgroGrid is formed by those parties, who participate in the sale, delivery and production of particular product or food trade unit.

To address the challenges of the interoperability, AgroGrid uses Portal technology, which offers a common, personalized, web-browser based, user-friendly, and secure access to AgroGrid services. To access the AgroGrid portal, running on the AgroGrid provider site, users need only a web browser and an account, obtained after registration.

In this section, we describe the AgroGrid's solution by describing AgroGrid platform and the process of dynamic supply chain building.

11.2.1 Composition of Dynamic Supply Chains

As already noted, a supply chain in AgroGrid is represented by a Virtual Organisation formed by those parties, who participate in the sale, delivery, and production of a particular product or food trade unit. The composition of supply chains in AgroGrid is based on market mechanisms – the law of supply and demand (Volk et al. 2009a). By using the AgroGrid platform, a company wanting to offer its capacities to the market, is able to publish them in the AgroGrid capacity offer registry, providing details on the product quality, quantity and pricing (optionally). The AgroGrid platform offers also the possibility to register requests for specific capacities in the capacity request registry. The other companies are now able to query and discover capacity offers, as well as capacity requests, stored in the AgroGrid capacity registry and retrieve the associated SLA-Template from the SLA-Template repository of the capacity provider. The SLA-Template contains in addition to the capacity data also pricing, environmental condition during transport and storage, possible penalties in case of SLA violation, delivery date, and in particular evaluation metrics.

The building of supply chains in AgroGrid is guided by a supply chain template, which defines roles (producer, consolidator, logistics, retailer, etc.) needed for building the product specific supply chain. A party wanting to create a supply chain, called supply chain manager (SC-Manager), selects in the first step from the list of available templates an appropriate supply chain template (e.g. for building a supply chain for apricots). If there is no such template already defined, the AgroGrid portal also offers possibilities to define new templates. After selection of a specific template, the system provides an overview of required roles and, after successful negotiation, also an overview of contracted parties with specific roles participating in the supply chain.

In the next step, the SC-Manager queries the capacity registry for a specific capacity (e.g., for apricots provided by an apricot producer) needed for building the supply chain. After selecting the required capacity from the capacity registry, the SC-Manager (who acts as a capacity requester) initiates the negotiation process by retrieving the SLA-Template from the capacity provider.

In the following negotiation step, the SC-Manager sends an SLA-offer to the capacity provider. The offer contains the SLA-Template with modified or unchanged SLA-terms. The provider may reject or accept the offer by sending an acceptance or rejection notification to the requester with the SLA.

After receiving an acceptance notification from the capacity provider with the accepted SLA, the system automatically sets up the SLA-Monitoring & Evaluator service, which is responsible for continuous monitoring and evaluation of established SLAs. As a result of the continuous monitoring and evaluation process the SLA-Evaluator service creates an SLA-evaluation report, which reflects the fulfilment of SLA, and, in case of a detected SLA violation it serves for the determination of penalty and compensation. The AgroGrid portal provides an overview of monitored SLAs and allows retrieving a specific SLA-evaluation report to approve fulfilment of contracted SLAs. After a SC-Manager has established an SLA with one party of the required role – for example an apricot provider –, he might select further capacities and initiate the negotiation process with more capacity providers (e.g., provider of logistics capacity) or even with capacity requester (e.g. retailer) in order to complete the building of the supply chain.

The described procedure allows composition of dynamic supply chains, by chaining of parties participating in sale, delivery, and production of particular product or food trade unit. Thereby, the dynamicity aspect for building of dynamic supply chains refers to the timely extension of the supply chain to include new partners, and to the possibility of removing or replacing supply chain members, whose performance consistently falls below acceptable norms, by new supply chain members.

11.2.2 AgroGrid Platform

AgroGrid's full lifecycle solution for *dynamic capacity markets* is based on a market place concept that allows companies in the agriculture food sector to offer and search for capacities, negotiate SLAs, and create dynamic supply chains (Volk et al. 2009b). A supply chain in AgroGrid is represented by a Virtual Organisation formed by those parties, who participate in one or more of the supply chain steps of a particular product or food trade unit. AgroGrid allows continuous monitoring and quality evaluation in order to ensure the safety of food delivered across all supply chains, based on distributed tracking and tracing capability of the GTNet® platform and the SLA-Monitoring & Evaluation component. As a result of continuous monitoring and evaluation through SLAs, the SLA-Monitoring & Evaluation component generates SLA evaluation reports, which reflects any occurred violation of negotiated SLAs.

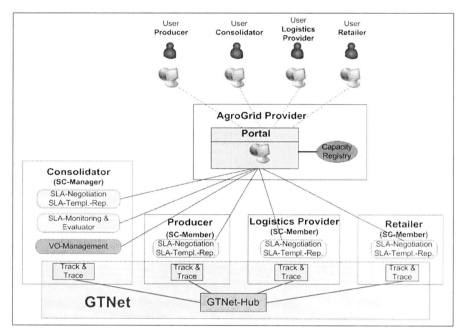

Fig. 11.2: AgroGrid – Platform

The solution provided by AgroGrid consists of the following components (see fig. 11.2): the *Portal*, the *VO-Management*, the *SLA-Negotiator*, the *SLA-Monitoring&Evaluator* and the *Track&Trace* component.

The *Portal* offers AgroGrid users a common, personalized, web-browser based, user-friendly, and secure interface to AgroGrid services. The authentication and authorisation mechanisms of the portal secure and personalise the web based access of the AgroGrid users. The portlets hosted on the portal of the AgroGrid provider form a graphical user interface to AgroGrid services and functionalities, allowing registering and discovering capacities, negotiating SLAs, building/managing supply chains, and accessing SLA evaluation reports.

The *SLA-Negotiator* component allows negotiation of SLAs between a capacity requester and a capacity provider. The negotiation of SLAs includes the negotiation of price, quantity, quality parameters of food to be delivered, environmental conditions during the transport or storage, and the compensation in case of SLA-violation. The negotiated parameters, like quantity, quality, as well as environmental conditions form SLA metrics, which are used by the SLA-Monitoring&Evaluator component for the evaluation of the SLA. The SLA-Negotiator is connected to the SLA-Template Repository, where SLA-Templates are stored. The SLA-Template reflects a capacity offered by a company on the market. The Globus Toolkit based SLA-Negotiator used in AgroGrid, was developed within the BEinGRID project and was adapted during the implementation of the AgroGrid platform.

The *VO-Management* component is used for the setup and management of partner memberships in supply chains. As already noted, a supply chain in AgroGrid is formed by those parties, who participate in the sale, delivery and production of particular product or food trade unit. A party wanting to create a new supply chain, adopts the role of a supply chain manager (SC-Manager), uses the VO-Management component for the management of parties participating in the supply chain, called supply chain members (SC-Member). Before a party can participate in a supply chain, it needs to negotiate a SLA with the supply chain manager. The .NET based VO-Management (called VO-Setup) component used for the realisation of the AgroGrid platform was developed within the BEinGRID project.

The *Track&Trace* component consists of an Enterprise Resource Planning system (ERP) and GTNet®'s distributed Traceability Information Exchange (TIX) databases. Users are able to choose whether they want to run their TIX by using their own hardware facilities or if they want to use a software as a service hosted by TraceTracker AG. In both cases, companies need to pay a license fee and they need to build a XML-file which describes all products and their relevant properties in general.

Later on, any ERP system can serve as a source of tracking and tracing information, as well as a source of monitoring information about quality and environmental conditions of food trade units during their production, storage, transportation or delivery. The tracking and tracing information, as well as monitoring information provided by the ERP is stored in the TIX database. The TIX also provides interfaces for querying traceability and monitoring information stored in the TIXs of the supply chain members. The access to TIXs of the supply chain members is mediated by a local TIX, and is secured by mechanisms provided by GTNet-Hub (Global Traceability Network-Hub) which interconnects all TIXs. The Traceability Information Exchange databases, as well as the GTNet-Hub are part of the TraceTracker's GTNet® platform and were coupled by the usage of the web service based interfaces to the other AgroGrid services, allowing querying the TIXs.

The *SLA-Monitoring&Evaluator* component is responsible for the automated monitoring and evaluation of negotiated SLAs. In order to obtain monitoring information of received food trade units, the component queries monitoring data stored in local TIX databases and in TIXs of the supply chain members. Later, the queried information is transformed into the metrics, as defined in the SLAs. The monitored SLA-metrics are compared and evaluated against the evaluation criteria defined in the SLAs by the SLA-Evaluator. In case of SLA violation detection, the

SLA-Evaluator notifies affected supply chain members about any violations that occur. The result of the SLA evaluation is stored in the evaluation report database and is accessible via the AgroGrid portal to supply chain members. The evaluation report serves for checking the successful SLA fulfilment, and, in case of a detected SLA violation it serves for the determination of penalty and compensation.

11.3 Added Value for the User

The described Grid computing concepts are used in AgroGrid in order to over-come the previously introduced challenges of the food industry. These concepts support important business objectives directly. From a user's point of view, this section provides an answer to what a user obtains from using AgroGrid, and what changes are needed in a user's daily work as well as in existing infrastructure to employ AgroGrid.

11.3.1 Application of Grid Concepts or: Why Grid?

Grid concepts in AgroGrid are used to break up traditional fixed boundaries in food supply chains in order to enable dynamic supply chain composition and to in crease the exploitation of production capacities. Besides, Grid concepts offer suitable solutions for composition and monitoring of supply chains. This means having Grid concepts ensuring an efficient and gap-free quality monitoring by using widely distributed data and, at the same time, helping to secure data ownership. Grid improves scalability of the overall solution – a very important characteristic against the background of the market size and the amount of traded goods.

The maintenance of accurate data for all partners is a crucial demand of compa-nies employing tracking and tracing solutions. While competitors in the market of tracking and tracing software solutions are numerous, these solutions often follow a central database approach (see table 11.2). One of the biggest success factors of TraceTracker's GTNet® is the distributed data management. A main challenge during the implementation of AgroGrid was to grasp data from these distributed traceability information exchange databases in order to detect SLA violations and to generate a SLA report.

Table 11.2: Competitors in the market of tracking and tracing software solutions

Competitor	Solution	Difference to GTNet/ AgroGrid
Trace One	Lifecycle management	Central Database
FXA	Internal traceability	Internal Database only
Historic Futures	Supply chain traceability	Central data registry
Yotta Mark	Product traceability and authentication	Central Database

Beside data management issues, Grid allows collaborative resource sharing across parties allocated all over the world and enables building of dynamic Virtual

Organisations as well as SLA-based negotiation, monitoring and evaluation. Table 11.3 gives an overview of which Grid or Grid-related concepts were used and what tasks they fulfill.

Table 11.3: Grid concepts and their roles in AgroGrid

Grid(-related) concept	Task in AgroGrid
Gridsphere Portal Server	User Management, Role Management, Rights Management, Portlet Container, Authorisation, Access point of all services
Service Level Agreements	Negotiation of SLAs, SLA-Template-Repository, SLA-Monitoring & Evaluation
Virtual Organisation	Management and visualisation of supply chains represented as VOs

Beside the use and integration of existing concepts, sector- and domain-specific concepts were developed and integrated in the AgroGrid solution. For example, AgroGrid provides a set of predefined templates for the description of supply chains. These templates can be created and managed within the AgroGrid portal and set out the right sequence of the companies in a VO.

11.3.2 Changes on the User-Side

AgroGrid offers a number of core benefits to AgroGrid users. In order to profit from these benefits, only a small number of changes on a user's site with respect to process and infrastructure adaptations is required. This is mainly due to the fact that, first, AgroGrid's Grid-enabled marketplace for production and logistics capacities is made available through the AgroGrid portal for which users only need Internet access and a standard browser. Heterogeneous and distributed tracking and tracing data are integrated through the GTNet®. Second, in addition to the collaboration with GTNet®, AgroGrid and GTNet® are marketed as a bundled solution. This implies that AgroGrid is promoted in the early market introduction phase towards existing GTNet® customers. Such customers already have most of the required local infrastructure available from a previous GTNet® installation, so that only smaller local changes have to take place. New users of AgroGrid will not have to change their whole processes or infrastructure. Since AgroGrid and GTNet® are sold as Software-as-a-Service, new customers will only need a common web browser and, of course, a license to access AgroGrid. GTNet® interoperates with all common ERP systems and user will be able to work with their graphical user interfaces they are familiar with. The only change in a user's day to day processes is that they are able to sell their overcapacities through the AgroGrid system instead of using telephone, fax or email. In further details, AgroGrid user changes are summarized as follows:

- AgroGrid users profit with AgroGrid from an efficient tool to manage product offering, transaction negotiations and actual purchase of available production capacities. This happens through the AgroGrid portal. This portal, which is based on Gridsphere, implements AgroGrid-specific portlets for all AgroGrid functionality needed. This includes, for instance, portlets for BaseVO management and VO visualisation, capacity publication and query, and SLA negotiation and SLA evaluation. For a user to access these portlets – and with them the core AgroGrid features – very little or no new investment is needed: As soon as a user account is opened, portlets are accessible via a standard browser through the Internet. No additional software or configuration is required locally.

- Thus, for a successful integration with GTNet®, and in order to profit from GTNet®'s tracking and tracing functionality, an installed and configured TIX is needed. All AgroGrid components can be installed locally on a company's level or they can be hosted by the AgroGrid Provider. The actual number of AgroGrid modules which can be deployed locally depends on a user's role within an AgroGrid VO. In the case the company acts as a VO coordinator, the respective AgroGrid modules for VO management, SLA template repository, SLA negotiation, SLA monitoring, and SLA evaluation have to be installed for active use in AgroGrid. Other AgroGrid VO members only require the modules for SLA template repository and SLA negotiation. Again, all components can be used as Software as a Service instead of being installed locally.

- In terms of process adaptations needed, all processes known to an existing GTNet® user remain unchanged. This refers in particular to the processes to upload and extract trade-related information to and from GTNet®. The actual capacity-related publication/lookup/booking processes plus all VO and SLA management processes will happen within the AgroGrid portal, which is designed with ease-of-use in mind so that those steps are clearly separated into easily differentiated tabs that allow for a short and easy learning period.

11.3.3 Discussion of the Added Value

AgroGrid users benefit from multifarious advantages in using AgroGrid. AgroGrid enables its users – companies in the food industry – to profit from a solution that facilitates dynamic production capacity markets in the agriculture food segment with the help of Virtual Organisation and Service Level Agreement management components and GTNet®'s fully integrated tracking and tracing functionality. To a good proportion, these user benefits base on AgroGrid's use of Grid-related principles, namely the use of resource sharing in VOs representing food supply chains, the comprehensive support of SLAs in the complete life-cycle, and the use of the Gridsphere portal server as a reliable, secure and user-friendly container for the implementation of all central AgroGrid services by means of AgroGrid portlets. Accordingly, the benefits for AgroGrid users include:

- Flexibility: AgroGrid users are enabled to offer production and logistics capacities to publish, and to source capacities from dynamic capacity networks through the AgroGrid market place. The AgroGrid market place facilitates increases a user's flexibility by means of on-demand visibility of available capacities.
- Efficiency: The AgroGrid portal aggregates portlets for all relevant AgroGrid services – ranging from capacity and VO to SLA management – in a user

friendly, secure web-based market place. AgroGrid's focus lays on a complete life cycle solution and ease of use makes its portal an efficient tool to manage capacity offerings, negotiations, and actual capacity sourcing.

- Cost reduction: AgroGrid users benefit from significant cost reductions by lowered transaction costs when using AgroGrid's market place. This means not only cost reductions in capacity sourcing, but also in quality management, since AgroGrid integrates tightly with GTNet®.
- Differentiation, less waste: AgroGrid users can better handle potential overcapacities or demand by trading even smaller, individualized quantities targeted at specific market segments in AgroGrid. Individualisation helps to differentiate from competitors, while smaller quantities help to reduce waste of perishable food.
- Confidence: AgroGrid users are enabled to assure consumers of food products high food quality and safety standards by means of GTNet®'s well known and trusted tracking and traceability functionality and AgroGrid's SLA evaluation reports.

11.4 Summary and Lessons Learnt

The purpose of the Business Experiment AgroGrid is reflected by the set of identified success criteria which include:

- Success criteria 1: to enable collaboration between companies throughout an agricultural food supply chain,
- Success criteria 2: to leverage open value chain services and
- Success criteria 3: to implement trust-building and commercialisation support mechanisms.

To do this, AgroGrid adopted the latest developments and implementations in the field of Grid computing to the agricultural food industry in order to solve sector-specific problems and prepare for future challenges. Furthermore, AgroGrid shows that concepts borrowed from the field of Grid Computing can also be applied to non-IT capacities like agricultural production or logistics. But AgroGrid also deals with traditional Grid Computing scenarios – in particular with distributed data storage and the sharing of tracking and tracing information for whole supply chains.

11.4.1 Technical Experiences

Since AgroGrid was built partly based on existing components, a lot of effort was put in integration and customisation work as well as in the building of a web-based graphical user interface to access all components through a single web portal. AgroGrid's users are able to interact with the whole system by using a standard web browser. The interplay of all components was oriented to meet the structural characteristics of the use case. For example, a Virtual Organisation in terms of AgroGrid is not an unordered set of service providers, but rather a number of companies assigned to individual supply chain roles and arranged in order to build up a linear supply chain over certain steps.

From a technical point of view, AgroGrid demonstrates that already existing Grid computing components can successfully be adopted to build up a working and promising business solution. Adoption, integration and customisation of available components are not a time consuming, risky and costly ventures. Because of their Service Oriented Architecture realised as web services, all components can be invoked easily, even if a web service was written in .NET (like the VO management component) and the corresponding AgroGrid portlet was implemented in Java.

11.4.2 Evaluation of the Business Scenario

To evaluate the outcomes of the one year project phase, a detailed application scenario was developed. In traditional fruit supply chains, participants are operating in fixed boundaries. Producers cooperate with a local consolidator to create a critical mass for economically efficient export activities. These consolidators are contracting logistic companies to transport apricots from local producers to retailers. Therefore, logistic companies offer special containers for shipping the fruits. During shipping, transport and delivery, the quality and environmental conditions of food-trade units are monitored. Monitoring data will be evaluated and stored in an (often) hand-written report.

AgroGrid provides an enhancement of this traditional way of collaboration (see fig. 11.3). All partners of a fruit supply chain are now able to publish their capacities in the AgroGrid system by filling in capacity-specific forms. In this first step, all offered capacities will be characterised by previously elaborated attributes. In a second step, a certain company (e.g. a retailer) requests capacities in order to fulfill a special customer demand or to replenish its own capacities. During the third step, AgroGrid supports all participants in the negotiation phase by offering capacity-specific SLA templates and by providing sending and retrieving facilities for SLA offerings. After a company has accepted an SLA offering, it becomes a contracted partner of the emerging VO. The current state of a VO is always visualised by a coloured graph in the VO visualisation portlet.

After all negotiations are completed, companies fulfill their SLA contracts and send their production data into GTNet® during the productive phase of the supply chain, meaning the VO. Later on, evaluation processes match all SLA agreements against real data sent to the TIX (Traceability Information Exchange database of GTNet®) of the corresponding partners (see arrows 4. and 5. in fig. 11.3). If SLA violations appear to have occurred, the corresponding trade units and their irregularity are shown in the according AgroGrid portlet. To get further information, a user is able to consult GTNet® to trace back the history of a specific trade unit.

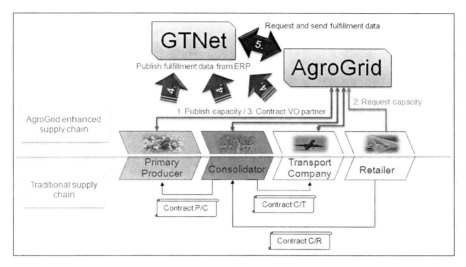

Fig. 11.3: Traditional and enhanced supply chains

During the evaluation phase, the described scenario was passed various times by different test users. Even untrained test persons were able to enter capacity characteristics, to perform SLA negotiations as well as SLA evaluations, and to backtrace trade units. The evaluation scenario shows that capacity offerings and demands are matched more precisely to reduce waste of perishable food and unused capacities. Retailers can now offer individualized food even in very small quantities. The use of Grid components in supply chain management leads to economically efficient exploitation of production capacities, while data ownership is secured.

11.4.3 Summary

To summarise the results of the evaluation phase in the Business Experiment, a self-assessment indicating progress towards meeting the success criteria was conducted. It can be concluded, that all major success criteria and metrics were met: The objective to enable collaboration between companies (success criteria 1) is fulfilled by choosing a proper way of interaction (i.e., by means of VOs) and by granting simple access to all AgroGrid services through a portal by using standard web browsers.

The goal to leverage open value chain services (success criteria 2) is fulfilled by using open standards such as web service technology and the Webservice-Agreement protocol for negotiation. In AgroGrid, authentication and authorisation are used to implement trust-building and commercialisation support mechanisms (success criteria 3), while charging and billing services have not yet been finalized. Additionally, the security concepts of the Gridsphere portal server and the GTNet® system are made use of. Additionally, the SLA concept used in AgroGrid allows continuous monitoring of SLAs, including important SLA parameters such as the amount and quality of trade units delivered and their temperature during transport and storage.

11.5 Outlook

After describing the Business Experiment, the technical and business background as well as all partners, this section provides some outlooks on the future of AgroGrid and its adoption to upcoming trends such as Cloud computing.

11.5.1 Outlook on the Next Steps

The first three years of the commercialisation phase are well planned in terms of possible clients, costs and revenues. To monitor the performance of the business and to mitigate risks, some key performance indicators were identified (see table 11.4). These indicators will be monitored continuously during the early start-up phase. If an indicator exceeds a certain level, the management of AgroGrid will take appropriate action to mitigate the risks.

Table 11.4: Key performance indicators

KPI	Measurement
Number of clients	Counting all companies recorded in the AgroGrid database.
Transaction number	Counting all closed and fulfilled SLA contracts within a measurement period
Transaction value	Sum up the value of all closed and fulfilled SLA contracts within a measurement period
Usage frequency	Number of logins, date/time of these logins and duration of system usage
Enterprise variety	Statistics of corporate objectives as a bar chart
Turnover ratio	Overall turnover divided by turnover using AgroGrid, both per period
System downtime	Downtime in seconds
Bugreport number	Counting all reported bugs within a measurement period

Since attracting a critical mass of customers in all the necessary supply chain roles is the dominant risk factor, the number of clients and the variety of enterprises are the most important indicators. In order to reach a critical mass of varying enterprises, AgroGrid will start with a clear focus on fruit supply chains because in this sector freshness and delivery time are very critical factors. A major focus will be put in promoting AgroGrid towards large retailers in the market – they will act as multipliers for the solution. Later, the product will be rolled out on the whole food industry.

In conclusion, AgroGrid is based on a very promising business model and it addresses a very interesting, challenging, and important industry with a huge annually turnover and a constant growth over the next years. Since changing consumer

demands, price pressure in the market and food quality as well as safety are identified as the leading factors, AgroGrid provides the right solution to move to new
ways in coordinating companies, reaching economically efficient exploitation of
capacities, accessing cost-effective mechanisms for collaboration, and ensuring end
to end gap-free food retraceability.

11.5.2 Upcoming Trends

One upcoming trend shaping the technology today is Cloud computing. "Gartner
defines Cloud Computing as a style of computing where massively scalable
IT-related capabilities are provided 'as a service' using Internet technologies to
multiple external customers" (Gartner 2008a). The business related aspects of
Cloud computing incorporates combination of IaaS (Infrastructure as a Service),
PaaS (Platform as a Service) and SaaS (Software as a Service) concepts. In addition
to IaaS, PaaS and SaaS, Horkan (2009) distinguishes between hosting, Managed
Service Provider (MSP) and Hosting 2.0 as further types of a Cloud, too.

From the technical point of view, the AgroGrid solution can easily be ported
into a "Cloud" environment, e.g., by hosting and at the same time executing all
AgroGrid services within a pool of easily usable and accessible virtualized resources. The ability of the Cloud to be scaled up or down to meet increases or decreases in workloads is called elasticity, and is one of the main features of a Cloud.
Hosting the AgroGrid's services in a Cloud would provide elasticity, improving the
scalability, availability and reliability of the AgroGrid solution, by acquisition of
new resources in case of increasing number of AgroGrid users, requests, or supply
chains to be monitored. The increased number of requests can be handled by increasing the number of TIX replications or service instances, running on additional
servers.

From the business point of view outsourcing of resources is one of the main
advantages of Cloud computing. Cloud users pay only for the usage of utilized resources in a pay-as-you-go manner (Armbrust et al. 2009), saving the maintenance
and ownership costs. Pay-as-you-go and elasticity are the main advantages of users
hosting AgroGrid services and TIXs in a Cloud. On the other hand, moving TIXs
to a Cloud raises new issues related to trustworthiness of the Cloud provider, and
in particular location of the data (esp. if the Cloud provider is located in a foreign
country).

From the AgroGrid provider's point of view, the AgroGrid portal and services
can be hosted on the IaaS Cloud, e.g. provided by Amazon, Sourceforge, Flexiscale,
Rackspace. Advantage are predictable costs and fast extensibility especially in the
start-up of the AgroGrid provider. On the other hand, this may lead to higher depen-
dency on one particular Cloud provider, as the middleware used in different Clouds
is in some cases provider specific.

In conclusion, moving the AgroGrid services to a Cloud brings benefits to the
end user as well as to AgroGrid provider making use of the main advantages of
a Cloud: elasticity and pay-as-you-go. GTNet®, with which AgroGrid services
interoperate, is available as an hosted variant today already. AgroGrid could be

redesigned for usage in an hosted variant on a virtualized server infrastructure (IaaS), an infrastructure software like ERP or DB software (PaaS), supply chain-specific code and services (SaaS), or operations (MSP) as well. AgroGrid as part of a Cloud could meet the requirements of a provider and the end users much better.

12 Virtual Hosting Environments for Online Gaming

David Bossard, Francesco D'Andria, Theo Dimitrakos, Angelo Gaeta

12.1 General Description

12.1.1 Background

The Virtual Hosting Environment (VHE) is an advanced Information and Communication Technologies (ICT) environment where business services can be integrated with one another across organisational boundaries and domains. The VHE also provides the means to virtualize the environment where the business services operate.

There are two keys areas to be considered as background for this experiment. The proof of concept aimed to provide a novel business service provision solution for online gaming. Online gaming relates to any form of game played over a network with one or more players. It involves in its simplest form a minimum of two computers (that of the player and the game server). In its more advanced form, it uses entire sets of servers, dedicated storage, and playing platforms for massive multiplayer online games (MMOG). The increasing reach of the Internet, the soaring number of connected homes, and the wider choice in technology have contributed to online gaming's rapid growth. The Internet now offers an ever richer palette of games. The gaming industry is thriving: this was true in 2006 at the start of this Business Experiment. According to report by PricewaterhouseCoopers (2009), it is even more true today. Their report estimates that between late 2008 and 2013, the entire gaming market will grow by an average of 7.4 %, jumping from $51.4 billion in 2008 to $73.5 billion in 2013 (PricewaterhouseCoopers 2009). A recent Eurotechnology Japan report states that the Japan Gaming sector alone is booming with the combined net annual income of Japan's top nine game companies overtaking the combined net income of Japan's top 19 electrical giants (Eurotechnology Japan 2009). Online gaming in particular is powering the growth. In the USA, online gaming grew 22% year on year, while console game sales are expected to drop by as much as 20% year on year (comScore 2009). One of the key reasons is the cheapness of online games by comparison to console alternatives. This fuels a greater consumer demand for more readily-available, cheaper, and richer games. In Total Telecom Magazine (2009), Strategy Analytics states "Global revenues from PC and video game software reached more than US$46.5 billion in 2008, of which $6.4 billion or 22% of total revenues was derived from online channels". In addition, "the online share of gaming is expected to continue to rise to an estimated one third of revenues in 2011/12" (Total Telecom Magazine 2009).

However, online gaming is a very demanding market that requires server farms, vast amounts of bandwidth, large storage capacities, rich web gaming portals, and

K. Stanoevska-Slabeva et al. (eds.), *Grid and Cloud Computing: A Business Perspective on Technology and Applications*, DOI 10.1007/978-3-642-05193-7_12,
© Springer-Verlag Berlin Heidelberg 2010

tools to manage fast-growing user communities. The online gaming industry can expect very fluctuating demands with gaming peaks and lows and irregular usage patterns. To address this, Service Providers (SP) could partner and support game developers to remove the infrastructure burden from them (Total Telecom Magazine 2009) and let them focus on what developers do best – write appealing, highly-interactive, and richly featured games for users to enjoy. SPs would then bring the hosting know-how along with support for a wide array of non-functional requirements such as security and Quality of Service (QoS).

With this in mind, this Business Experiment has analysed the current state of the art (see sect. 12.1.2). It designed a new architecture that supports online gaming providers. It also unlocks internal capabilities at different SP sites to offer them externally as Value-Adding Services (VAS). Such VAS can include billing services, Customer Relationship Management (CRM), or VoIP services (BT 2009b). This has given birth to the Virtual Hosting Environment (VHE) (see sect. 12.2). The VHE is a service-oriented modular architecture able to deliver extensible, flexible, and adaptive scenarios both for online gaming and other service-oriented businesses.

Indeed, online gaming is not the only area that can benefit from the VHE. Any enterprise wishing to embrace the Internet and offer capabilities as a service could benefit from the VHE. Today's organisations are undergoing major changes in the way they conduct business. This requires their IT infrastructure be rethought. Enterprises are increasingly pervasive with a mobile workforce, a rising number of business collaborations with other organisations, and a rising number of externalized infrastructure and services. Many services not seen as core to the business are being outsourced. This is the case for instance of CRM, communications tools (email, VOIP, virtual intranets), and even mission-critical applications such as security. In fact, it is estimated that in the light of today's growing complexity, Small and Medium Enterprises (SMEs) will no longer be able to afford to implement some of the business functions they need and should resort to third-party solutions. In particular, this is the case with security (McAfee 2006). Even worse, many SMEs may not be correctly assessing the risks involved in doing online business while at the same time they "have become very reliant on the Internet" (McAfee 2006). Online access and availability has become very important to the running of businesses.

12.1.2 Limitations of the Current Solution

Current gaming platforms and online gaming providers are built on top of a very static architecture: each online gaming provider buys, runs, and manages its own dedicated game servers. This requires a large initial investment for any new entrant and makes it harder to penetrate the market. It also entails high running costs both from a management and operation aspect as from a maintenance and hardware aspect. In addition, it is extremely difficult to correctly scale the infrastructure as online gaming targets millions of users that will often connect from the same geographical region at roughly the same time for variable periods of time. This generates extreme peaks and lows in demand that impact gaming performance, QoS and ultimately user experience and satisfaction. It shifts the load across the entire world at different times and would ideally require a geographically-distributed solution.

The online gaming providers' infrastructure is often poorly utilized due to architectural limitations. This can generate ongoing financial losses in addition to the high cost of the initial investment.

Each online gaming provider also needs to implement each core function needed for the running of its business. This includes the hosting and execution of games at the lower end of the overall online game provision; the load balancing between different servers; the monitoring of QoS metrics, service delivery, and customer satisfaction; overall system security and secure messaging; and appealing rich internet applications (RIA) to manage user communities with rich content that drives the overall business. The distributed nature of online gaming, the rising number of users and connections greatly augments the complexity of the systems which in turn will drive online gaming providers to design and adopt easier-to-manage solutions.

On the other hand, service providers currently often only offer communication services, generally limited to the provision of internet and telephony to businesses. However, Total Telecom Magazine (2009) states "service providers could have an opportunity to take some of the infrastructure burden away from games developers and create a new revenue stream. To date network operators have shown more than a tentative interest in online gaming as a new revenue stream. But stellar growth in the gaming market and signs that content companies don't want to manage the whole service end to end, means there could be a greater opportunity for telcos to capitalise on their infrastructure."

The current solution doesn't easily allow for additional VAS to be plugged into it. It is therefore difficult for SPs to provide and bill for such services. The aim of the VHE will therefore be to offer a modular, extensible, pluggable architecture where service providers, businesses, end users, and hosting environments can be brought together to deliver higher-value services.

12.1.3 Requirements for a New Service-Oriented Architecture

In order to address the issues created by static architectures, there is a need to design from scratch a new architecture that can enable the dynamic composition and exposure of Software-as-Services to end customers. Requirements can be grouped into different themes: high-level business requirements, infrastructure requirements, service exposure requirements, governance requirements, and non-functional requirements.

Overall, the key aim of the solution is to develop an architecture that clearly segregates between the actual operations of a business service from the hosting of that service, the network aspects, and the non-functional aspects. The solution should let different providers focus on those areas where they excel.

From a high-level, business perspective, the main requirement is to achieve a new dynamic system that allows cross-enterprise business interactions. This system should be flexible enough so that it can accurately reflect the value chains that exist between the different business partners. The system should offer adequate tools to offer and measure different levels of QoS based on pre-agreed Service-Level Agreement (SLA) contracts.

The solution put forward should enable each organisation using a Service-Oriented Infrastructure (SOI) to define its own policies to drive their infrastructure. The solution should bring visibility into the execution of these policies. It should also bring visibility and ease-of-management into organisations' relationships with customers, suppliers, and partners.

The solution should be able to leverage existing third-party VAS such as SLA and security services. In particular, it should guarantee QoS to the end customer along with correct billing and QoS measurements. In addition to being able to connect to VAS, the solution should enable organisations to offer their own internal capabilities as VAS: the architecture should enable the secure and controlled exposure of in-house software as services to external customers following the Software-as-a-Service (SaaS) paradigm.

From a core infrastructure perspective, the solution should enable a scalable, extensible, and manageable system capable of reducing IT cost through service reuse and optimization. To achieve this, the architecture should offer a manageable hosting environment where applications can be contextualized, virtualized, and run on the most adequate hosts. It should be possible to combine these environments in clusters or matrixes to provide increased performance. These environments should be highly configurable and manageable to give the end-user (an organisation using these resources) maximized control over its services.

From a security perspective, the solution should support the operation and life-cycle management of trust federations of common capabilities (CC) and business services. By federation, we mean an aggregation of users and services together with an underpinning circle of trust defining the relationship between the different participating partners.

The solution should enable a management and governance model that spans across layers and organisational boundaries in order to achieve a correct picture of the infrastructure, its state, and the services exposed. The governance framework should enable the ability to manage the full policy lifecycle. It should provide the means to audit policies and sub-systems and should be able to prove the compliance of the solution with local regulations, corporate rules, as well as legal constraints both at national and international levels.

Applied to the Online Gaming scenario, these requirements confirm the trend identified in Total Telecom Magazine (2009). Game developers should focus on editing and developing games while buying or renting hosting resources from specialists e.g. Amazon EC2 (http://aws.amazon.com/ec2/). This also confirms the model identified by McAfee. SMEs will either not understand the risks linked with online business models or will not have the means and dedication to invest in an adequately secure infrastructure in order to ensure its business is adequately protected.

The requirements are further detailed in Brossard et al. (2008), Brossard and Prieto Martínez (2009) and Dimitrakos et al. (2009b).

12.1.4 The Business Experiment – Partners and Work Performed

Five key partners took part in the design and development of the VHE for online gaming. These partners are Andago of Spain, ATOS Origin of Spain, BT Group plc of the UK, the Centre of Research in Pure and Applied Mathematics (CRMPA) of Italy, and the University of Rey Juan Carlos (URJC) of Spain.

Andago provided the gaming platform and the business use cases. In particular they fed the initial requirements stemming from the business world and the online gaming sector. Andago also provided (in conjunction with URJC) the resources on which to test the solution developed.

ATOS implemented the service-level agreement (SLA) (monitoring and evaluation) subsystem for the VHE. More information can be found in D'Andria et al. (2008) and in section 12.2.1.4. In particular, ATOS focused on the following issues:

- Automatic resources "negotiation" through an "SLA-based" service advertisement and discovery mechanism.
- Monitoring of agreements, considering network related QoS and the network availability itself as a relevant component of the value chain for service provisioning.
- Platform independent agreement evaluation against the Service Level Objectives (SLO) inside the collaboration contract at run-time.

In addition to leading the overall experiment, BT provided the security services and the technical know-how to integrate them. These services include the federation manager, the identity broker (SOI-STS), the authorization service (SOI-AuthZ-PDP), and the secure messaging gateway (SOI-SMG) detailed in section 12.2.1.3 and in Gaeta et al. (2008), Brossard et al. (2008), and (Brossard and Prieto Martínez 2009). BT also developed the governance gateway (SOI-GGW) which allows the secure management of the infrastructure and full policy lifecycle management.

CRMPA led the integration task of the experiment and also provided the foundation for the hosting environment based on the GrASP middleware (http://www.eu-grasp.net) (Gaeta et al. 2008).

Lastly, URJC integrated the Andago Game Platform (AGP) with GrASP to work in a VHE. URJC focused their efforts on the design and implementation of appropriate integration architecture between both technologies (AGP and GrASP) to provide support for the new business model based on Grid services.

12.1.5 Scenario Description

A network-centric application provider, which in the application example used in this experiment, is an on-line collaborative game platform provider (we shall call it Andago), engages in a contract with the VHE operator (BEMOL) that allows the application provider to use other applications, resources and infrastructure services offered by BEMOL or other parties in order to enhance their user experience. In our example Andago uses game titles from a Game Application Provider; Game Servers offered by other parties (Sunny and Saygah for instance).

Andago can then initiate the creation of a Virtual Organisation (VO) that allows Andago to create instances of a game title from the Game Application Provider on the Game services offered by Sunny Data Centres. Andago use Sunny computational resources in Spain in order to offer collaborative on-line games to Andago's gamer communities. As Andago's customer base expands they decide to expand their VO by amending their contract with the operator (BEMOL) and introducing more game servers this time offered by Saygah. Their decision to expand may be in reaction to surge of use or it may reflect a customer base expansion in the UK, a region for which Saygah Data Centres can offer better QoS than Sunny.

As Andago's customer base expands, they also need to enhance the business intelligence of their network-centric application. Andago may choose to use advanced identity management services offered to the VHE by CHOIR and distributed access management services offered by BEMOL Security. These are network-hosted services that allow Andago to define their own profiles of standards-compliant identity assertions and access control policies. Other business partners of Andago (such as Saygah Data Centres) may choose to use other identity providers (say BEMOL Security) depending on their preferences. The VHE infrastructure ensures compatibility between the different infrastructure services in place. In addition to security services, Andago may want to set-up an SLA framework to measure the QoS that Sunny and Saygah are delivering. It therefore invites ARPEGGIO Quality Services which will deliver a set of SLA monitors and an SLA evaluator to be used as VAS in the VHE.

Different customer relationships over the VHE may be more appropriate for different charging models. For example, Saygah Data Centres and Sunny Data Centres may be charging Andago following a "pay-per-use" model. CHOIR, on the other hand, as an Identity Provider may be charging Andago on the basis of the size or duration of the VO. Finally BEMOL, as a VHE operator, may be charging Andago on a "pay-as-you-grow" fashion based on the portfolio of VHE capabilities that are made available to Andago, while BEMOL may be charging Sunny Data Centres and Saygah Data Centres based on a percentage of their resource utilisation via the VHE and CHOIR a flat fee on the number of customers gained. Such dynamics require very flexible accounting mechanisms offered by the VHE infrastructure in order to allow the various stakeholders to retrieve and correlate chargeable events accurately.

This is a major shift from current state-of-the-art solutions where an online games provider such as Andago would have to invest in hardware and other infrastructure, architect its security and billing solutions, in addition to providing the end-user interfaces, web portals and communities. By delegating hosting issues to specialized providers (Sunny and Saygah), and by delegating security and SLA needs to third-party VAS providers (BEMOL Security, CHOIR, ARPEGGIO Quality Services), Andago can focus on its core business: the provision of an appealing user gaming platform.

12.2 Overview of the Virtual Hosting Environment

The VHE is an advanced Information and Communication Technologies (ICT) environment where business services can be integrated with one another across organisational boundaries and domains. The VHE also provides the means to virtualize the environment where the business services operate. As such, the VHE enables new Software-as-a-Service models that exploit economies of scale for the business service and infrastructure providers; and reduce time-to-market margins by enabling fast service composition and business flexibility.

The virtualisation of hosting environments refers to the federation of a set of distributed hosting environments for execution of an application and the possibility to provide a single access point (e.g. a Gateway) to this set of federated hosting environments.

In the following paragraphs, we will describe the solution developed in this Business Experiment and how it applies to the online gaming scenario.

12.2.1 The Virtual Hosting Environment: Architecture & Implementation

The approach taken in the VHE is that put forward by the Service Oriented Architecture (SOA) paradigm. From an implementation's perspective, this means the experiment has referred to the Web Service Framework roadmap (IBM 2009a) which is currently supported by several commercial SOA platforms and implements service interface specifications and protocols in the WS-* stack that are being standardised mainly in OASIS and W3C.

The core implementation is therefore based on the convergence of Grid and Web Services technology and complies with implementations of the WS-* and WSRF/WSDM protocol stack as well as associated mission-specific standards such as SAML and XACML.

12.2.1.1 Key Concepts

There are four key concepts in the virtual hosting environment (Brossard and Prieto Martínez 2009). These concepts are:

1. The hosting environments
2. The Business-to-Business (B2B) gateways
3. The value-adding infrastructure services (e.g. security and SLA services), and
4. The VO management service

The hosting environment typically represents the physical infrastructure where the applications (for instance the games) are being deployed, instantiated, and executed. It should be possible to manage the hosting environments closely, and monitor the use of resources in order to extract QoS information. Generally, hosting environments can include servers, application gateways, data stores, etc. The instantiation of an application refers to the creation of a unique segregated instance with (possibly) allocated separate resources (CPU, storage) and separate data stores and state. This instance can then be individually served to customers or organisations.

On the one hand, the B2B gateway acts as an integration point at the edge of the organisation, supporting the virtualisation and secure exposure of application services and enhancing the functionality of these application services, and, on the other hand, by aggregating infrastructure services to implement common non-functional aspects. The latter include QoS obligations, identity federation, access and usage control, etc.

Value-adding services are applications that can be offered as a service over the network and that have as a primary function the support of new application virtualization within different collaborations or contexts. Typically VAS services address critical technical areas that are difficult to achieve for a given organisation for lack of investment, time, know-how, or due to corporate strategies (McAfee 2006). VAS services include identity services, access control services, policy servers, security monitors, SLA evaluators, and so on. In this experiment, the key focus was on security (identity management and bridging, access control, secure policy enforcement) and SLA (SLA monitor, SLA evaluator, SLA-based service selection). Another important VAS is that of the governance gateway which offers the ability to manage business services, infrastructure profiles and full policy life-cycle management during the collaboration lifetime. Other VAS include presence or telephony services e.g. VoIP. An overview of the VAS used in this experiment is given in sections 12.2.1.3 and 12.2.1.4. In addition, we encourage the readers to refer to Gaeta et al. (2008), D'Andria et al. (2008), Brossard et al. (2008) and Dimitrakos et al. (2009a).

The Virtual Organisation Management Service (VOMS) contains a set of services used in the setup of collaborations between different organisations. Typically an organisation will identify a business opportunity and key requirements and technical needs (be it hosting, security, or more complex needs e.g. business processes).

The figure above illustrates the static architectural view of a typical deployment of the entire VHE with several partners as per the scenario elicited in section 12.1.5. Each key component that constitutes the VHE is illustrated: The VOM services are split among partners and the VHE provider. The hosting environments are provided – as per the scenario – by Sunny and Saygah. The game to be run is in Sunny's and Saygah's service pool and will be deployed on their hosting environments. Andago contains its own game web portal which will expose the gaming management interface and user control pane to its end users, the gamers.

In this scenario, the security VAS are provided by CHOIR and BEMOL Security. ARPEGGIO provides the SLA services that will monitor the QoS during the delivery of the services to the end user.

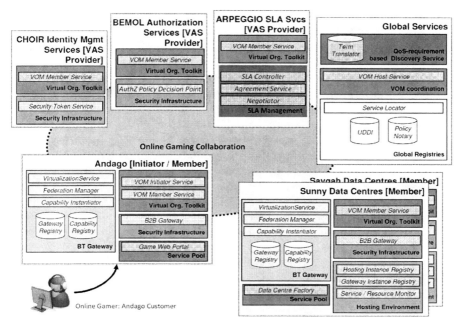

Fig. 12.1: Architectural perspective of the online gaming scenario with the hosting environments, the gateways, the VAS, and the VOMS (Virtual Organisation Toolkit)

The B2B gateways at each participating partner (Andago, Sunny, and Saygah) allow each partner to securely connect to the collaboration and expose their services in a contextualized way. Each participating partner also has a service gateway which handles the instantiation and virtualization of the application instances – in this case the Data Centre factories which will be used to create, host, and run new games instances at either of Sunny or Saygah.

12.2.1.2 Four Steps towards Managed Dynamic Collaborations

Using VOMS, the organisation can follow a rigorous four-step process to create and manage collaborations implemented over the B2B gateway, the VAS infrastructure services, the VOMS, and the hosting environments. These four steps are VO identification, formation, operation, and dissolution. The VOM Coordination Services provided by the VHE operator help liaise between the different partners' VOM member services and manage the lifecycle of the given collaboration (see fig. 12.1).

During the first phase, the organisation identifies relevant partners based on service types they offer and the QoS they guarantee for each service. QoS here relates to high-level customer expectations e.g. a 'gold service experience'. These high-level QoS (HL-QoS) are then translated into lower-level QoS (LL-QoS) such as service latency, CPU usage, and so on depending on the business rules defined. At this time, high-level contracts have been drafted from which lower-level policies and rules can be derived.

In the VO formation phase, the originating partner sends out invitations to the relevant business partners it wishes to invite. An invitation contains the high-level contract or agreement that governs the new collaboration as well as any other low-level policies and rules the originating partner may wish other partners to enforce such as global access control policies. At this point invited partners may accept (or not, as they wish). In a typical online gaming collaboration, the originator may invite hosting environments, game title providers, user base providers, web portals, identity management providers, SLA monitoring providers, and so on. In the online gaming scenario, Andago invites Sunny and Saygah to take part in a gaming collaboration where Sunny and Saygah will be responsible for hosting and executing game instances. Andago also invites ARPEGGIO, BEMOL, and CHOIR to take part in the collaboration as IT solutions providers. BEMOL and CHOIR, for instance, provide security solutions as VAS in the collaboration.

The third phase deals with the operation of the VO. During this phase, new business services previously selected in the VO formation phase can now be instantiated, configured, contextualized, and exposed through the B2B service gateways to the consumers inside the collaboration. The required supporting infrastructure (the VAS) may also be instantiated, configured, and exposed to the collaboration. Instantiation of a business service involves creating an altogether new segregated instance of the service for a particular customer (be it a single user or an organisation), configuring the logical host on which to run the instance (CPU, memory, storage rules and restrictions), configuring the supporting VAS (security, QoS, SLA), exposing the instance to the collaboration, and updating the service instance registries maintained by the VOMS. This step of instantiation, configuration, and contextualization is often called virtualization hence the name Virtual Hosting Environment.

The final phase, VO dissolution, focuses on the removal of the collaboration, the destruction of all created service instances (business and VAS), the removal of configuration files and the reversion to the previous known stable state. In particular, VO dissolution must ensure all systems involved remain in a coherent state and that the registries correctly reflect the business state.

The following figure summarizes the VO lifecycle.

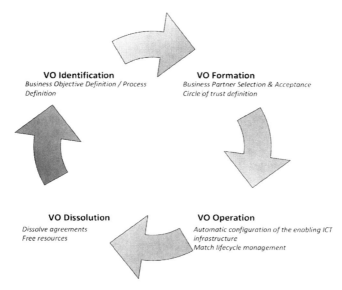

VO Identification
Business Objective Definition / Process Definition

VO Formation
Business Partner Selection & Acceptance Circle of trust definition

VO Dissolution
Dissolve agreements Free resources

VO Operation
Automatic configuration of the enabling ICT infrastructure Match lifecycle management

Fig. 12.2: The VO Lifecycle

12.2.1.3 The Security Value-Adding Services

The Security value-adding services used in this experiment were developed by the Trust & Security Theme of the BEinGRID project. This theme includes technical innovation that addresses areas where a perceived and actual lack of security appears to inhabit commercial adoption of SOI technologies. It includes solutions for brokering identities and entitlements across enterprises, managing access to shared resources, analyzing and reacting to security events in a distributed infrastructure, and securing multi-tenancy hosting. These innovations underpin solutions offered in VOM and several other categories.

Out of the work done in this theme, four capabilities have been retained for use in this experiment.

The first capability is a security token service (SOI-STS) which provides Identity and Federation management: it allows, on the one hand, the management of the lifecycle of circles of trust between providers, and therefore the life-cycle management of federation of trust realms, and on the other hand, managing the life-cycle of identities and privileges of users and resources within such federations of trust realms. The obvious benefits of offering these as network-hosted services that can be integrated with application services through the VHE include:

- Facilitating the creation of communities of identity providers that enable identity brokerage and management by supporting open standards such as Liberty Alliance, SAML and WS-Federation, and therefore giving rise to new means of revenue generation. Indeed the SOI-STS can be exposed in the SaaS approach and sold to external customers.

- Enabling the customer to choose the identity provider that is more appropriate for a specific collaboration instead of being locked into what is incorporated in their SOA platform by a middleware vendor or starting expensive product integration projects that give them identity provision and federation, at a very high cost, for the specific application at hand.

The second capability is an Authorization Service (SOI-AuthZ-PDP) which supports distributed access control. It is a policy-based, rule-based access control service which implements XACML, the eXtended Access Control Markup Language (an OASIS standard aimed at defining an access control language to express rich access control rules). It allows the distribution of delegated administrative authority across the value chain. It allows managing the distribution of administrative authority among multiple partners (e.g. providers of applications, of application hosting, of identity services, etc.) and the management of constraints about the scope within which each administrative authority can operate.

The delegated access control mechanism explored in this experiment allows finely granular control on the delegation of administrative authority. In particular, management and access policy can be signed on behalf of different administrators and evaluated at run time against delegation constraints that discount parts of the polices and resolve conflicts in accordance with the identity and role of each administrator. This allows for example the VHE operator to profile or constrain the policies that an Application Service Provider (ASP) administrator can define, and their period of validity. The ASP administrator can then define whatever access policies fit their application best, including policies that allow a collaboration manager to fine tune the certain aspects of the access for a limited period of time. For example, the VHE operator may have constrained that the ASP cannot deny access to information about the services it provides to another legitimate customer of the VHE. The VHE operation may have also constrained that an ASP can only define policies about services offered in those collaborations they can join according to their subscription to the VHE. Then the ASP will have full control of access to the applications they offer in collaborations that they are allowed to join but will not be able to hide information about the service they offer within the VHE. In addition to access policies about the services they offer in those collaborations, they may also define a constraint that allows the collaboration manager to fine tune access to resources during a promotion period. Therefore the collaboration manager could override a policy denying game service access to "bronze" members to a "limited-edition" game but only during the promotion period.

This capability offers an essential service managing distribution of the administration tasks across the value chain while assuring accountability and non-repudiation of administrative actions during the operation of a distributed infrastructure.

Thirdly, the secure messaging gateway (SOI-SMG) is a network- or perimeter-hosted policy enforcement point that can be itself configured through an extensible policy language. It brings together selected functionalities from XML firewalls, application gateways, content inspection and transformation engines, light-weight enterprise service / event bus, and network resource management. It can securely expose services on the basis of network traffic, message content, and application data. It acts as a message interceptor, decorator, router and enforcer. It is also the integration node in an SOA deployment (as in this scenario). The SOI-SMG being policy-based allows for rich, highly adaptive scenarios. The SOI-SMG can be used in several collaborations concurrently while maintaining clear message flow segregation.

Lastly, the governance gateway (SOI-GGW) focuses on the management and governance of infrastructure and capability profiles. In particular, it provides the ability to define security infrastructure profiles that associate the business service to be exposed with a unique combination of virtual service endpoint and collaboration context, and with

- A collection of one or more application gateways (SOI-SMG),
- A collection of zero or more VAS (SOI-STS, SOI-AuthZ-PDP…),
- A collection of security policy templates to apply for each VAS
- A configuration management process reflecting a common policy management life-cycle

It also provides a process to manage the life-cycle of the business service being exposed in accordance with a selected profile. This process includes sub-processes for exposing the service in the given context, binding the corresponding value-adding security services and managing the applicable policy instances for each of these value-adding security services.

These capabilities integrate as illustrated in the figure below. The integrated view illustrates part of the operational phase of the gaming scenario.

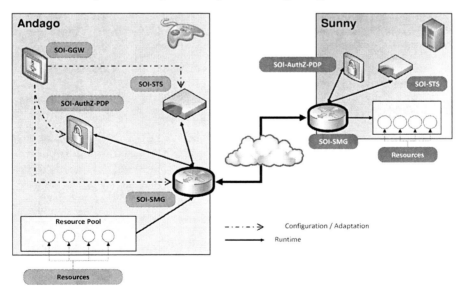

Fig. 12.3: An integrated view of the Security VAS

Figure 12.3 proposes a zoom on the security infrastructure being used in the proposed architecture as illustrated in figure 12.2. This figure abstracts away the organisations which offer the services. Figure 12.3 clearly shows that the SOI-SMG is the underlying VAS to the B2B security gateway mentioned in section 12.2.1.1. Once correctly configured on a per-service, per-context basis, it integrates several value-adding security services namely the identity broker (SOI-STS) and the authorization service (SOI-AuthZ-PDP) to protect service invocations from Andago's services to Sunny's services where the game instances are being executed. In particular the SOI-SMG at Andago will check that the initial request comes from a valid user who is authorized to proceed with such a request. This involves checking for the identity of the requestor, checking whether they are a member of the current collaboration, and checking whether there is an existing identity mapping definition for that particular identity. If so, Andago's SOI-STS delivers a virtual identity token which is then used for authentication by Sunny where the token is validated and checked for identity claims that describe the initial requestor and which can be used for access control decisions at Sunny's SOI-AuthZ-PDP. Details of this interaction are further explained in section 12.2.2 as well as in Brossard et al. (2008) and Dimitrakos et al. (2009b). This service-oriented model brings context-aware, content-aware security to the application layer and as such brings flexibility and enables dynamic service composition models.

12.2.1.4 The SLA Value-Adding Services

The SLA value-adding services consider two well differentiated phases: firstly, the advertisement and discovery of the Business Service / SLA Contract and, secondly, the monitoring and evaluation of its fulfilment at run-time. In the experiment the L&D subsystem extends the classical Universal Description, Discovery and Integration (UDDI) directory functionalities in two areas:

- It allows the publication of business services against the directory through an automatic mechanism.
- It allows the classification of business on the basis of metadata that describes QoS information contained in the associated SLA pre-contract.

In the gaming scenario, when a Game Provider deploys a new game, he also publishes an SLA Template (or SLA pre-contract) associated to that game with specific QoS that should be guaranteed. These QoS parameters cover infrastructure, performance and network parameters, such as CPU use, latency or memory, which will be called low level (LL) parameters. The game provider then defines an XML-based mapping policy which maps the LL-QoS into high level (HL), human understandable, QoS parameters.

At search time when the on-line game (OLG) clients (Gamers) want to look for a service (game), the "human understandable" HL QoS parameters are specified as search criteria: e.g. Graphic Resolution or Available Resources. Using the mapping capability provided by the VHE the L&D, the Service Directory is queried for potential Service Providers that are able to offer the most suitable service to the client as shown in the following figure. Finally the business service (in this scenario, a match for a given game) and its associated SLA Contract are delivered to the Gamer.

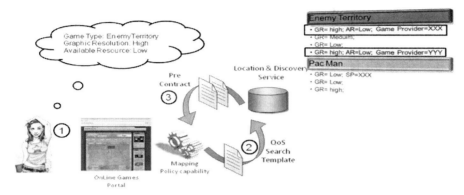

Fig. 12.4: High-level to Low-level QoS requirements mapping

After the business service has been delivered, it is necessary to ensure that the contractual terms are respected. This is done though the Monitoring and Evaluation subsystem (M&E). The M&E subsystem is logically divided into three main blocks:

- Application-specific monitoring: offers the ability to retrieve at run-time information about the users participating in a game, and other general information about the match like its lifecycle, number of users playing the match and some game statistics;
- Infrastructure monitoring: offers the ability to monitor resources virtualized as Grid services. In this experiment, it is possible to monitor parameters like the CPU cycle and the memory consumed by the match (service instance) at runtime;
- Evaluation layer: offers the ability to collect (through the two above mentioned modules) the monitored values in order to verify whether the measurements are within the thresholds defined in the SLA contract assigned to every player. Whenever the execution of a match does not satisfy these SLA conditions, the module will launch a notification event (using a WS-Notification mechanism) about this potential breach of contract.
More information can be found in D'Andria et al. (2008).

12.2.2 Online Gaming Scenario at Runtime

The gaming scenario is perhaps best told from the end user's perspective. In online gaming, a user typically wants to play a game online within a community of liked-minded players. He wants to take part in various games where other players play as well as he or she does. Response time and availability are therefore critical. So is the overall security of the underlying systems. The player's interaction starts when he goes to the Andago website to play a game. Provided he has a valid account, he can log into Andago's web portal which manages users, games, and online communities. On the richly-enabled website, the user can choose a game he wishes to play. Andago decides to advertise certain game titles depending on agreements with game title publishers. Up to this point, all interactions take part solely between Andago and the end user and therefore neither the VHE nor its enabling B2B gateways are in play. However the richness of Andago's offering is a direct consequence of its ability to form dynamic collaborations with different provider. Once the player has selected a game, e.g. EnemyTerritory, he can choose a match to take part in. This is where the VHE and the B2B gateways kick in. A match is in fact a given specific VO with a virtualized exposed application instance for one of the game servers (GS) selected e.g. either Sunny or Saygah.

Once the player has selected a match, Andago will kick-start the virtualization of its own client application which liaises between the Andago platform and the hosting environment's virtualized service. In this scenario, Andago exposes a management client called Agasy. Therefore at this stage Andago is virtualising and exposing a contextualized instance of the Agasy at its B2B gateway. The Agasy instance will be exchanging management and monitoring messages with the virtualized game watcher instance at either Sunny or Saygah. This watcher continuously monitors the state of the running game instance on the host server and sends back gaming operation statistics to the Agasy instance. Every time the client instance running behind Andago's B2B gateway makes a call to the virtualized watcher instance at either Sunny or Saygah, the request goes:

- through Andago's gateway where
  - it is checked and decorated with the appropriate virtual identity (e.g., a SAML token) issued by the SOI-STS for the given instance
  - checked against client-side authorization rules
  - encrypted for transport between the partners' gateways
  - sent to the partner's gateway, i.e. Sunny or Saygah

- through the receiving partner's gateway where
  - the SAML token is extracted and sent to the STS for validation
  - the STS validates the virtual identity (SAML token) and returns the associated identity attributes for the given requestor
  - the gateway decrypts the message
  - the gateway requests an authorization decision from the SOI-AuthZ-PDP based on the XACML attributes extracted from the SAML token and based on the originating client and targeted service
  - the gateway forwards the request to the internal service i.e. the watcher

During the execution of the sequence of these interactions, the relevant infrastructure services, in particular the SOI-SMG and the application instances, feed events into the SLA monitoring services in order to evaluate the status of the infrastructure and to determine whether any service provider is breaching the agreed contract.

Thanks to the B2B gateway, the message exchange is secured and therefore allows Andago to monitor the hosting environments. It can determine how much to pay Saygah and Sunny depending on the usage as well as on the experience delivered (reliable hosting or not for instance).

12.3 Business Benefits

12.3.1 Customer Benefits in Online Gaming

There are different customer types that can benefit from the VHE approach. Firstly, the end user or gamer will indirectly benefit from the VHE as he will be given a wider range of games at different levels of quality with more adequate and competitive pricing models.

Secondly, traditional service providers (SP) who contented themselves with providing raw communications services (typical of ISPs) will now be able to offer additional capabilities as services in a SaaS approach. Such services include, as already mentioned, identity and access control management services, encryption services, SLA services, CRM services, telecommunications services (call-backs, the sending of SMS, etc), and generally any capability the enterprise has internally and is willing to share with external customers in order to generate revenue. This has been clearly identified in Total Telecom Magazine (2009). In particular it highlights that the "huge cost of developing massive multiplayer online games (MMOG) could mean an increasing opportunity for network infrastructure and data warehousing service providers as games publishers increasingly try to move away from providing the end-to-end 'vertical'".

Thirdly, game developers and web gaming platforms also benefit from the VHE approach as they can focus on developing new game titles and creating appealing user platforms without having to worry about the details of operating the platform, the game, or any of the underlying infrastructure along with the non-functional requirements (such as security and QoS) these bring. Again, Total Telecom Magazine states that "because MMOGs are persistent online games that are commonly played by hundreds or thousands of players on one hardware server at the same time, support costs can be high". These costs need to be controlled and driven down. Piers Harding-Rolls (a senior analyst at Screen Digest) states that "a popular game might have tens of servers each with a few thousand players". This is the main cause for the expensive infrastructure and maintenance when owned and operated by the game developer. A pay-as-you-grow or pay-as-you-go provision model can help reduce such costs.

12.3.2 The VHE as an Enabler of the SOA Approach

The VHE enables the customer to adopt a low risk approach to SOA deployment and increases Return on Investment (RoI). The VHE provides common, shared technologies that enable business processes to be added and changed easily. Expensive infrastructure is pooled, decreasing the support and maintenance costs, allowing for a greatly reduced capital outlay, and increasing utilisation of the IT resource. Implementing a service-oriented design facilitates increased collaboration with both customers and suppliers, and offers opportunities for a higher degree of service composition and process automation across the value chain. The VHE also offers common capabilities meeting non-functional requirements such as:

- Business collaboration management,
- Service publication, service categorization and discovery based on high-level QoS requirements,
- Process driven service composition,
- Federated identity and access management,
- SLA monitoring and evaluation, and
- Secure messaging and content validation, content-based routing.

This experiment validates the use of VHE as an enabler of collaborative online gaming services. Validation is achieved by implementing a gaming platform (provided by Andago) on the top of a VHE specialisation for on-line collaborative gaming. The VHE helps businesses to improve their "concept-to-market" development cycle. This is achieved by leveraging the common capability integration and process-driven service and resource composition that is enabled by the VHE infrastructure. The VHE should enable a 25% – 50% reduction of the concept-to-market cycle, especially in cases where services are composed for the first time in response to a new market need (Sawnhey 2005). The VHE should also help businesses optimise their "right first time" ratio by leveraging the flexibility offered by policy-based management of the VHE infrastructure and its ability for autonomic adaptation in response to contextual changes. The VHE should allow an 80% or higher "right first time" ratio for exposing composite services on the VHE, especially in cases where reconfiguration is required in order to respond to changes of service usage or access requirements (Sawnhey 2005). The VHE proposition offers the potential to treat both IT and business functions as a series of interconnected services—from activities like HR and travel that serve employees, to sales, to managing customer identity and access, to delivery and other activities that serve customers. It offers organisations new ways to selectively outsource, to quickly configure and reconfigure these services to continually maximize efficiency, even as their business world changes.

From a customer's perspective SOI provides a very compelling story, incorporating the attractive aspects of SOA with flexible, cost effective infrastructure. Current estimates (IDC 2006) are that between 50 – 80% of enterprises are planning and deploying SOA to achieve the following:

- *Service reuse*: accelerated implementation of new business functions and changes to existing ones, lower effort and risk, reduced cost, quicker implementation;
- *Composite applications built by combining services*: *Rapid response* to changing market requirements and *first-to-market* competitive advantage. *Optimization of end-to-end processes* rather than just individual activities

- *Loosely coupled systems*: greater flexibility, increased implementation agility, improved process efficiency, and a higher degree of automation.
- *Standards-based end-to-end security*: greater interoperability; controlled exposure of business functions to business partners; managing (and hiding) infrastructure complexity; guaranteed compliance with higher-level enterprise policies including the implementation of *regulatory requirements* and ability to *prove compliance* with these.

VHE customers can select productised components from a menu of options, each with its own service level (speed, capacity and/or availability) and pricing model. Under the VHE, customers' demands are becoming more service-based and Service Level Agreements and Guarantees (SLAs & SLGs), as well as Identity, Security and Access policies, are more focused on business requirements. Instead of defining network or application availability related guarantees, customers will require a range of service level performance options based upon end user requirements and business metrics.

12.3.3 Business Benefits in Other Market Sectors

Essentially, the VHE product is a network-centric Service Oriented Infrastructure to be used by enterprise networks. Enterprise network scenarios range from defence coalitions, to multi-site finance institutions, multi-party logistics support, and aggregation of entertainment and media services. The VHE allows enterprises to expose interfaces to internally-hosted services in such a way that they can be combined easily and securely with services contributed by other business partners on demand. The three main markets in priority are:

- Defence coalitions (e.g. coalitions between NATO members)
- Multi-provider VAS integration for entertainment and gaming (such as BT and Sony's Go! Messenger offering (BT 2009a))
- Large-scale corporations with a multi-site IT infrastructure including those arising from a series of mergers and acquisitions

One motive for emphasising large corporations and coalitions as early adopters stems from the up-take of an SOA strategy in such organisations and the willingness of some of these customers to make a substantial investment on innovation in order to solve challenges in the Managed (IT) Infrastructure Services area. Once an operational infrastructure is established, we expect it will also be particularly valuable for smaller companies who want to earn money out of innovative web services. In the future, we envisage the enterprise networks using the VHE platform being clusters of SMEs within a given market sector. However, in the short term, the VHE offering is being driven by the needs and investment of large corporate customers and government departments (especially defence).

12.4 Lessons Learnt

Over the course of the two years during which the Business Experiment ran, several lessons have been learnt as to the choice and development of the technology, the chosen approaches, the architecture put forward. Additional lessons relate to the customer's expectations and its management.

12.4.1 Organisations' Main Motivation to Migrate to SOA

In his SOA Maturity Model, Theo Beack, Chief SOA Architect at SoftwareAG, summarizes the main issues faced when interfacing with new customers: "Organisations are all inundated with information about SOA and the steps [this] require[s]…" (Beack 2006). The first lesson to retain is that SOA confuses many decision makers when wondering whether to make a strategic move which may halt or hinder an enterprise's IT operations over a significant period of time during which the transition takes place.

To avoid this adverse reaction, the customer, be it the online gaming platform provider or any IT enterprise, needs to have the key benefits delivered by the VHE clearly explained. The latter brings a clear roadmap to SOA adoption along with the adequate tools and an architecture that allows growth and expansion. It is important to accompany enterprises in their migration by supporting them with a clear plan. The VHE should first provide a point of reference which is the main aim of the SOA realization. Based on that reference, the organisation should create a common vision and understanding of what it wants to realize with SOA and what it means for its IT operations and business in general. In a later stage, the organisation should identify gaps between its current state of the art and what it wants to achieve. Lastly, before deciding to proceed, it should prioritize and measure the impact of SOA and the VHE on its business and in particular try to measure the Return on Investment (RoI) to determine whether it is worthwhile. An additional stage in this plan should consider, prioritize and plan actions for improvement of the architecture being put forward. Only with the adequate framework will enterprises become less reluctant and start adopting the VHE.

Another key aspect that is increasingly proving useful to incite enterprises to adopt an SOA strategy is the ability to cut operation costs (mainly electricity used in running servers and the necessary cooling equipment) and the linked environmental concern. A recent article in the Wall Street & Technology Journal (2009) highlights that more and more Wall St. firms are turning to SOA architectures and virtualization technologies to cut their electric bill and become greener. This approach is helping them to save their energy consumption and generally helps them reduce manpower and "do more with less". This is in line with current IT budgets which are suffering massive cuts due to the 2009 recession. Where enterprises were once reluctant to evolve to an SOA or VHE approach, the current financial situation is forcing them to.

Enterprises can also particularly benefit from this approach by generating profits from once locked-in value-adding services. BT, for instance, has launched in March

2009 a virtualised infrastructure service which involves the virtualisation of servers, storage, networks and security delivered to customers via an online portal as Cloud-based services (ZDNet UK 2009). By doing so, BT is in fact offering capabilities it already provides internally for its own operations and is optimizing resource usages and selling them to generate additional revenue. Other common capabilities included in the telecommunications sector are Voice over IP (VoIP) services, call-backs and call flows, text message services such as the ones offered by Ribbit (http://www.ribbit.com/). Going to other organisation with success stories – such as BT's – will help them in their own adoption of the VHE and the SOA paradigm in general.

12.4.2 Risks Associated to SOA

Changing to an open, service-oriented model comes with technical pitfalls addressed in the VHE but that should not be overlooked by organisations. In particular, a distributed system with multiple components that potentially span across different organisational domains needs adequate management tools: governance is therefore critical to control this complexity. This governance process should be based on a well-defined set of interface guidelines and policies.

Secondly, the governance process should provide the means to manage those policies that matter and provide tools to manage the entire lifecycle of the policies from its initial template stages to their execution. Policies should have issuers. The latter should not be able to repudiate the policies in order to ensure compliance with regulations and laws both inside the enterprise, within the dynamic collaboration, and within national and international legal frameworks.

Thirdly accurate governance should come with the identification of asset owners, administrators and generally speaking those responsible for maintaining the services with which an enterprise is to integrate.

Lastly, from a more technical perspective, if SOA is to be fully achieved, particular care is to be put on the definition of service interfaces and contracts. In particular, those interfaces should enable loose coupling.

12.5 Conclusion

In the past, many companies' strategic business planning relied upon forecasts of future market conditions and customer needs over time periods of one to five years. In the stable business environment that then existed, companies could take their time to plan and develop a suitable IT infrastructure because market conditions and customer needs were relatively stable. But in today's uncertain business conditions, it is difficult for companies to look that far into the future, with any certainty. Instead they have to spot trends early and respond more quickly than competitors to new opportunities and threats. However, many enterprises are finding that their ability to innovate and execute new business strategies is being constrained by the inability of their IT infrastructure to support these new strategic initiatives. If so, these customers need to transform their existing inflexible IT infrastructures into more flexible and agile infrastructures that can support new and innovative business strategies in shorter time scales.

In response to such customer needs and insights, this experiment has developed the VHE proposition. The VHE offers the potential to treat both IT and business functions as a series of interconnected services. It is an attempt to offer organisations new ways to selectively outsource, to quickly configure and reconfigure these services and to continually maximize efficiency, even as their business world changes. VHE is an enhanced Service Oriented Infrastructure (SOI) that is built on the fusion of:

- The SOA for ensuring composition of loosely coupled services
- The virtualisation and distributed management of ICT resources based on Grid computing
- The management of Network resources based on a federated architecture.

The pull for the VHE has mainly come from two areas: the need for enterprises to become more flexible in order to adapt to evolving business models leading to new revenue-generating opportunities and the increasing pressure to reduce operating costs.

Other reasons come from the need to reduce organisations' environmental impact by reducing energy consumption as stated in Wall Street & Technology (2009).

Between the completion of this experiment in June of 2008 and now, the Grid SOA paradigm has evolved into the Cloud computing proposition. Many leading IT organisations including telecommunications providers such as BT and Orange are investing in Cloud computing proposals. Indeed, Gartner predict 22% growth in 2009, with revenues reaching $9.6bn and rising to $16bn by 2013 in the Cloud computing market (MicroScope 2009). A trend toward Cloud computing is to be expected in the light of the challenges faced by major Wall St firms. The VHE approach taken in this experiment has been built in such a flexible way that it can be easily migrated towards a Cloud approach with little or no effort.

Cloud computing will also impact security services because we expect to see a new Security-as-a-Service model emerge. With technology dissolving traditional network boundaries and companies changing their operational business models, Cloud-based security will be essential. The work in identity and access management done in BEinGRID and this experiment fit naturally into the Cloud.

The results of this experiment are extremely encouraging. There is a very dynamic market with very high expectations for new SOA-oriented visions in order to pursue new business opportunities, cut IT operation costs, and fuel the corporate green agenda which is becoming important in Corporate Social Responsibility (CSR) strategies. We believe large IT corporations (consultancy firms, telecommunications providers) should lead the way into the Cloud computing paradigm. The partners of this experiment and in particular ATOS and BT can leverage the results of this experiment to strengthen their respective proposals.

13 Organizational and Governance Challenges for Grid Computing in Companies – Summary of Findings from Business Experiments

Katarina Stanoevska-Slabeva, Thomas Wozniak

13.1 Introduction

Grid computing originated in eScience where it is applied to support scientific tasks requiring high performance computing and collaborative scientific efforts. The Business Experiments presented in chapters 9 to 12 and the remaining 21 experiments of the BEinGRID project (BEinGRID Booklet 2009) demonstrated the applicability of Grid computing in business environments and provided an outlook towards the application of Cloud computing in companies.

Besides illustrating and testing technical Grid innovations and developments specifically dedicated to business usage of Grids, services and an outlook to Cloud computing, the Business Experiments provided an insight of the potential benefits and challenges of these technologies for business purposes. One benefit of Grid computing for companies is enabling high performance computing (HPC) either through access to external HPC resources or through creating internal Grids based on existing company computing resources. The access to HPC enables significant acceleration of business tasks that require high computing power. Such tasks are mainly simulation tasks as part of product development, design and engineering activities or other tasks as treatment or risk calculation in health and financial organizations respectively.

Another benefit of Grid computing for business purposes is the support for efficient inter- and intra-company collaboration by enabling both the establishment of virtual organizations (VO) and the sharing of resources and data within them. Application areas for Grid-enabled VO are for example collaborations within supply chains, inter-company collaborative engineering or common offerings within complex online sites.

Based on the results from the Business Experiments, it became evident that companies can benefit from Grid computing not only by enabling savings on infrastructure costs. Grid computing also allows companies to create new value and to achieve competitive advantage.

As Fellows and Barr (2007) from the market research company "The 451 Group" state it: "Grids are evolving beyond high-performance computing (HPC) and compute tasks in order to support broader organizing principles driving enterprise IT evolution". Faster and more accurate product design for example lowers time-to-market and strengthens the innovation capabilities and competitiveness of companies. Similar effects are achieved through the ability to quickly establish necessary business alliances within supply chains or other inter-company collaboration efforts in a safe and trustable way.

However, the Business Experiments also revealed the organizational challenges and obstacles for companies that want to apply Grid or Cloud computing on a large scale. Grid and Cloud computing imply major changes in the way how information technology is used and governed in companies.

This chapter provides another analytical view on the Business Experiments and summarizes the findings with regards to organizational and governance challenges of Grid and Cloud computing in organizations. These aspects are considered separately for the case of application of Grid as utility and high performance computing and for the case of using Grid computing to support virtual organizations.

The chapter is structured as follows: section 13.2 summarizes the organizational challenges related to utility and high performance computing, while section 13.3 summarizes the findings related to resource sharing within virtual organizations. Section 13.4 concludes the chapter with a summary.

13.2 Organizational Challenges Related to Application of Utility and High Performance Computing

The BEinGRID project involved 15 Business Experiments that illustrated the application of Grid computing for enabling efficient support for tasks requiring high computing power. Two of these Business Experiments were presented in detail in the previous chapters:

- The BEinEIMRT Business Experiment (see chapter 9) illustrated the potential of applying external HPC resources for calculation of radiotherapy cancer treatment planning in hospitals based on the Monte Carlo methodology. The starting point for the Business Experiment was an existing application for radiotherapy calculation that was Grid-enabled in the Business Experiment. The application was enhanced in the Business Experiment so that it can utilize external HPC resources and it can be offered either in a Software-as-a-Service (SaaS) mode or it can be deployed on internal computing clusters. The deployment of the Grid-enabled radiotherapy planning application resulted in a decrease of the time-to-solution to a level that can be acceptable for daily work at the hospital. For example, the execution time of a treatment verification was reduced from 193 hours to only 4, this means, from more than one week to an acceptable time for a day of work.
- The Ship Building Business Experiment (see chapter 10) illustrated the use of external computing resources for collaborative ship simulation and engineering based on the SaaS paradigm. Similar to the BEinEIMRT Business Experiment described above, the starting point for the Business Experiment was an existing application for Ship Design and Integration System (SESIS) that was Grid-enabled in the Business Experiment. One of the participants in the Business Experiment provided the external utility computing resources. The new Grid-enabled collaborative simulation solution was tested for simulating the impact

of different combination of materials for a new funnel in sandwich technology for fire safety on ships. The test of the solution showed that the computing time for a required simulation of 60 minutes real time of fire that needs approximately one month of computing time on a single PC can be reduced to one day on a 32-node cluster. The experiment also showed the technical feasibility of sourcing external computing resources.

The two experiments had several common characteristics and problem areas:

- Tasks that require high computing power and are crucial part of the core activities of the organizations involved – treatment calculation in hospitals and collaborative product engineering at the shipyard.
- Lack of own infrastructure and knowledge that can support tasks requiring high performance computing.
- Support of tasks with demand for high performance computing with applications that are not designed for use in a Grid environment.

Similar characteristics have been observed also with other BEinGRID Business Experiments for example in the BE addressing computational fluid dynamics simulation in the automotive industry (BE01 2009) or the BE considering engineering and business processes in metal forming in manufacturing (BE08 2009) (for more examples see BEinGRID Booklet 2009). All experiments were able to provide a proof that computing intensive tasks can be accelerated considerably by using Grid computing either by sourcing external computing power through utility computing or by creating internal clusters.

However, the Business Experiments revealed also that application of utility computing or external high computing resources requires considerable changes in the way how information and communication technology is handled in organisations.

First of all, the experiments showed that in general usage of HPC, or IaaS in case of Clouds, requires Grid-enabled applications. This means that the application deployed on a Grid needs to be able to parallelize and distribute jobs among available resources – independent of the fact if the resources are internal or external. Availability of utility computing on the market per se is somehow irrelevant, if there are no applications that can take advantage of it. Through the Business Experiments it became evident that in order to be able to use Grid computing, an initial investment is necessary for the adjustment, i.e. Grid-enablement, of existing software applications. This initial investment needs to be considered by the external Independent Software Provider (ISP) or by the company itself in case of own applications. The Grid-enabled application can then be deployed either in a SaaS manner or on company internal Grids (see the BEinEIMRT Business Experiment). Both approaches require substantial organizational and IT governance changes.

The usage based on SaaS implies that internal resources and licenses for the application are combined with a SaaS pay-per-use licenses and usage. The access of the application in a SaaS manner requires new contracts and license agreements with the software vendor providing it (see for example Stanoevska-Slabeva et al. 2008).

Thereby the applications under consideration are very specialized and expensive similar to the applications described in chapters 9 and 10. Due to the low number of users, such applications are usually offered with licensing models that are valid for use on one computer on which the application runs and a certain period of time (usually a year). As soon as the application is obtained in a SaaS manner, different licensing relationships need to be established. A move towards licenses that abstract from the fact on which machine the application is running or which allow an ad hoc transfer of jobs from the application to available resources internally or externally is necessary. Even though many software vendors have already started to evolve towards pay-per-use and similar licensing and payment models, there are still not many applications available that are suitable for Grid environments.

The second aspect that needs to be considered by user companies is the choice of the external utility computing providers and the establishment of contractual relationships with them. This means that in case the user company is interested in a SaaS version of a HPC application, it might require two new contracts, one to the SaaS provider and one to the utility computing provider. From the perspective of the user company a better solution is clearly a contractual relationship to only one of the providers. Usually this is the SaaS provider who is the main contact point to the user company and who hides the complexity of the underlying infrastructure by establishing bilateral relationships to one or several utility computing providers.

Major legal aspects that need to be considered are (see also chapter 7): fees that apply as well as Service Level Agreements (SLA) including Quality of Service (QoS) in terms of availability, performance, downtime and service suspension and support services, privacy, security, and confidentiality.

The access of external HPC infrastructure furthermore implies changes in IT governance of companies, in particular with respect to:

- Definition of criteria for the choice of external utility computing and SaaS providers.
- Establishment of rules when external resources can be used and by whom.
- Establishment of guidelines for contractual relationships with the utility computing and SaaS providers.
- Choice and application of tools to monitor the execution of SLA and provided QoS in a complex mixed internal and external monitoring environment.
- Consideration of security and definition of security policies. These policies need to include at least the following aspects: secure communication of input and resulting data among the end user and external provider, access policies defining who in the company has the right to access external data and under which conditions, and policies for storage of data on external resources.
- Consideration of privacy risks and definition of privacy policies. Special care should be taken for particularly sensitive data – for example patient or customer data. Consideration of privacy includes a range of questions related to communication, storage and processing of data. The BEinEIMRT Business Experiment for example anonymised and encrypted the patient data before sending it to the external providers. The end user company needs to assure that even though the

data might be processed on computers spread over several continents and countries the privacy rules valid in his country are applied.

Overall many new governance rules need to be established and their execution needs to be monitored in an efficient way. This is difficult to achieve by manual monitoring. Thus, the availability of support for coding policies in monitoring tools and automatic execution of the governance policies is an important aspect. Potential software modules providing this functionality are described in chapter 8. Without automatic monitoring, the gain in computing speed will result in a loss of time for management and governance tasks. Thus, support for monitoring of internal resources needs to be extended with support for monitoring of external resources. All this implies additional costs and investments that need to be compared to the potential gains of Grid computing.

To summarize, the introduction of HPC based on external resources in form of utility computing or deployed on internal Grids results in advantages but also additional costs and requires considerable organizational and governance changes for the organization. The potential gains of Grid computing can be summarized as follows:

- Significant acceleration of tasks that require high performance computing and based on that time-to-solution.
- Increased flexibility and scalability of available resources based on the possibility to add external resources in an ad hoc manner according to demand. This also results in higher agility and flexibility of related business processes.
- Lower IT infrastructure and maintenance costs as part of the demand is covered by external resources that are consumed on a pay-per-use basis.
- Conversion of fixed investment costs into variable costs that occur only if external infrastructure is actually used.

The potential gains may be partially offset by some potential costs:

- Investment in Grid enablement of own applications or switch to pay-per-use licenses. This might include also costs for Grid middleware, which is used for enhancing the application.
- Connection and communication costs to the utility computing and SaaS provider.
- Investment in new monitoring tools and capabilities of employees to be able to manage a heterogeneous IT environment consisting of external and internal resources.
- Costs related to change of processes.
- Costs related to meeting higher requirements related to security and privacy aspects.

In each case a careful Total Cost of Ownership (TCO) calculation needs to be performed in order to disclose if the gains from evolving to utility computing and SaaS in financial terms are higher than incurring costs related to it. For example, the case of the BE BEinEIMRT clearly shows the advantage of external resources for hospitals. On the contrary, in his attempt to quantify the gains of Grid computing,

Gray (2003) comes to the conclusion that Grid applications must be really compute-intensive, or will otherwise not be economical.

Compared to that, the question of most cost-effective investment in cases similar to the Ship Building BE example might be different. The Ship Building BE demonstrated the benefits of Grid computing on the example of one of many simulation tasks during the design of a ship. The volume of compute-intensive tasks required for the complete virtual design and build of a ship is much higher. Thus, a more favourable solution might be an investment in bundling own available resources into an internal Grid infrastructure. For example, Opitz et al. (2008) show that a solution based on cycle stealing from existing resources has the potential for considerable costs savings.

The examples above illustrate that for a sound HPC Grid computing investment decision, several options need to be compared: sourcing from external utility computing and SaaS providers, transforming the existing internally available infrastructure into a Grid infrastructure and investing in a specially dedicated internal Grid computing infrastructure.

13.3 Organizational Challenges Related to Application of Grid Computing for Virtual Organization Support

Support for building virtual organizations (VOs) is the second application area of Grid computing in companies illustrated by Business Experiments. The main goal of Grid-based VOs is to enable resource and data sharing as well as coordinated problem solving in dynamic, multi-institutional collaborations (see also Foster et al. 2008) among several cooperating companies. Two Business Experiments illustrated the application of Grid-based VOs in companies in this book:

- The AgroGrid Business Experiment (see chapter 11) provided a Grid-based solution for supporting collaboration among companies within supply chains in the agricultural industry. The presented solution provides a Grid-enabled market place that allows companies operating in agriculture food markets to offer and source capacities, to negotiate quality of food to be delivered, to establish contracts, to track and trace contract execution and to create dynamic supply chain-related VOs.
- The VHE Business Experiment (see chapter 12) was dedicated to the development of a generic Grid-based and service-oriented virtual hosting environment (VHE), where business services can be integrated with one another across organizational boundaries and domains. The environment supports service-based cross-enterprise interaction by leveraging the services available at the different organizations. It allows for an easy and flexible exposure and offering of services and usage within supply chains. The solution enables a management and governance model that spans across resource layers and organizational boundaries in order to achieve a correct picture of the infrastructure, its state and the services exposed. It provides the means to audit policies and sub-systems and is able to prove the compliance of the solution with local regulation, corporate

rules, as well as legal constraints both at national and international levels. The generic VHE was tested with a use case in online gaming.

The two cases have the following common characteristics and problem areas:

- The need to establish quickly and efficiently in a trustable manner collaboration with business partners, without centralising involved resources and data.
- No solution that provide support for efficient, secure and trustable sharing of data and execution of collaborative business processes without fostering centralization of data and resources.

The two Business Experiments illustrated the potential for supporting VO based on Grid and service orientation. Substantial benefits revealed were:

- Ad hoc establishment of VO among cooperating companies.
- Faster and more accurate establishment of a collaboration environment that takes advantage of available core competencies, resources and services of involved business partners and enables more efficient resource sharing and collaboration.

Similar to the application of HPC, the application of VO requires substantial changes that need to be addressed by the involved organization. This includes the overall decision for participation in VO, the decisions which data and in which form it will be made available in a VO and which partners are suitable for a VO collaboration. Closely related to this is the need to clearly define security policies regarding: who can access the services, in which form services can be accessed, which services are exposed in the environment, which data is exchanged, which SLAs and QoS are required.

13.4 Summary and Conclusion

13.4.1 Summary of Findings

The Business Experiments presented in this book illustrated two potential application areas of Grid computing in companies:

- High performance computing (HPC) either through external utility computing and SaaS or through internal Grids,
- Efficient inter-company collaboration and data and resource sharing within a virtual organization (VO).

Both application areas revealed potential for substantial benefits:

- Improved core processes and tasks, which have strategic importance for the user companies.
- Cut of infrastructure and maintenance costs and transfer of capital expenditures in operational expenditures.
- Increased flexibility and scalability of available resources and by that increased agility and flexibility of business processes.

The Business Experiments illustrated that Grid computing is not only optimizing the management of ICT in companies, but that it can also provide strategic advantage to companies. Thus, the introduction of Grid is a strategic decision that is not only a matter of the IT department, but must be taken and supported by top management. The operationalization of the strategic decision is then a task of the IT department.

The introduction of Grid requires substantial organizational and governance changes and regulations that can be summarized in the following thematic areas:

- Sourcing and deployment of IT infrastructure:
  - Choice and decision which processes and resources might by outsourced, i.e. supported by external infrastructure.
  - Justification when, how and why access to external resources is needed.
  - Company rules for selecting and establishing relationships with external utility computing, SaaS and VO providers.
  - Rules and policies for using of SaaS offered by Clouds by employees.
  - Guidelines and templates for defining the contractual relationships with external providers.

- Security and privacy policies:
  - Policies for secure communication with external providers: the SaaS, utility computing, and VO provider.
  - Access policies – who and under which condition is allowed to access external resources.
  - Policies for storage of data on external resources.
  - Privacy policies specialized for a grid environment.

Furthermore, integrated monitoring support for an environment with mixed internal and external resources is required.

In summary, the introduction of Grid computing in companies is a substantial change process that requires change in the mindset how IT is organized and managed in organizations. It is typically a stepwise and evolutionary process that provides the companies sufficient time to adjust and accommodate changes inferred by each evolutionary step.

13.4.2 Evolution from Grid to Cloud Computing

While the applicability of Grid computing is still under consideration and evaluation in companies, Cloud computing is creating a new hype and opportunity. The definition and differences of Grid and Cloud computing are still subject to debate in science and their applicability in business is raising increasing attention in industry. According to Foster et al. (2008): *"... Cloud Computing not only overlaps with Grid Computing, it is indeed evolved out of Grid Computing and relies on Grid Computing as its backbone and infrastructure support. The evolution has been a result of a shift in focus from an infrastructure that delivers storage and compute resources (such is the case in Grids) to one that is economy based aiming to deliver more abstract resources and services (such is the case in Clouds)"*. The experiences made with the Business Experiments in the BEinGRID project show a strong support for this evolutionary relationship among Grids and Clouds. The evolution from Grids to Clouds resulted from the concrete requirements of the players involved in a Grid ecosystem, in particular in the case of HPC application of Grid computing.

As the Business Experiments presented in chapters 9 and 10 illustrated, the establishment of HPC offerings on the market requires a functioning ecosystem consisting of utility computing providers, SaaS provides and users. In particular, the first two players are strongly interrelated and interdependent. The utility computing providers emerge mainly from technology providers as for example Sun, IBM, HP and others. New entrants to the market as Amazon with its EC2 offerings are for the moment rather an exception. A common characteristic of these providers is strong technical knowledge and availability of major data and server farms. While these providers have a strong knowledge in providing infrastructure with high quality, they lack at the same time applications that can run on the available infrastructure. Thus, availability of utility computing offerings alone is not sufficient. There also need to be Grid-enabled applications that can run on them. Such Grid-enabled applications are provided by independent software vendors (ISV) that are switching to the SaaS paradigm. However, while they are building knowledge how to best turn applications into SaaS, they are lacking the knowledge and resources to build up Grid infrastructure on which SaaS applications can run. Thus, utility computing and SaaS providers have complementary needs and requirements. Utility computing providers need to provide their offerings in a manner that makes it easy for SaaS to develop their applications on top of the available infrastructure. The example of Sun, one of the first movers in the utility computing market, shows that only utility computing offerings might not be sufficient. A clear interface for SaaS providers and developers is required (see also Fellows 2009). Utility computing providers have to move in the direction of SaaS and provide open environments on which SaaS applications can be developed and run. The findings from the Business Experiments in the BEinGRID project showed a similar tendency. To support faster growth of SaaS offerings and their adoption, access to utility computing is required (see also Stanoevska-Slabeva at al. 2008a).

The three levels of Cloud computing – Iaas, PaaS and SaaS – offer the vertical integration needed to support the complementary needs of utility and SaaS providers (see fig. 13.1).

The infrastructure on the lowest level is represented through defined interfaces and in a virtualized manner in form of a platform for SaaS developers. The PaaS level provides the necessary development environment for SaaS developers to develop and test SaaS applications and to source infrastructure from the IaaS layer in a flexible and scalable manner. Finally, the SaaS layer presents the combined offering to the end user. The end users, the third players in the ecosystem, are interested in flexible applications. This means, the more modular and combinable the services are the more interesting for end user companies. Thus, provisioning of the services in small, interconnectable pieces, for example mash-ups (see also Foster et al. 2008, Hoyer and Stanoevska-Slabeva 2009), would provide the necessary flexibility for the end user and allow for horizontal integration within and among different SaaS offerings. All three layers of emerging Cloud offerings have the potential to meet the needs of the utility computing, SaaS and user ecosystem. Such offerings evolved from Grid and SaaS developments and rely on Grid computing on the lowest layer. Overall, the need of end users to access HPC and Grids over SaaS applications is one important driver for the emerging Clouds.

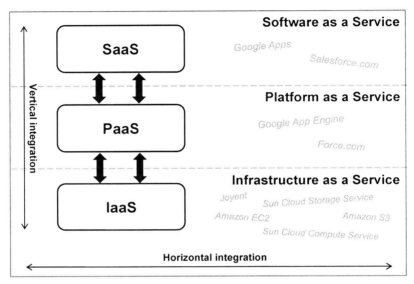

Fig. 13.1: Vertical integration across and horizontal integration within Cloud layers

The relation between Grid-based VOs, as described above and Clouds is less clearly visible. Clouds provide integration within the Cloud, but support for integration of resources of independent participants is rather weak. They also provide a rather simple storage of data and do not necessarily support for data sharing and processing. Support for VOs clearly requires horizontal integration, in many cases according to a defined workflow – for example a supply chain workflow. VOs are typically driven by one company coordinating the remaining participants. As a result, it might be expected that Grid-supported VOs might be driven by external company Clouds that provide integrating platforms for partner companies, which are similar to the VHE presented in chapter 12.

Part IV: Practical Guidelines

14 Practical Guidelines for Evolving IT Infrastructure towards Grids and Clouds

Katarina Stanoevska-Slabeva, Thomas Wozniak, Volker Hoyer

14.1 Introduction

In the previous chapters of this book the foundation of Grid and Cloud Computing were described and their application in companies was illustrated with examples. Grid Computing enables sharing of and access to distributed and heterogeneous computing resources as well as establishment of VOs. Through virtualization, heterogeneous pools of servers, storage systems and networks are pooled together into a virtualized system that is exposed to the user as a single computing entity. This entity can be centrally monitored and assigned to computing tasks. Overall, Grid Computing enables a virtualization layer that is placed between the heterogeneous infrastructure and the specific user application using it. Grid Computing potentially results in higher flexibility of computing resources and their more efficient utilization, and by that, enables an environmentally friendlier IT management in companies.

Cloud Computing evolved from and builds upon the convergence of Grid Computing and SOC. It has the potential to substantially change the way how computing resources are consumed. Core features of Cloud Computing are integrated support for IaaS, PaaS and SaaS as well as user-friendly and service-oriented interfaces for developers and users. Cloud Computing offers a new, easy-to-use way for increasing scalability and flexibility of own IT resources on demand. Sudden peaks can be accommodated with access to external resources provided in a pay-per-use manner without additional investments in hardware, data centres and related human resources required for maintenance and support. Cloud Computing provides also new opportunities for Independent Software Vendors. They can develop innovative business models and offer their software in a SaaS manner without building up the necessary infrastructure.

The examples provided throughout this book show that there is high potential of Grid and Cloud Computing to provide value for companies in two areas:

1. Management and utilization of IT resources
2. Business process agility.

From the perspective of IT management, Grid and Cloud Computing can increase scalability, flexibility and cost-effectiveness of IT infrastructure in use. From the business process perspective, the companies can increase their agility, enable new innovative processes and based on that increase their innovation capabilities and competitiveness.

K. Stanoevska-Slabeva et al. (eds.), *Grid and Cloud Computing: A Business Perspective on Technology and Applications*, DOI 10.1007/978-3-642-05193-7_14,
© Springer-Verlag Berlin Heidelberg 2010

However, the examples described throughout the book (see Part III of the book) also illustrate that Grids and Clouds, by their very nature, are based on complex technologies and result in substantial changes across organizations. Thus, the introduction of Grid and Cloud Computing in companies is a complex and difficult endeavour. Besides mastering the technical complexity, companies also have to consider cultural, legal, IT policy, and regulatory obstacles that often prove even more difficult to overcome. While there are plenty of market study reports describing the market potential and opportunities of Grid and Cloud Computing, there is less literature on problems facing companies while dealing with these technologies as well as on guidelines how to effectively overcome them.

Based on the experiences from the BEinGRID project (see also chapter 13) and a summary from literature, this chapter provides guidelines for efficient implementation of Grids and Clouds in companies. Given the overall target of this book, the proposed guidelines focus rather on organizational, human and project management aspects than on technical aspects of a potential Grid and Cloud Computing application in organizations.

In the next section first, a state-of-the-art overview of Grid and Cloud Computing adoption in companies is given. Then, in section 14.3 practical guidelines for Grid and Cloud implementation are proposed. Each major step proposed in the implementation guidelines is then explained in more detail in the subsequent sections.

14.2 State-of-the-art of Grid and Cloud Computing Adoption in Practice

Before describing the practical guidelines for evolving IT infrastructures towards Grid and Cloud Computing, the goal of this section is to provide an overview of the state-of-the-art of their adoption in companies. In particular, an indication is provided how companies consider Grid and Cloud Technologies in practice, how these technologies are applied and what major problems and obstacles the companies have been confronted with, while adopting them. The summary of findings resulting from a literature review should provide a broader picture and enhance results already presented in chapter 13.

14.2.1 Status and Adoption of Grid Computing in Practice

While there is no lack of market studies about the potential of Grid Computing, the availability of empirical data on the actual use and current status of the adoption of the technology is rather limited.

This section summarizes the key findings of a recent and comprehensive study on the adoption of Grid technology in German companies published by Messerschmidt (2009). The study by Messerschmidt (2009) was based on a survey conducted in Mai and June 2008. Thereby, the main focus was on the financial industry and the results from the survey stemming from the financial industry were explicitly emphasized in the report and compared to the results related to other industries.

The survey only included participants who work for a company of at least 50 employees and who hold at least the position of a team leader. In addition, survey participants were required to meet one of the following two criteria: a) be entitled to decide on the use of IT budget, or be in the position to influence planning of IT purchase; b) be involved in tasks that require extensive IT resources at least once a year. 369 people participated in the survey. Most of them (54%) worked for companies with at least 250 employees.

Those survey results that can most likely serve as an indication for the current status of general industry adoption of Grid are presented below (Messerschmidt 2009):

- **Grid technology is not very well known.** Almost half of survey participants (48%) heard of the term "Grid Computing" for the first time from the survey. 22% became aware of Grid Computing within one year prior to the survey. A quarter of participants have known Grid technology since 2 to 5 years. 5% have known it for longer than 5 years.
- **Current usage of Grid technology is very limited.** 81% of participants stated Grid technology is currently not used in their company.
- **Grid is predominantly used to obtain additional IT resources.** 53 companies (14%) use Grid to obtain additional IT resources (see also fig. 14.1). 8 companies (2%) use Grid to provide/share idle IT resources. 9 companies (3%) use Grid to obtain additional IT resources and also to provide/share idle IT resources.
- **Grid is mostly used internally or in mixed environments.** As figure 14.1 shows, the majority of those companies using Grid (in total 70 companies) do so internally (31 companies) or in mixed environments (internally and externally) (25 companies).

The survey results presented above and in figure 14.1 provide also indications for which type of Grid companies use. The different types of Grids are described in detail and illustrated with examples in section 3.5.2 in chapter 3.

Type of involvement \ Scope of integration	With regard to scope of integration and type of involvement, indication for **Utility Grids**			
	Internal	**External**	**Internal & External**	**Total**
Obtaining additional IT resources	24 A1	12 B1	17 C1	53
Providing/sharing idle IT resources	3 A2	1 B2	4 C2	8
Obtaining additional IT resources and providing/ sharing idle IT resources	4 A3	1 B3	4 C3	9
Total	31	14	25	N=70

With regard to scope of integration, indication for deployment of **Enterprise Grids**

With regard to scope of integration and type of involvement, indication for **Virtual Organizations**

Fig. 14.1: Grid usage by scope of integration and type of involvement (adapted from Messerschmidt 2009)

The internal use of Grid technology serves as an indication for the potential deployment of Enterprise Grids (see sec. 3.5.2.2). Thus, up to 44% of the total 70 Grid deployments in the study sample may be Enterprise Grids. Alternatively, that would be up to 8% of the studies total sample. It is possible that the percentage of Enterprise Grids in the study sample is higher than that, as some of the companies in cells C1, C2 and C3 (see fig. 14.1) may also operate an Enterprise Grid.

Grid technology exclusively used for obtaining additional IT resources from an external provider is an indication that a Utility Grid (see sec. 3.5.2.3) may be in play, i.e. the IT resources are obtained from a third party that operates a Utility Grid. So, up to 17% of the total 70 companies that use Grid may do so through an Utility Grid owned and operated by a third party. Alternatively, that would be just above 3% of the total study sample. It is possible that the percentage of Utility Grid users in the study sample is higher than that, as some of the companies in cells B3, C1 and C3 (see fig. 14.1) may also obtain IT resources from a Utility Grid.

Obtaining, while also providing IT resources across company borders, is one characteristic of a VO (see sec. 3.5.2.4). It can therefore be taken as an indication that the 5 companies in cells B3 and C3 (see fig. 14.1) may be part of a VO. In addition to sharing of heterogeneous recourses across company borders, a defining characteristic of a VO is a common goal among the VO members. If this is not in place, the sharing of resources may rather take place ad hoc and does not result in longer-term relationships between the involved companies. From the available survey data, the existence of a common goal among potential VO members in the study sample cannot be judged.

Messerschmidt (2009) also analysed the main reasons why companies implement Grid technology. Most companies use Grid to improve existing processes. In particular, the main reasons for using Grid technology are:

- Speeding up of processes (33% financial services, 34% remaining industries)
- Higher flexibility of IT resources (30% financial services, 26% remaining industries),
- Increasing efficiency of existing processes (30% financial services, 27% remaining industries),
- More efficient utilization of IT resources (30% financial services, 28% remaining industries), and
- Cost reduction (27% financial services, 33% remaining industries).

The use of Grid technology is rather less driven by a potential enhancement of existing customer offerings or creation of new customer offerings (21% financial services, 24% remaining industries). This also means that there is still low awareness of the strategic potential of Grid technology for establishment of new processes as well as increased agility and competitiveness.

Sustainability and Green IT are no primary usage reasons yet. Only 15% of financial services and 21% of remaining industries consider Green IT as an important reason for Grid usage. However, Green IT and sustainability can be expected to gain importance in the coming years as the need for computing and storage is constantly increasing and data centres increasingly contribute to total volume of greenhouse emissions (see also section 1.3 in chapter 1).

Since not any IT task or process may be able to benefit from Grid technology to the same extent, the type and technical profile of IT tasks performed in a company determines the readiness for and overall benefits a company can obtain from using Grid technology. In general, tasks and processes that can be decomposed into subprocesses that can then be run in parallel are suited to be performed in a Grid environment. Decomposable tasks can benefit from both increased computational power of an IT resource and from a greater number of IT resources allocated to perform the task (Messerschmidt 2009). Table 14.1 shows the results of the survey related to the profile of tasks performed in companies regarding their decomposability.

Table 14.1: Technical profile of IT tasks performed in companies (Messerschmidt 2009)

	Financial services industry	Remaining industries
Decomposition into sub-processes possible	64%	61%
% of tasks that can benefit from increased computing power of one server	35%	31%
% of tasks that can benefit from an increased number of servers	31%	29%
Decomposition into sub-processes **not** possible	36%	39%
% of tasks that can benefit from increased computing power of one server	19%	24%
% of tasks that can benefit from an increased number of servers	18%	23%

Across all industries, in more than 60% of all cases some of the tasks can be decomposed into sub-processes. For the financial services industry, in companies where some tasks are decomposable, 35% of tasks could benefit from greater computing performance of a single resource and 31% from a greater number of resources allocated to the task. Both can be achieved via a Grid. Sub-processes could be spread over a great number of client PCs that individually have low performance, but collectively, as a Grid, provide significant compute performance that can drastically reduce the computation time of a task. Table 14.1 also shows that in companies where tasks are not decomposable, the number of tasks that could benefit from a Grid is relatively lower.

The majority of IT computing tasks in the respondent companies – 75% – are database queries and 81% of computing tasks are requests for data storage, while only 36% are dedicated to Web applications. Only 32% of the tasks are dedicated to high performance processing tasks and 23% are dedicated to redundant calculations in order to increase the accuracy.

This type of tasks are different compared to HPC tasks, which are typically the main target tasks of Grid Computing and illustrate the different needs in industry compared to eScience. The 36% of Web Application indicate a substantial potential for Cloud Computing as Web applications are suitable to be run on Clouds.

The survey revealed also that a substantial number of companies (58%) needed up to 12 months for building the Grid until the Grid was operational; after two years a cumulative 92% of companies were able to use the Grid. In only 10% of the companies the implementation of the Grid solution took longer than three years (Messerschmidt 2009). This confirms that the introduction of Grid Computing is a complex and long-lasting process.

The survey involved also questions related to the technical and non-technical obstacles for introducing Grid Computing. The 81% of the companies participating in the survey that are not using Grid Computing mentioned the following major technical obstacles (Messerschmidt 2009):

- Missing Know how
- Security risks in particular associated with data transfer
- Grid technology is considered not to be appropriate for the company needs
- Costly and complex integration with the existing IT infrastructure
- Complexity of Grid Technology
- Doubts in the reliability of Grid Technology
- Missing offerings of Grid resources on the market
- Insufficient quality of the own network
- Insufficient quality of own IT resources

The major non-technical obstacles selected by the survey participants are (Messerschmidt 2009):

- Lower security
- Unclarified legal aspects related to liability of involved players
- No trust in unknown transaction partners
- Low awareness for Grid Technology in general
- Legal constrains – some processes or data are per law prohibited to be performed in other countries
- Difficulties to find the right partner
- Missing payment systems
- Legal constraints with respect to processes that cannot be performed outside the company
- Internal and legal regulations do not allow some processes to run in parallel on the same machine or to run in parallel with processes from other companies
- Service Level Agreements not established yet
- Costs involved with the introduction of Grid Technology are higher than potential gains
- Certain processes can, according to law, not be performed in other company departments.

Overall, the survey results and also the results presented in this book in form of case studies, show that the adoption of Grid Computing in companies on a broader scale just started and that there are still considerable obstacles that need to be overcome.

14.2.2 Status of and Obstacles for Cloud Computing Adoption in Practice

Cloud Computing is compared to Grid Computing a newer phenomenon. As is typical for emerging and hyped technologies, it is mainly discussed in terms of opportunities and challenges related to it. However, also first reports about experiences in practice as well as empirical studies are starting to be published. A recent survey conducted by Applied Research and F5 Networks (F5 Networks 2009) provides promising empirical data. F5 Networks surveyed 250 companies during the period of June and July 2009. The target respondents were personnel of Enterprise IT departments of companies with at least 2500 employees that hold a position of managing director in the following domains: network, information security, architecture and development.

The survey revealed that in spite there is awareness for Cloud Computing in most of the companies, there is no agreement yet what exactly the defining features of Cloud Computing are. Despite of that according to the results of the survey it seems that Cloud Computing is becoming widespread: 99% of the respondents claimed that they are discussing or implementing Cloud Computing and 82% report that they are in some stage of trial, implementation, or use of public clouds. According to the report furthermore "*66 percent of respondents report they have a dedicated budget for cloud. Additionally, 71 percent of respondents expect cloud computing to grow in the next two years.*" (F5 Networks 2009). These are rather encouraging numbers regarding Cloud Computing adoption, even though they have to be interpreted carefully. The summary report of the study available online does not mention which Cloud Services (IaaS, PaaS or SaaS) are in use.

According to the report, major needs of companies driving the usage of Cloud Computing are: the efficiency of IT (according to 71% of the respondents) and reduction of capital costs and easing staffing issues (according to 68% of respondents) (F5 Networks 2009).

Further clarification which companies are using public Clouds is provided by the analysis of published case studies of Cloud providers. For example, at the case study subpage of its Web Services Site (http://aws.amazon.com/solutions/case-studies/), Amazon provides an overview of short case studies of companies using its Cloud services. The majority of the customers presented there are rather young Internet companies. Such Internet companies start on a green field and can build their infrastructure from the beginning based on the Cloud Computing paradigm. Even more, the availability of computing power on demands gives them the opportunity to start and grow fast without investments in infrastructure. For traditional companies, Cloud Computing proves to be more challenging. Only few traditional companies are present on the Amazon case study list as for example The Washington Post that uses the Amazon Web Services to turn online Hilary Clinton's White House schedule during her husband's time in office, with more than 17'000 searchable pages (see also The Economist 2008). Another example described by The Economist (2008) is NASDAQ who uses the Amazon Web Services for providing its service related to historical stock market information, called Market Replay. Both applications are not critical with respect to data security and privacy. Thus, it seems that traditional companies are using Clouds only where no critical and sensitive data is involved. Major concerns related to implementation of Cloud Computing besides those mentioned in Chapter 4 are:

- *Security and privacy of data* as well as international regulation related to them
- *International and company regulation regarding data storage* – current Cloud providers do not offer the possibility to monitor where the data is.
- *SLA agreements with Cloud providers* – currently available SLA agreement involve generic terms in terms of availability, support and similar aspects, but are not able to cover individual needs.

Overall, Cloud Computing seems to have a faster adoption than Grid Computing. On the one hand this is due to the fact that, in particular Internet start-ups can build their application on top of it. Furthermore the more modularized offerings of the Clouds on IaaS, PaaS and SaaS level provide a wider and more customized choice. Another factor that positively drives the adoption of Cloud Computing is the support also for other applications then mainly HPC based applications. For a higher adoption of Cloud Computing by traditional companies, higher maturity of the technology in terms of security, reliability, automatic monitoring of individual SLAs as well as established standards are necessary.

14.3 Practical Guidelines for Introducing Grid and Cloud Computing in Companies

The institutionalization of Grid and Cloud Computing in companies, in particular across several organizational domains, is a complex task. It results in substantial changes how IT is used, managed and consumed (see also Murch 2004 and Gentzsch 2007). These changes do not only affect the IT department, but also the whole company. A new mindset and attitude of employees towards IT, based on sharing and acceptance of external IT resources is required. Such substantial changes cannot be easily introduced in one step. A stepwise and evolutionary approach towards companywide introduction of Grid and Cloud Computing is required, which provides companies sufficient time to adjust and accommodate changes inferred by each evolutionary step (Murch 2004).

Evolutionary changes are enabled with the modularity and service-orientation of the basic technology. In chapter 3, a potential development path towards Grid and Cloud Computing based on different scope of these technologies was sketched (see also figure 14.2).

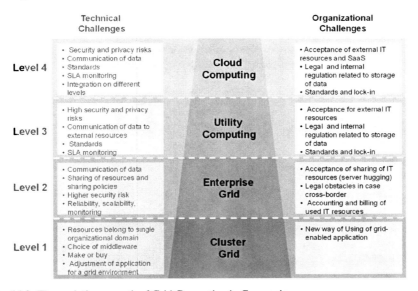

Fig. 14.2: The evolutionary path of Grid Computing in Companies

A first step towards an Enterprise Grid and Cloud infrastructure is the establishment of Cluster Grids. Cluster Grids are located within one organizational domain and do not affect the whole organization. They are a good starting point, as they enable the companies to accumulate know-how, and to experience the advantages of the technology with low exposure to the risks.

The next step is to connect Cluster Grids with IT infrastructure from different organizational domains into an Enterprise Grid. Technically this imposes higher challenges in terms of support for: integration of heterogeneous physical resources and data, security and privacy in distributed environments, automation of resource sharing policies, and communication in a distributed environment. From a human perspective, a new positive attitude of employees towards acceptance of resources sharing and adjustment of processes is required. From an organizational and IT governance perspective, new rules and policies need to be defined that regulate: the resource sharing and the distribution of management functions among organizational units involved in the Grid as well as security and privacy aspects of data sharing and communication within the Grid.

The third and forth step is inclusion of external resources as Utility Computing and Cloud Computing. Also in the last two steps besides technical, additional organizational and governance challenges arise. The establishment of a culture favouring the acceptance of external resources and applications, the introduction of policies for choice of external providers, or for regulating security and privacy aspects related to communication of data to the external provider are some examples of the possible challenges.

Overall, a successful introduction of Grid computing requires changes in the employees' culture, attitude, mindset and the companies' processes and IT governance. To assure success, a well organized project and change management as well as a comprehensive communications strategy is needed.

Given the findings above, practical guidelines integrating the technical stages of Grid and Cloud introduction with supporting change management and IT governance aspects are proposed below and visualized in figure 14.3:

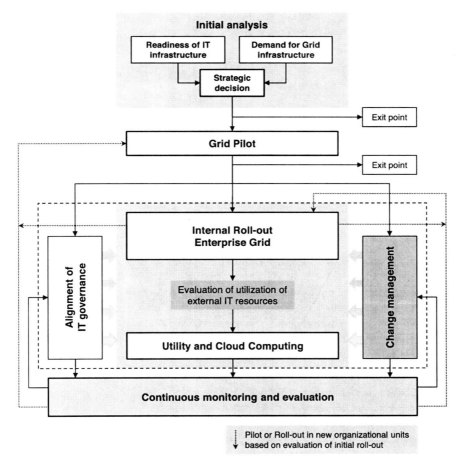

Fig. 14.3: Practical Guidelines for implementation of Grid and Cloud Computing in companies

The core technology-oriented activities of a Grid and Cloud Computing introduction process are the following:

1. Initial analysis
2. Pilot Implementation
3. Internal interconnection (internal roll-out)
4. Integration of Utility and Cloud Computing
5. Continuous monitoring and evaluation

Besides the technology related core activities in the introduction process, there is a need for supporting organizational and change management processes. On the one hand, the IT governance needs to be adjusted to reflect and guide the changed way of consuming of IT resources, on the other hand, all phases in the introductory process need to be accompanied with extensive change management. The adjustment of the

IT governance policies should reflect the changed situation and support the attitude towards sharing own resources and using external resources. The change management process should be designed in a way to address all affected parties in the company (management, employees in the IT department and end users), and to include a comprehensive communication plan.

14.3.1 Technical Implementation Activities

14.3.1.1 Initial Analysis of Demand and Readiness for Grid and Cloud Computing

Grid and Cloud Computing has the potential to provide many advantages, but not in any case. An initial analysis is necessary that should provide a first check if Grid and Cloud Computing are suitable and possible solutions in the specific context of a company (Murch 2004 and Gentzsch 2007). The initial analysis involves the following activities:

- Check of the demand for grid computing based on the strategic objectives of the company
- Assessment of the readiness of the company's infrastructure for Grid and Cloud Computing and based on that, an estimation of needed action and investments to improve its readiness
- Identification and conception of the business case for Grid and Cloud Computing
- Preparation of an initial business, implementation and project plan.

Each of the above listed activities will be described in detail below:

Checking the demand for Grid Computing: The initial analysis for the demand of Grid and Cloud Computing in a company has two perspectives: a business and a technology perspective. The institutionalization of Grid and Clouds in a company needs to be justified with concrete business needs and aligned to the business strategy of the company. Thus, a first step of the analysis is the assessment of the company's strategic goals and based on that deduction of requirements upon business processes necessary to achieve them. The requirements of the business processes need to be compared with the potential and opportunities provided by Grid and Cloud technology. This very first analysis step should ensure that the introduction of Grid and Cloud Computing is strategy and business driven.

The analysis from the technology perspective is dedicated to the evaluation of the existing IT support for the identified strategic business processes. The goal is the identification of gaps and opportunities for improvement based on Grid and Cloud technology. The most important aspects in this context are:

- Are there any type of tasks and business processes that require high computing capacity or additional scalable and flexible IT infrastructure and cannot be supported with the available infrastructure? For example, the case of Novartis described in chapter 3, showed that some important tasks that have direct impact on the innovation capability of the company became possible only after the establishment of the Enterprise Grid.

- How many of the existing tasks and processes with strategic importance would profit from higher processing and storage capacity of the existing infrastructure?
- How many of the existing tasks and processes with strategic importance do need more servers and storage capacity?

Checking the readiness for Grid and Cloud Computing: The check of the readiness for Grid and Cloud Computing concerns mainly the existing infrastructure. It involves in particular the analysis of: grid suitability of existing applications, quality of the existing infrastructure and of the existing network.

- *Analysis of the grid suitability of existing applications.* A Grid infrastructure can only be successful if there are suitable applications running on it. This means that an important analysis that needs to be done is, if the existing application that might benefit from Grid and Cloud Computing can be grid-enabled, i.e. adjusted to run in parallel or to be modularized in smaller subprograms. The less applications available that can be parallelised the lower the added value of Grid and Cloud Computing.
- *Analysis of the quality of the existing infrastructure.* Old infrastructure with low availability and old software might not be appropriate as a starting point for Grids and Clouds. The higher the heterogeneity of the existing infrastructure the higher the risk of failure. Given this, it is important to check, if and in which scope an initial investment for standardizing the infrastructure might be necessary.
- *Analysis of the quality of the existing network* – for example the available bandwidth of the network. For Computing Grids, where only computing instructions are transferred, a local network with lower bandwidth might be sufficient (see the Novartis example in chapter 3). Data Grids might require high bandwidth and higher security (for example the HP rendering centre described in chapter 3 was connected with the user company over a high security optical network).

The readiness of a company for Grid and Cloud Computing might also be affected by the level of standardization and smoothness of business processes involved. An important question is how well standardized and automated the involved business processes are. The higher the degree of automation and the lower the number of media breaks within the process, the higher the potential of Grid and Cloud Computing is.

Identification and definition of the business case: Based on the first two steps of the initial analysis it should become clear if Grid and Cloud Computing is suitable for the company. However, to achieve definitive certainty if Grid and Cloud Computing is applicable, it is necessary to quantify the potential gains and to analyse if it would also result in financial gains. Thus, a concrete business case for Grid and Cloud Computing needs to be identified and defined. First of all this means a priorization of the identified opportunities for introduction of Grids and Clouds and then quantification of a potential return on investment in a business case. The business case comprises a quantification and comparison of required investments and costs with potential gains from Grid and Cloud Computing. An important aspect that needs to be considered during the development of the business case is that it takes time until investments in Grid and Cloud Computing result in financial gains.

To summarize: the initial analysis evaluates the potential of Grids and Clouds to support business strategies, determines whether the corporation is ready to embark on Grid and Cloud programs, defines where to focus efforts to gain the maximum benefits, and quantifies potential benefits of Grids and Clouds in a business case. The result of the grid assessment can be used to determine the overall company's Grid and Cloud Computing goals, a Grid and Cloud Computing strategy, and the most cost-effective domains in which to focus Grid and Cloud efforts. They furthermore, serve as the basis for recommending action and developing a detailed implementation plan (Murch 2004).

14.3.1.2 Strategic Decision to Introduce Grid and Cloud Computing

As Grid Computing is complex and results in considerable changes for the company and the projects are long-lasting and costly, a final decision whether to institutionalize Grid and Cloud Computing needs to be taken on the highest management level of the organization and has strategic character. The results of the initial analysis, in particular the developed business case, are input to the strategic decision making process related to Grid and Cloud Computing. The identified business case should be presented in a way to clearly show current deficiencies, the potential and specific benefits of the technology, the risks associated with its introduction, the necessary investments and the expected return on investment. Other important information is: the expected changes and the duration of the project. Of high importance is also the management of expectations and of realistic assessment when the Grid or Cloud solution will become operative and after which period of time the return on investment might be expected.

If a positive decision is made to go for Grid and Cloud Computing, at this stage of the process it is also important to assure management support for the whole duration of the project. An ideal situation would be to have one representative of top management as main project owner. Visible interest of top management representatives and frequent communication of the importance of the project and its results helps to motivate employees and to introduce change with less overall objection.

14.3.1.3 Pilot Implementation

It is recommendable to apply an evolutionary approach and start with a pilot implementation of Grids and Clouds. The pilot should be suitable to provide a proof of the advantages of Grid and Cloud Computing for the company and to provide input for the next steps of implementation. In a company with no Grid experience a typical starting point in the evolution towards Grid and Cloud infrastructures is the introduction of Cluster Grids. Cluster Grids of several organizational units serve as a foundation for a pilot interconnection of them in an Enterprise Grid.

14.3.1.4 Internal Interconnection

In case the pilot in one organizational domain is successful the next stage is the internal interconnection of resources from different units of the company with Grid and Cloud Computing, i.e. evolution towards an Enterprise Grid. Enterprise Grid means the interconnection of the infrastructure from different domains and departments in the company. In an extreme case, an Enterprise Grid might interconnect the whole enterprise infrastructure. The evolution towards an Enterprise Grid is in itself a complex process, which should be justified by business needs and approached step-by-step. This means to start from the beginning of the introduction process and to first evaluate which tasks and processes require Enterprise Grids, to identify an initial pilot implementation, to extend the pilot and to adjust IT governance and policies (see also figure 14.2).

As described in the section 14.3.1.1 at the beginning the business needs for Enterprise Grids need to be evaluated. Typically processes that might span over several organizational units at different physical location, or collaborative tasks are an indication for suitability of Enterprise Grids. Global, intra-company processes that need adequate and efficient IT support might be considerably improved by the support of Enterprise Grids. For example, global companies need to decompose their highly complex processes into modular components of a workflow which run on the infrastructure of several company locations. Such global processes usually require on-demand availability and access to suitable IT resources. *"Application of grid technology in these processes, guarantees seamless integration of and communication among all distributed components and provides transparent and secure access to sensitive company information and other proprietary assets, world-wide"* (Gentzsch 2007). The application of Enterprise Grids to support such processes has the potential to considerably improve their effectiveness, productivity and time-to-market and at the same time to reduce costs.

After the suitable business processes for Enterprise Grids are identified, the implementation of the Enterprise Grid should be approached step-by-step. In case the identified business process is complex, it is recommendable to start with a pilot involving two to maximum three locations. The experiences gained with the pilot can be applied to grow the Enterprise Grid by subsequently involving additional locations.

The institutionalization of the Enterprise Grid should be supported by adjustment of IT governance and policies (see section 14.3.2.1) and by change management (see section 14.3.2.2).

14.3.1.5 Inclusion of External Resources

A successful pilot and roll-out in the company provides a good technical foundation for integration of the internal Grid with external resources. Thus, the next evolutionary step might be the integration and resource sharing with external Utility Computing and Cloud providers or with other partner companies in so called Partner Grids. However, the step towards external Utility and Cloud Computing is again a substantial strategic decision and needs to be business driven. First suitable processes that can be outsourced and run on external structure need to be identified. As mentioned in chapter 14.2.2 traditional companies are reluctant to run critical processes or data on external infrastructure. Besides security and privacy concerns, the application of Utility and Cloud Computing for many processes might be impeded by legal regulation determining whether data and processes might be deployed on infrastructure in different countries. In general, suitable processes that can be run on external resources are:

- Processes and applications that often have unpredictable peaks for computing and storage resources. Example of such processes and applications are online sites where demand for resources might be influenced by different seasons or marketing activities of the company.
- Processes and applications involving non-critical data, but which have high storage consume and require high online availability.
- Processes and applications that require HPC.

After suitable processes are identified, in a next step a thorough return on investment calculation is necessary if usage of external resources indeed results in cost savings and financial gains.

Also in the case of Utility and Cloud Computing, it is advisable to start with a pilot implementation. The usage of external resources should be supported by adjustment of IT governance (see section 14.3.2.1) and policies and by change management (see section 14.3.2.2).

14.3.1.6 Continuous monitoring and Evaluation

Grids and Clouds once institionalised in a company are like a living organism that can frequently be adjusted according to changing business needs and technical developments. To enable adjustment of the Grid, a management cycle needs to be established for constantly measuring both the performance of the Grid or Cloud and its strategic fit. Thus, as soon as the Grid or Cloud is established also a monitoring concept needs to be put in place. The components of the monitoring system are: Grid and Cloud metrics, monitoring and analysis procedures and decision making processes. The monitoring of the Grid or Cloud should be from two perspectives:

- Technical performance and
- Strategic alignment and fit.

Technical monitoring involves measurement of technical performance indicators such as availability, performance and response time as well as problem management and monitoring. Another rather strategic technical aspect of Grid and Cloud monitoring is also the long-term capacity planning and adjustment (Murch 2009). The monitoring of the strategic alignment involves observation of changing business needs and evaluation of the necessity for respective change and strategic re-alignment of the Grid or Cloud.

14.3.2 Supporting Implementation Activities

14.3.2.1 Adjustment of IT Governance

In general IT governance is considered as specification of *"... the decision rights and accountability frameworks to encourage desirable behavior in the use of IT"* (Weill & Ross 2004). In this sense, effective IT governance must address the following three main questions (Weill & Ross 2004):

- What decisions must be made to ensure effective management of IT?
- Who should make these decisions?
- How will these decisions be made and monitored?

Thus, Grid and Cloud IT governance involves policies and rules guiding the usage of IT resources in companies and a description of the management structure of the Grid or Cloud. On the path of a company from traditional computing to Grid and Cloud Computing substantial organizational changes result that require an adequate change in both parts of the IT governance.

The scope of adjustment of the company's IT governance concept depends on the level of introduction of Grid and Cloud Computing. On the Cluster Grid level there is almost no need for changing the IT governance policy. The Cluster Grids are integrated in one IT domain and are not connected outside the domain. The change towards Cluster Grids affects therefore a limited number of applications and users and basically does not affect the existing governance structure.

The IT governance situation changes on the level of Enterprise Grids and requires its considerable adjustment. On the Enterprise Grid level the following adjustments are necessary:

- Which part of the existing infrastructure and under which rules is made available to the Enterprise Grid at each of the involved domains
- Clear division of IT management tasks among the involved organizational units
- Clear rules which processes with which priority can run on the Grid
- How is the usage metered and how is the usage paid for
- New security and privacy policies.

When Utility and Cloud Computing gets involved, the necessary IT governance changes concern mainly rules for sourcing and deployment of external IT infrastructure and adjustment of security and privacy policies. These changers are described in detail below:

- Adjustment of IT Governance with policies regulating the sourcing and deployment of IT infrastructure:
  - Definition of rules for choice and decision making regarding the question which processes and resources might by outsourced, i.e. supported by external infrastructure.
  - Definition of rules for assessment when, how and why access to external resources is needed.

- – Definition of company rules for selecting and establishing relationships with external Utility computing, SaaS and VO providers.
- – Definition of rules and policies for using of SaaS offered by Clouds by employees.
- – Definition of guidelines and templates for defining the contractual relationships with external providers.
- Adjustment of IT Governance with security and privacy policies:
  - – Definition of policies for secure communication with external providers: the SaaS, Utility Computing, and VO provider.
  - – Definition of access policies – who and under which condition is allowed to access external resources.
  - – Definition of policies for storage of data on external resources.
  - – Definition of privacy policies specialized for a grid environment.

Furthermore, integrated monitoring support for an environment with mixed internal and external resources is required.

14.3.2.2 Change Management

People usually have negative attitudes and perceptions towards change. Often change provokes fears, stress, frustration and denial of change. In order to avoid the negative effects of change processes in companies, it is necessary to support them with change management activities. *"Change management means to plan, initiate, realize, control, and finally stabilize change processes on both, corporate and personal level."* (Recklies 2009).

As already described above, the introduction of Grid and Cloud Computing results in substantial changes for employees in the IT department, for end users and for IT managers of a company. Given this, each substantial change or evolutionary step on the path towards Grid and Cloud Computing should be accompanied with related change management measures.

The main reason for negative attitude of employees towards change is mainly the lack of information or incomplete information about what kind of change is going on and how it will affect their personal situation in terms of tasks, workload, or responsibilities. To avoid the appearance of fears, the main components of change management are:

- Activities for user involvement
- Communication activities
- Training activities.

The goal of change management is to keep employees informed about the change, to make employees to participate in the change process, and to help employees to master the changed environment. In general, change management activities accompany the actual change process and can be classified in three phases:

- *Initiation phase* – where the most important goal is to involve employees and to create awareness for the problem that requires change and the possible solutions.

- *Project phase* – where the change is actually starting to be introduced. In this second phase the actual consequences of the change become visible as the project progresses. At this stage it is important to diagnose employees' resistance to change and to enable and support the employees' transition through the change process. With a comprehensive communication strategy it is important to keep employees and management informed.
- *Stabilization phase* – in which the new solution is stabilized. Major change management activities at this stage are training for employees and support for establishment of the new processes.

The necessary change management activities during the introduction of Grid and Cloud Computing in the three above mentioned phases are:

- *Initiation phase:* First it is important to identify all employees that might be affected by the introduction of Grid and Cloud Computing. Typically these are employees and managers of the involved IT department, end users and the company management. Specific action need to be taken to create awareness for current problem areas and for the potential of Grid and Cloud Computing to provide a solution for them. Possible activities to involve employees and to create awareness are: organization of common workshops to discuss the problem, presentations about Grid and Cloud Computing, provision of information to successful cases studies of successful Grid and Cloud Computing implementation and similar.
- *Project phase:* One major instrument of change management in this phase is a comprehensive communication strategy. A communication plan needs to be developed with communication activities addressing the employees and reporting about the progress of the project. The communication measures might include a mixture of instruments as for example: blogs, project wikis, project newsletters, face-to-face meetings and personal discussion rounds.
- *Stabilization phase:* In the stabilization phase it is of high importance to have the new IT governance in place on time and to establish grid-training programs for all involved employees. It is also important to establish support activities and to guide the employees through the new solution.

14.4 Summary and Conclusion

This book started with a vision of using computing as utility in a way as simple as using electricity. This vision implies that, if the Utility Computing infrastructure is in place, we do not have to worry about hardware on which our application runs, about software updates, standards, system software, sufficient storage and similar. The availability and maturing of Grid and Cloud Computing is an important milestone in achieving this vision.

References

AbdelSalam H, Maly K, Mukkamala R, Zubair M, Kaminsky D (2009) Towards Energy Efficient Change Management in a Cloud Computing Environment. In: Proceedings of the 3rd International Conference on Autonomous Infrastructure, Management and Security: Scalability of Networks and Services (AIMS 2009), pp. 161-166, Lecture Notes in Computer Science (LNCS 5637). Springer, Heidelberg. doi:10.1007/978-3-642-02627-0_13

Allee V (2002) A Value Network Approach for Modeling and Measuring Intangibles. White paper, Open Value Networks. http://www.value-networks.com/howToGuides/A_ValueNetwork_Approach.pdf. Accessed 9 August 2009

Amazon S3 (2009) Amazon Simple Storage Service (Amazon S3). Amazon Web Services http://aws.amazon.com/s3/. Accessed 9 August 2009

Amazon Web Services (2009) Amazon Elastic Compute Cloud (Amazon EC2). http://aws.amazon.com/ec2/. Accessed 14 July 2009

Angelis G, Gritzalis S, Lambrinoudakis C (2004) Mechanisms for Controlling Access in the Global Grid Environment. Internet Research 14(5):347-352. doi:10.1108/10662240410566935

Armbrust M, Fox A, Griffith R, Joseph AD, Katz RH, Konwinski A, Lee G, Patterson DA, Rabkin A, Stoica I, Zaharia M (2009) Above the Clouds – A Berkeley View of Cloud. Technical report UCB/EECS-2009-28, EECS Department, University of Berkeley, California, 10 February 2009. http://www.eecs.berkeley.edu/Pubs/TechRpts/2009/EECS-2009-28.html. Accessed: 15 June 2009

Arrington M (2006) Amazon: Grid Storage Web Service Launches. TechCrunch. http://www.techcrunch.com/2006/03/14/amazon-Grid-storage-web-service-launches/. Accessed 14 July 2009

Baker M, Buyya R, Laforenza D (2002) Grids and Grid technologies for wide-area distributed computing. Softw. Pract. Exper. 32(15):1437-1466. doi:10.1002/spe.488

BE01 (2009) Business Experiment 1: Computational Fluid Dynamics and Computer Aided Design. BEinGRID. http://www.beingrid.eu/be1.html. Accessed 10 August 2009

BE02 (2009) Business Experiment 2: Movie Post-Production Workflow. BEinGRID. http://www.beingrid.eu/be2.html. Accessed 10 August 2009

BE06 (2009) Business Experiment 6: Ground Water Modelling. BEinGRID. http://www.beingrid.eu/be6.html. Accessed 1 July 2009

BE08 (2009) Business Experiment 8: Integration of Engineering and Business Processes in Metal Forming. BEinGRID. http://www.beingrid.eu/be8.html. Accessed 10 August 2009

BE13 (2009) Business Experiment 13: Virtual Laboratory for Textile. BEinGRID. http://www.beingrid.eu/be13.html. Accessed 1 July 2009

BE23 (2009) Business Experiment 23: Workflows on Web2.0 for Grid enabled infrastructures in complex Enterprises (WOW2GREEN). BEinGRID. http://www.beingrid.eu/wow2green.html. Accessed 1 July 2009

BE24 (2009) Business Experiment 24: Grid technologies for affordable data synchronization and SME integration within B2B networks (GRID2(B2B)). BEinGRID. http://www.beingrid.eu/be24.html. Accessed 10 August 2009

Beack T (2006) SOA Maturity Model: Compass on the SOA Journey. SOAInstitute.org. http://www.soainstitute.org/articles/article/article/soa-maturity-model-compass-on-the-soa-journey.html. Accessed: 30 July 2009

Beale H, Kötz H, Hartkamp A, Tallon D (eds) (2002) Cases, Materials and Text on Contract Law. Hart Publishing, Oxford

BEinGRID Booklet (2009) Better Business Using Grid Solutions: Eighteen Successful Case Studies from BEinGRID. http://www.beingrid.eu/casestudies.html. Accessed 1 July 2009

Belady CL (2007) In the data center, power and cooling costs more than the IT equipment it supports. ElectronicsCooling 13(1). http://electronics-cooling.com/articles/2007/feb/a3/. Accessed 06 August 2009

Bennett K, Layzell P, Budgen D, Brereton P, Macaulay L, Munro M (2000) Service-based software: the future for flexible software. Seventh Asia-Pacific Software Engineering Conference (APSEC'00), apsec, pp. 214. doi:10.1109/APSEC.2000.896702

Benoist G, Martins C (2008) The agricultural holdings – Structural data. In: Agricultural statistics, Main results 2006-2007, pp. 25-66. eurostat report, European Commission. http://epp.eurostat.ec.europa.eu/cache/ITY_OFFPUB/KS-ED-08-001/EN/KS-ED-08-001-EN.PDF. doi:10.2785/13552

Berman F, Hey T (2004) The scientific imperative, Chapter 2. In: Foster I, Kesselman C (eds) The Grid: Blueprint for a New Computing Infrastructure, 2nd ed. Morgan Kaufman, San Francisco, CA

Berry D (2007) Grid Computing challenges current software licensing models. ComputerworldUK. http://www.computerworlduk.com/technology/servers-data-centre/grid-utility/opinion/index.cfm?articleid=493. Accessed 15 March 2009

Berstis V (2002) Fundamentals of Grid Computing. IBM RedBooks Paper. http://www.redbooks.ibm.com/redpapers/pdfs/redp3613.pdf. Accessed 21 August 2009

Biddick M (2008) Service-Level Agreements Come of Age. InformationWeek, issue 1 December 2008. http://www.informationweek.com/news/services/business/showArticle.jhtml?articleID=212200435. Accessed 20 August 2009

Boccaletti G, Löffler M, and Oppenheim JM (2008) How IT can cut carbon emissions. McKinsey Quarterly, October 2008, McKinsey & Company. http://www.mckinseyquarterly.com/How_IT_can_cut_carbon_emissions_2221. Accessed 20 August 2009

Boden T (2004) The Grid Enterprise — Structuring the Agile Business of the Future. BT Technology Journal 22(1):107-117. doi:10.1023/B:BTTJ.0000015501.06794.97

Bourbonnais S, Gogate VM, Haas LM, Horman RW, Malaika S, Narang I, Raman V (2004) Towards an information infrastructure for the grid. IBM Syst. J. 43(4):665-688

Brodkin J (2008) Gartner: Seven cloud-computing security risks. InfoWorld, 2 July 2008. http://www.infoworld.com/article/08/07/02/Gartner_Seven_cloudcomputing_security_risks_1.html. Accessed 25 February 2009

Brossard D, Dimitrakos T, Colombo M (2008) Common Capabilities for Trust & Security in Service Oriented Infrastructures. In: Cunningham P, Cunningham M (eds) Collaboration and the Knowledge Economy: Issues, Applications, Case Studies, 5th vol. IOS Press, Amsterdam

Brossard D, Karanastasis S (2009) A note on integrating common capabilities from Security and Portals. July 2009. To appear at Gridipedia Technical White Papers. http://www.gridipedia.eu/technicalwhitepapers.html

Brossard D, Prieto Martínez JL (2009) A Virtual Hosting Environment for Distributed Online Gaming. In: Proceedings of the 3rd IFIP WG 11.11 International Conference on Trust Management (IFIPTM 2009), pp. 314-317, IFIP Advances in Information and Communication Technology (AICT 300). Springer, Boston. doi:10.1007/978-3-642-02056-8_23

BT (2009a) BT and Sony unveil PSP tool. BT Innovation news. http://www.btplc.com/Innovation/News/psp.html. Accessed: 24 June 2009

BT (2009b) BT Service Development Kit and Ribbit. http://www.ribbit.com/. Accessed: 24 June 2009

Bugeiro MG, Mouriño JC, Gómez A, Váquez C, Huedo E, Llorente IM, Rodríguez-Silva DA (2009) Integration of SLAs with GridWay in BEinEIMRT project. In: Proceedings of the 3rd Iberian Grid Infrastructure Conference (IBERGRID 2009). Netbiblo

Buyya R, Abramson D, Venugopal S (2005) The Grid Economy. In: Proceedings of the IEEE, 93(3), pp. 698-714. doi: 10.1109/JPROC.2004.842784

Cain MW (2008) E-Mail and the Cloud. Gartner, 6 June 2008

Castro-Leon E, Munter J (2005) Grid Computing Looking Forward. Intel white paper. http://cache-www.intel.com/cd/00/00/20/57/205719_205719.pdf. Accessed 9 August 2009

Cern (2006) Grid: More bytes for science. http://public.web.cern.ch/public/en/Spotlight/SpotlightGrid-en.html. Accessed 19 March 2009

Chesbrough H, Rosenbloom RS (2002) The role of business model in capturing value from innovation: evidence from Xerox Corporation's technology spin-off companies. Industrial and Corporate Change 11(3):529-555

Coleman MP, Alexe DM, Albreht T, McKee M (eds) (2008) Responding to the challenge of cancer in Europe. National and University Library, Ljubljana, Slovenia. http://www.euro.who.int/Document/E91137.pdf

comScore (2009) Online Gaming Continues Strong Growth in U.S. as Consumers Increasingly Opt for Free Entertainment Alternatives. comScore press release, 10 July 2009. http://www.comscore.com/Press_Events/Press_Releases/2009/7/Online_Gaming_Continues_Strong_Growth_in_U.S._as_Consumers_Increasingly_Opt_for_Free_Entertainment_Alternatives. Accessed 29 July 2009

Cooter R, Ulen T (2004) Law and Economics. Pearson Addison Wesley, Boston

D'Andria F, Jiménez S, Biette M, Brossard D, Madsen L, Orciuoli F (2008) Dynamic SLA and Trust for Next Generation Business Models in Grid. In: Cunningham P, Cunningham M (eds) Collaboration and the Knowledge Economy: Issues, Applications, Case Studies, 5th vol. IOS Press, Amsterdam

Desai B, Currie W (2003) Application Service Providers: A Model in Evolution. In: Proceedings of the 5th International Conference on Electronic Commerce (ICEC'03), Vol. 50, pp. 174-180. ACM, New York, NY. doi:10.1145/948005.948028

Dimitrakos T, Djordjevic I, Milosevic Z, Jøsang A, Phillips CI (2003) Contract Performance Assessment for Secure and Dynamic Virtual Collaborations. In: Proceedings of the 7th International Conference on Enterprise Distributed Object Computing (EDOC 2003), pp. 62-75. IEEE Computer Society, Washington, DC

Dimitrakos T, Wilson M, Ristol S (2004) TrustCoM – A Trust and Contract Management Framework enabling Secure Collaborations in Dynamic Virtual Organisations. ERCIM News, No. 59, October 2004

Dimitrakos T, Martrat J, Wesner S (2009a) Service Oriented Infrastructures and Cloud Service Platforms for the Enterprise: A selection of common capabilities validated in real-life business trials by the BEinGRID consortium. Springer, Heidelberg, to be published in 2009

Dimitrakos T, Brossard D, de Leusse P (2009b) Securing business operations in SOA. In BT Technology Journal Vol. 26, no. 2, April 2009

Directive 2007/47/EC of the European Parliament and of the Council of 5 September 2007. Official Journal of the European Union, L 247/21, 21 September 2007. http://eur-lex.europa.eu/LexUriServ/LexUriServ.do?uri=OJ:L:2007:247:0021:0055:EN:PDF. Accessed 7 August 2009

EGEE (2008) An EGEE Comparative Study: Grids and Clouds – Evolution or Revolution?. Enabling Grids for E-sciencE (EGEE) report, 11 June 2008. https://edms.cern.ch/document/925013/. Accessed 20 August 2009

EGEE (2009) Objectives, The Enabling Grids for e-sciencE (EGEE) Project. http://www.eu-egee.org/index.php?id=104. Accessed 12 August 2009

ENISA (2009) An SME perspective on Cloud Computing – Questionnaire, June 2009 – for more information please contact ENISA via http://www.enisa.europa.eu/

Entrepreneur (2003) Linux Networx Cluster Speeds Development Of Diagnostics. Entrepeneur.com, 1 July 2003. http://www.entrepreneur.com/tradejournals/article/103446134.html. Accessed 15 August 2009

Eurotechnology Japan (2009) Games sector overtakes electrical. eurotechnology.japan.blog, 13 July 2009. http://eurotechnology.com/blog/2009/07/japans-games-sector-overtakes.html. Accessed 31 July 2009

Eymann T (2008) Cloud computing. Enzyklopädie der Wirtschaftsinformatik. http://www.enzyklopaedie-der-wirtschaftsinformatik.de/wi-enzyklopaedie/lexikon/uebergreifendes/Kontext-und-Grundlagen/Markt/Softwaremarkt/Geschaftsmodell-(fur-Software-und-Services)/Cloud-Computing. Accessed: 10 June 2009

F5 Networks (2009) Cloud Computing Survey Results June – July 2009. www.f5.com/pdf/reports/cloud-computing-survey-results-2009.pdf. Accessed: 01 September 2009

Fellows W (2008) Partly Cloudy – Blue-Sky Thinking About Cloud Computing. 451 Position Paper, Executive Overview, The 451 Group. www.451group.com/reports/executive_summary.php?id=619. Accessed: 10 June 2009

Fellows W (2009) Sun in the cloud: IaaS gets to market as first Open Cloud Platform offering. Market Insight Service report, The 451 Group

Fellows W, Barr J (2007) 2008 preview – Enterprise Computing Strategies. Market Insight Service report, The 451 Group

Ferlay J, Autier P, Boniol M, Heanue M, Colombet M, Boyle P (2007) Estimates of the cancer incidence and mortality in Europe in 2006. Ann. Oncol, 18(3):581-592

Forrester (2009) Market Overview: IT Security In 2009. Forrester Research report, 22 April (updated 29 May) 2009. http://www.forrester.com/Research/Document/Excerpt/0,7211,47598,00. html

Foster I, Kesselman C (1998) Computational Grids. http://citeseerx.ist.psu.edu/viewdoc/ summary?doi=10.1.1.36.4939

Foster I, Kesselman, C, Tuecke S (2001) The Anatomy of the Grid: Enabling Scalable Virtual Organization. International Journal of High Performance Computing Applications 15(3):200-222

Foster I (2002) What is the Grid? A Three Points Checklist. Argonne National Laboratory & University of Chicago, 20 July 2002. http://www.mcs.anl.gov/~itf/Articles/WhatIsTheGrid. pdf. Accessed 9 August 2009

Foster I, Kesselman C, Nick JM, Tuecke S (2002) Grid Services for Distributed System Integration. Computer 35(6):37-46. doi:10.1109/MC.2002.1009167

Foster I, Kesselman C (2004) Concepts and Architecture. In: Foster I, Kesselman C (eds) The GRID: Blueprint for a New Computing Infrastructure, 2nd edn, pp. 37-63. Morgan Kaufmann, San Francisco, CA

Foster I, Kesselman C (2004) Preface to the Second Edition. In: Foster I, Kesselman C (eds) The GRID: Blueprint for a New Computing Infrastructure, 2nd edn. Morgan Kaufmann, San Francisco, CA

Foster I, Zhao Y, Raicu I, Lu S (2008) Cloud Computing and Grid Computing 360-Degree Compared. In: Grid Computing Environments Workshop (GCE'08). doi:10.1109/GCE.2008.4738445

Gaeta A, Orciuoli F, Capuano N, Brossard D, Dimitrakos T (2008) A Service Oriented Architecture to Support the Federation Lifecycle Management in a Secure B2B Environment. In: Cunningham P, Cunningham M (eds) Collaboration and the Knowledge Economy: Issues, Applications, Case Studies, 5th vol. IOS Press, Amsterdam

Gantz JF, Chute C, Manfrediz A, Minton S, Reinsel D, Schlichting W, Toncheva A (2008) The Diverse and Exploding Digital Universe. IDC white paper, March 2008. http://www.emc.com/ collateral/analyst-reports/diverse-exploding-digital-universe.pdf

Gantz, J, Boyd A, Dowling, S (2009) Cutting the Clutter: Tackling Information Overload At the Source. IDC white paper, March 2009. http://www.xerox.com/downloads/usa/en/n/nr_IDC_ White_Paper_on_Information_Overload.pdf

Garfinkel SL (2007) An Evaluation of Amazon's Grid Computing Services: EC2, S3 and SQS. Harvard University. http://simson.net/clips/academic/2007.Harvard.S3.pdf. Accessed 14 July 2009

Gartner (2008a) Gartner Says Cloud Computing Will Be As Influential As E-business. Gartner press release, 26 June 2008. http://www.gartner.com/it/page.jsp?id=707508. Accessed 20 August 2009

Gartner (2008b) Gartner Says Contrasting Views on Cloud Computing Are Creating Confusion. Gartner press release, 29 September 2008. http://www.gartner.com/it/page.jsp?id=766215. Accessed: 9 June 2009

Gartner (2008c) Gartner Says Worldwide SaaS Revenue in the Enterprise Application Markets Will Grow 27 Per Cent in 2008. Gartner press release, 22 October 2008. http://www.gartner. com/it/page.jsp?id=783212. Accessed 24 August 2009

Gartner (2009) Forecast: IT Security Services, Worldwide – see also press release: Gartner Says Worldwide Security Software Revenue Grew 18.6% in 2008: Appliance-Based Products Saw Fastest Growth. http://www.gartner.com/it/page.jsp?id=1031712. Accessed 24 June 2009

Geiger A (2006) Service Grids – von der Vision zur Realität. In: Barth T, Schüll A (eds) Grid Computing: Konzepte, Technologien, Anwendungen, pp. 17-32. Vieweg+Teubner, Wiesbaden

Gens F (2008) Defining "Cloud Services" and "Cloud Computing". IDC eXchange, 23 September 2008. http://blogs.idc.com/ie/?p=190. Accessed: 9 June 2009

Gentzsch W (2007) Top 10 Rules for Building a Sustainable Grid. http://www.gridforum.org/TLS/index.php. Accessed 24 July 2009

Geuer-Pollmann C (2005) How to Make a Federation Manageable. In: Proceedings of the 9th IFIP TC-6 TC-11 Conference on Communications and Multimedia Security (CMS 2005), pp. 330-338, Lecture Notes in Computer Science (LNCS 3677). Springer, Heidelberg. doi:10.1007/11552055_43

Gibson S (2004) eBay: Sold on Grid. Eweek, 30 August 2004. http://www.eweek.com/c/a/Web-Services-Web-20-and-SOA/eBay-Sold-on-Grid/. Accessed 15 March 2009

Gil P (2009) Beginners Guide to eBay: Buying and Selling. Netforbeginners. http://netforbeginners.about.com/cs/buyingselling/a/eBay101.htm. Accessed 15 March 2009

Gillett FE, Brown EG, Staten J, Lee C (2008) Future View: The New Tech Ecosystems Of Cloud, Cloud Services, And Cloud Computing. Forrester Research document excerpt, 28 August 2008. http://www.forrester.com/Research/Document/Excerpt/0,7211,45073,00.html. Accessed: 16 June 2009

Gillies L (2001) A Review of the New Jurisdiction Rules for Electronic Consumer Contracts Within the European Union. J. Inf. Law. Tech. (1). http://www2.warwick.ac.uk/fac/soc/law/elj/jilt/2001_1/gillies. Accessed 25 February 2009

Gohring N (2006) Attack hits Sun public grid service on day one. Networkworld, 23 March 2006. http://www.networkworld.com/news/2006/032306-attack-sun-public-grid.html. Accessed 21 July 2009

Gómez A, Fernández Sánchez C, Mouriño Gallego JC, López Cacheiro J, González Castaño FJ, Rodríguez-Silva D, Domínguez Carrera L, González Martínez D, Pena García J, Gómez Rodríguez F, González Castaño D, Pombar Cameán M (2007) Monte Carlo Verification of IMRT treatment plans on Grid. In: From Genes to Personalized HealthCare: Grid Solutions for the Life Sciences – Proceedings of HealthGrid 2007, pp. 105-114, Studies in Health Technology and Informatics, Vol. 126. IOS Press, Amsterdam

Gottfrid D (2008a) Self-service, Prorated Super Computing Fun!. The New York Times Open Blog, 1 November 2007. http://open.blogs.nytimes.com/2007/11/01/self-service-prorated-super-computing-fun/. Accessed 21 July 2009

Gottfrid D (2008b) The New York Times Archives + Amazon Web Services = TimesMachine. The New York Times Open Blog, 21 May 2008. http://open.blogs.nytimes.com/2008/05/21/the-new-york-times-archives-amazon-web-services-timesmachine/. Accessed 21 July 2009

Goyal B, Lawande S (2005) Grid Revolution: An Introduction to Enterprise Grid Computing. McGraw-Hill, Emeryville, CA

Gray J (2003) Distributed Computing Economics. Technical Report, MSR-TR-2003-24, Microsoft Research, March 2003. http://research.microsoft.com/pubs/70001/tr-2003-24.pdf

Gridipedia (2008) Grid Players. http://www.Gridipedia.eu/Gridplayers.html. Accessed 14 July 2009

Gridipedia (2009) Value chains and networks. http://www.gridipedia.eu/valuechainsandnetworks.html. Accessed: 23 July 2009

Gridipedia (2009a) VO Management. http://www.gridipedia.eu/vo-article.html. Accessed 1 July 2009

Gridipedia (2009b) Security. http://www.gridipedia.eu/grid-security.html. Accessed 1 July 2009

Gridiepedia (2009c) The Vine Toolkit. http://www.gridipedia.eu/thevinetoolkit.html. Accessed 10 August 2009

GT4 (2009) Globus Toolkit version 4. http://www.globus.org/toolkit/. Accessed 1 July 2009

Harms U, Rehm H-J, Rueter T, Wittmann H (2006) Grid Computing für virtualisierte Infrastrukturen. In: Barth T, Schüll A (eds) Grid Computing: Konzepte, Technologien, Anwendungen, pp. 1-15. Vieweg+Teubner, Wiesbaden

Harris D (2008) Why 'Grid' Doesn't Sell. On-Demand Enterprise blog, 24 March 2008. http://www.on-demandenterprise.com/blogs/26058979.html. Accessed 20 August 2009

Hof RD (2006) Jeff Bezos' Risky Bet. BusinessWeek, 13 November 2006. http://www.businessweek.com/print/magazine/content/06_46/b4009001.htm. Accessed 18 May 2009

Horkan W (2009) Cloud Relationship Model. Sun Startup Essentials. http://blogs.sun.com/startups /entry/cloud_relationship_model. Accessed 8 July 2009

Hoyer V, Stanoevska-Slabeva K (2009) Generic Business Model Types for Enterprise Mashup Intermediaries. In: Proceedings of the 15th Americas Conference on Information Systems (AMCIS 2009), San Francisco, C

HP Labs (2004) HP Labs goes Hollywood. HP Labs News, April 2004. http://www.hpl.hp.com/ news/2004/apr-jun/nab.html. Accessed 15 August 2009

Huedo E, Montero RS, Llorente IM (2004) A Framework for Adaptive Execution on Grids. Softw. Pract. Exper. 34(7):631-651. doi:10.1002/spe.584

IAEA (2009) Directory of Radiotherapy Centers (DIRAC). International Atomic Energy Agency (IAEA). http://www-naweb.iaea.org/nahu/dirac/query3.asp. Accessed 17 January 2009

IBM (2006) Web services federation language v1.1. IBM, December 2006. http://www.ibm.com/ developerworks/library/specification/ws-fed/

IBM (2008) IBM Server Optimization and Integration Services – VMware server virtualization. http://www-935.ibm.com/services/in/gts/pdf/ssd03022usen.pdf. Accessed 18 August 2009

IBM (2009a) Seeding the Clouds: Key Infrastructure Elements for Cloud Computing. ftp://ftp.soft-ware.ibm.com/common/ssi/sa/wh/n/oiw03022usen/OIW03022USEN.PDF. Accessed 9 August 2009

IBM (2009b) Standards and Web Services. http://www.ibm.com/developerworks/webservices/ standards/. Accessed: 24 June 2009

IDC (2005) European Infrastructure Management Services Market, Forecast and Analysis, 2005 – 2009. IDC report, April 2005

IDC (2006) Systems Integrator Approaches for Service Oriented Architecture Implementations. IDC report, May 2006

IDC (2008a) IT Cloud Services User Survey, pt.2: Top Benefits & Challenges. IDC exchange, 2 October 2008. http://blogs.idc.com/ie/?p=210. Accessed 12 August 2009

IDC (2008b) IDC Finds Cloud Computing Entering Period of Accelerating Adoption and Poised to Capture IT Spending Growth Over the Next Five Years. IDC press release, 20 October 2008. http://idc.com/getdoc.jsp?containerId=prUS21480708. Accessed 20 August 2009

IDC (2008c) IDC Predictions 2009: An Economic Pressure Cooker Will Accelerate the IT Industry Transformation. IDC report, December 2008

IGD (2009) IGD – The Food & Grocery Experts. http://www.igd.com. Accessed 26 June 2009

Ilic A, Staake T, Fleisch E (2009) Using Sensor Information to Reduce the Carbon Footprint of Perishable Goods. IEEE Pervasive Computing 8(1):22–29. doi:10.1109/MPRV.2009.20

InfoCard (2009) Information Card Ecosystem, Overview. Information Card Foundation. http:// informationcard.net/quick-overview. Accessed 1 July 2009

Insight Research (2006) Grid Computing: A Vertical Market Perspective 2006-2011. Report, Executive Summary. The Insight Research Corporation. http://www.insight-corp.com/reports/ grid06.asp

Intel (2003) Distributed Desktop Grid, PC Refresh Help Novartis Enhance Innovation. Intel Business Center Case Study. http://www.univaud.com/about/resources/files/cs-novartis.pdf. Accessed 20 August 2009

Jha S, Merzky A, Fox G (2008) Clouds Provide Grids with Higher-Levels of Abstraction and Explicit Support for Usage Modes. Presentation for OpenGridForum (OFG) 23. http://www. ogf.org/OGF23/materials/1272/grids_hla_cloud.pdf. Accessed 20 August 2009

Johnson B (2008) CERN: The brains behind the operation. The Guardian, 30 June 2008. http:// www.guardian.co.uk/science/2008/jun/30/cern.computer.technology. Accessed 15 March 2009

Jøsang A, Keser C, Dimitrakos T (2005) Can we manage trust?. In: Proceedings of the 3rd International Conference on Trust Management (iTrust 2005), pp. 93-107, Lecture Notes in Computer Science (LNCS 3477). Springer, Heidelberg. doi:10.1007/11429760_7

Joseph J, Ernest M, Fellenstein C (2004) Evolution of Grid Computing Architecture and Grid Adoption Models. IBM Syst. J. 43(4):624-644

Kantor LS, Lipton K, Manchester A, Oliveira V (1997) Estimating and Addressing America's Food Losses. FoodReview 20(1) 2–12

Kaplan JM, Löffler M, Roberts RP (2004) Managing Next-Generation IT Infrastructure. McKinsey on Business Technology, Winter 2004. http://www.mckinsey.com/clientservice/bto/point ofview/pdf/MoIT3_nextgenIT.pdf

Keating S (2004) Cluster, Grid Computing: Greater than Sum of Parts. Drug Discovery & Development Online, 16 September 2004. http://www.univaud.com/about/news/news_2004/091404_jjdrugdev.pdf. Accessed 15 August 2009

Kourpas E (2006) Grid Computing: Past, Present and Future – An Innovation Perspective. IBM white paper

Leff A, Rayfield J, Dias DM (2003) Service-Level Agreements and Commercial Grids. IEEE Internet Computing 7(4):44-50. doi:10.1109/MIC.2003.1215659

Leible S (2006) Negotiation and Conclusion of the Contract: Formal and Substantive Validity, Choice-of-Court and Choice-of-Law Clauses – An Introduction. In: Schulz A (ed) Legal Aspects of an E-commerce Transaction: International Conference in The Hague, 26 and 27 October 2004, pp. 57-71. Sellier, Munich

Licklider JCR (1960) Man-Computer Symbiosis. IRE Transactions on Human Factors in Electronics, HFE-1:4-11. http://groups.csail.mit.edu/medg/people/psz/Licklider.html

Lilienthal M (2009) Grid Computing – Die nächste Generation des Resource Sharing. In: Hinz O, Beck R, Skiera B, König W (eds) Grid Computing in der Finanzindustrie, pp. 16-29. Books on Demand, Norderstedt

Llorente IM, Montero RS, Huedo E (2005) A Loosely Coupled Vision for Computational Grids. IEEE Distributed Systems Online, 6(5):2. doi:10.1109/MDSO.2005.25

Llorente IM (2008a) Cloud Computing for on-Demand Resource Provisioning. Presentation on the International Research Workshop on High Performance Computing and Grids (HPCC08), July 2008. http://www.reservoir-fp7.eu/twiki/pub/Reservoir/PresentationsPage/Cloud_Computing_for_on-Demand_Resource_Provisioning.pdf, access date: 18 July 2008

Llorente IM (2008b) A Virtual Infrastructure Layer for Cluster and Grid Computing. DSA (Distributed Systems Architecture) Research Group blog, 14 April 2008. http://blog.dsa-research.org/?p=39. Accessed 20 August 2009

Lohr S (2009) When Cloud Computing Doesn't Make Sense. The New York Times Bits Blog,15 April 2009. http://bits.blogs.nytimes.com/2009/04/15/when-cloud-computing-doesnt-make-sense. Accessed 12 August 2009

MacFarland A (2006) eBay Infrastructure — A Prototype for the Future. The Clipper Group Observer, 9 November 2006. http://www.clipper.com/research/TCG2006097.pdf. Accessed 15 March 2009

McAfee (2006) Does Size Matter? The security challenge of the SMB. McAfee report. http://www.mcafee.com/us/local_content/reports/does_size_matter_en_v2.pdf. Accessed 31 July 2009

McKinsey (2004) Power Unbound: The Emerging Importance of Grid Computing. McKinsey & Company white paper. http://www.mckinsey.com/clientservice/bto/pointofview/pdf/Grid_computing_white_paper.pdf

McKinsey (2009) Clearing the Air on Cloud Computing. McKinsey & Company report

Meliksetian DS, Prost J, Bahl AS, Boutboul I, Currier DP, Fibra S, Girard J, Kassab KM, Lepesant J, Malone C, Manesco P (2004) Design and Implementation of an Enterprise Grid. IBM Syst. J. 43(4):646-664

Menken I (2008) Cloud Computing – The Complete Cornerstone Guide to Cloud Computing Best Practices. Emereo

Merrill Lynch (2008) The Cloud Wars: $100+ billion at stake. Merrill Lynch research note, May 2008

Mertz SA, Eschinger C, Eid T, Pring B (2007) Dataquest Insight: SaaS Demand Set to Outpace Enterprise Application Software Market Growth. Gartner RAS Core Research Note, 3 August 2007

Messerschmidt CM (2009) Grid-Technologie in deutschen Unternehmen – eine empirische Studie. In: Hinz O, Beck R, Skiera B, König W (eds) Grid Computing in der Finanzindustrie, pp. 30-67. Books on Demand, Norderstedt

MicroScope (2009) Channel equipped for cloud security. http://cde.cerosmedia.com/1B4a320 f3eb2f96012.cde/page/16. Accessed 31 July 2009

Miller M (2008) Cloud Computing: Web-Based Applications That Change the Way You Work and Collaborate Online. Que Publishing, Indianapolis

Mittilä T, Lehtinen K (2005) Customizing the Application Service Provider Offering. http://www.ebrc.fi/kuvat/1066.pdf. Accessed 23 August 2009

Montagnat J, Frohner A, Jouvenot D, Pera C, Peter Kunszt P, Koblitz B, Santos N, Loomis C, Texier R, Lingrand D, Guio P, Brito da Rocha R, Sobreira de Almeida A, Farkas Z (2008) A Secure Grid Medical Data Manager Interfaced to the gLite Middleware. Journal of Grid Computing 6(1):45-59

Mouriño Gallego JC, Gómez A, Fernández Sánchez C, González Castaño FJ, Rodríguez Silva DA, Pena García J, Gómez Rodríguez F, González Castaño D, Pombar Cameán M (2007) The eIMRT Project: Planning and Verification of IMRT treatments on Grid. In: Proceedings of the 1st Iberian Grid Infrastructure Conference (IBERGRID 2007)

Murch R (2004) Grid Computing: Is It Right for Your Company? informIT. http://www.informit.com/articles/article.aspx?p=340735. Accessed: 24 August 2009

NESSI-Grid (2006) Deliverables D.1.1 & D.1.3 – Grid Vision and Strategic Research Agenda. Official deliverable of the project NESSI-Grid FP6-033638. http://www.nessi-europe.com/Nessi/LinkClick.aspx?fileticket=8ZXAmjsvpeA%3D&tabid=234&mid=930. Accessed 9 August 2009

Next Generation GRIDs Expert Group (2006) Future for European Grids: GRIDs and Service Oriented Knoewledge Utilities – Vision and Research Directions 2010 and Beyond. Next Generation GRIDs Expert Group Report 3. ftp://ftp.cordis.europa.eu/pub/ist/docs/grids/ngg3_eg_final.pdf. Accessed 20 August 2009

NZZ (2003) Schlafende PC mutieren zum Supercomputer. NZZ Online, 7 November 2003. http://www.nzz.ch/2003/11/07/em/article97JEJ.html. Accessed 20 August 2009

OASIS (2007) OASIS WS-Trust specification v1.3. http://docs.oasis-open.org/ws-sx/ws-trust/200512

OCCI (2009) OGF Open Cloud Computing Interface (OCCI) Working Group. http://www.occi-wg.org/doku.php. Accessed 19 August 2009

Opitz A, König H, Szamlewska A (2008) What Does Grid Computing Cost? J. Grid Comput., 6(4): 385-397. doi: 10.1007/s10723-008-9098-8

O'Reilly T (2008) Web 2.0 and Cloud Computing, O'Reilly Radar, 26 October 2008. http://radar.oreilly.com/2008/10/web-20-and-cloud-computing.html. Accessed: 15 June 2009

Osterwalder A (2004) The Business Model Ontology – a proposition in a design science approach. PhD thesis, HEC Lausanne. http://www.hec.unil.ch/aosterwa/PhD/. Accessed 15 March 2009

Overby E, Bharadwaj A, Sambamurthy (2006) Enterprise agility and the enabling role of information technology. Eur. J. Inf. Syst. 15(2): 120-131. doi:10.1057/palgrave.ejis.3000600

Padgett J, Djemame K, Dew P (2005) Grid Service Level Agreements Combining Resource Reservation and Predictive Run-time Adaptation. In: Proceedings of the UK e-Science All Hands Meeting 2005. http://www.allhands.org.uk/2005/proceedings/papers/526.pdf. Accessed 25 February 2009

Papazoglou MP, Traverso, P, Dustdar S, Leymann F, Kraemer BJ (2006) Service-Oriented Computing: A Research Roadmap. In: Cubera F, Kraemer BJ, Papazoglou MP (eds) Service Oriented Computing (SOC). Dagstuhl Seminar Proceedings Internationales Begegnungs- und Forschungszentrum fuer Informatik (IBFI), Schloss Dagstuhl, Germany. http://drops.dagstuhl.de/opus/volltexte/2006/524/

Papazoglou MP, Traverso P, Dustdar S, Leymann F (2007). Service-Oriented Computing: State of the Art and Research Challenges. Computer 40(11):38-45. doi:10.1109/MC.2007.400

Parrilli DM (2008) The Server as Permanent Establishment in International Grids. In: Proceedings of the 5th International Workshop on Grid Economics and Business Models (GECON 2008), pp. 89-102, Lecture Notes in Computer Science (LNCS 5206). Springer, Heidelberg

Parrilli DM, Stanoevska-Slabeva K, Thanos G (2008) Software as a Service (SaaS) Through a Grid Network: Business and Legal Implications and Challenges. In: Cunningham P, Cunningham M (eds) Collaboration and the Knowledge Economy: Issues, Applications, Case Studies, 5th vol. IOS Press, Amsterdam

Pena J, González-Castaño DM, Gómez F, Gago-Arias A, González-Castaño FJ, Rodríguez-Silva D, Gomez A, Mouriño C, Pombar M, Sánchez M (2009) eIMRT: a web platform for the verification and optimization of radiation treatment plans. Journal of Applied Clinical Medical Physics, to be published in 2009

Peterovic O, Kittl C, Teksten RD (2001) Developing Business Models for eBusiness. In: Proceedings of the International Conference on Electronic Commerce, Vienna (ICEC '01)

Pil FK, Holweg M (2006) Evolving From Value Chain to Value Grid. MIT Sloan Management Review 47(4):72-80

Porter M (1985) Competitive Advantage: Creating and Sustaining Superior Performance. Free Press, New York

PricewaterhouseCoopers (2009) Global Entertainment and Media Outlook: 2009-2013. http://www.pwc.com/gx/en/global-entertainment-media-outlook/index.jhtml

Quigley C (1997) European Community Contract Law: The Effect of EC Legislation on Contractual Rights, Obligations and Remedies. Kluwer Law International, Alphen a/d Rijn

Quocirca (2003) Business Grid Computing. Quocirca report. http://www.quocirca.com/pages/analysis/reports/view/store250/item1515/

Raekow Y, Simmendinger C, Grabowski P (2009) An Improved License Management for Grid and High Performance, July 2009. To appear at Gridipedia Technical White Papers http://www.gridipedia.eu/technicalwhitepapers.html

Raekow Y, Simmendinger C, Krämer-Fuhrmann O (2009) License management in grid and high performance computing. Computer Science – R&D 23(3-4): 275-281. doi:10.1007/s00450-009-0078-4

Rajic H, Brobst R, Chan W, Ferstl F, Gardiner J, Haas A, Nitzberg B, Rajic H, Templeton D, Tröger P (2008) Distributed Resource Management Application API Specification 1.0. http://www.ogf.org/documents/GFD.133.pdf. Accessed: 29 June 2009

Ranger S (2005) World's biggest grid seeks secrets of the universe. CNET. http://news.cnet.com/Worlds-biggest-grid-seeks-secrets-of-the-universe/2100-1008_3-5970641.html?tag=nefd.top. Accessed 15 March 2009

Rappa MA (2004) The Utility Business Model and the Future of Computing Services. IBM Syst. J. 43(1):32-42

Reese G (2009) Cloud Application Architectures. O'Reilly Media, Sebastopol, CA

Reinefeld A, Schintke F (2004) Dienste und Standards für das Grid Computing. In: von Knop J, Haferkamp W (eds) 18. DFN Arbeitstagung über Kommunikationsnetze, Düsseldorf, Lecture Notes in Informatics, Series of the German Informatics Society (GI), Vol. P-55, pp. 293-304. http://subs.emis.de/LNI/Proceedings/Proceedings55/GI-Proceedings.55-19.pdf

Resch M (2006) Grid at the Interface of Industry and Research. In: Barth T, Schüll A (eds) Grid Computing: Konzepte, Technologien, Anwendungen, pp. 85-96. Vieweg+Teubner, Wiesbaden

RightScale (2008) Define Cloud Computing. RightScale Blog, 26 May 2008. http://blog.rightscale.com/2008/05/26/define-cloud-computing/. Accessed: 9 Jun 2009

Rissanen E, Firozabadi BS (2004) Administrative Delegation in XACML. In: Proceedings of the W3C Workshop on Constraints and Capabilities for Web Services, Redwood Shores, CA

Rosenberg I, Juan A (2009) The BEinGRID SLA framework. Report. http://www.gridipedia.eu/slawhitepaper.html. Accessed 1 July 2009

Roth C (2008) SaaS Implementation Survey: Where, When, and How to Use SaaS. Burton Group, Utah

Salamone S (2003) Gridlock is a Good Thing at Novartis. Bio-ITWorld.com, 15 October 2003. http://www.bio-itworld.com/archive/101003/novartis. Accessed 20 August 2009

SAML (2005) Assertions and Protocols for the OASIS Security Assertion Markup Language (SAML) V2.0. OASIS Standard, 15 March 2005. Document ID: saml-core-2.0-os. http://docs.oasis-open.org/security/saml/v2.0/saml-core-2.0-os.pdf. Accessed 1 July 2009

Sanjeepan V, Matsunaga A, Zhu L, Lam H, Fortes JAB (2005) A Service-Oriented, Scalable Approach to Grid-Enabling of Legacy Scientific Applications. In: Proceedings of the IEEE International Conference on Web Services (ICWS '05), pp. 553-560. ICWS. IEEE Computer Society, Washington, DC. doi:10.1109/ICWS.2005.17

Sawhney M (2005) Technology is the secret of an agile advantage. Financial Times, 24 August 2005, p. 8

Schommer P, Harms T, Gottschlich H (2007) LOHAS – Lifestyle of Health and Sustainability. Report, Ernst & Young

Schrödter S, Gosch T (2008) SESIS – Ship Design and Simulation System. In: Proceedings of the 7th International Conference on Computer and IT Applications in the Maritime Industries (COMPIT '08), pp. 163-173. http://www.anast.ulg.ac.be/COMPIT08/Files/Proceeding_Compit08.pdf

Schwartz J (2006) The Network is the Computer. Jonathan's Blog, 20 March 2006. http://blogs.sun.com/jonathan/entry/the_network_is_the_computer. Accessed: 24 June 2009

Siegel ES, Ford BR, Bornstein JM (1993) The Ernst & Young Business Plan Guide. John Wiley and Sons, New York

SIIA (2001) Software as a Service: Strategic Backgrounder. Software & Information Industry's (SIIA) eBusiness Division white paper. http://www.siia.net/estore/ssb-01.pdf. Accessed: 15 June 2009

Singer M (2004a) Sun's Utility Grid Play: Act II. Grid ComputingPlanet.com, 19 October 2004. http://www.Gridcomputingplanet.com/news/article.php/3423701. Accessed 14 July 2009

Singer M (2004b) Sun's Utility Grid To Open for Business. InternetNews.com, 21 September 2004. http://www.internetnews.com/ent-news/article.php/3410541. Accessed 14 July 2009

Smith M, Friese T, Freisleben B (2006) Model Driven Development of Service-Oriented Grid Applications. In: Barth T, Schüll A (eds) Grid Computing: Konzepte, Technologien, Anwendungen, pp. 193-213. Vieweg+Teubner, Wiesbaden

Sotomayor B, Montero RS, Llorente IM, Foster I (2008) Capacity Leasing in Cloud Systems using the OpenNebula Engine. In: Workshop on Cloud Computing and its Applications 2008 (CCA08), Chicago, Illinois, USA, October, 2008 Cornell University Library, in press

Stanoevska-Slabeva K, Talamanca CF, Thanos GA, Zsigri C (2007) Development of a Generic Value Chain for the Grid Industry. In: Proceedings of the 4th International Workshop on Grid Economics and Business Models (GECON 2007), pp. 44-57, Lecture Notes in Computer Science (LNCS 4685). Springer, Heidelberg

Stanoevska-Slabeva K, Bijlsma M, Fleck M, Hakonen M, Lönnblad J, Rook L, Vartiainen M, Verburg R (2008) Final Report Part A: Results from Case Studies. Report of the Study NEW GLOBAL. http://www.mcm.unisg.ch/content/blogcategory/77/193/lang,de/

Stanoevska-Slabeva K, Parrilli DM, Thanos G (2008a) BEinGRID: Development of Business Models for the Grid Industry. In: Proceedings of the 5th International Workshop on Grid Economics and Business Models (GECON 2008), pp. 140-151, Lecture Notes in Computer Science (LNCS 5206). Springer, Heidelberg

Stanoevska-Slabeva K, Parrilli DM, Thanos GA (2008b) Defining Efficient Business Models for Grid-enabled Applications. In: Cunningham P, Cunningham M (eds) Collaboration and the Knowledge Economy: Issues, Applications, Case Studies, 5th vol. IOS Press, Amsterdam

Storskrubb E (2008) Civil Procedure and EU Law: A Policy Area Uncovered. Oxford University Press, Oxford

Sun (2007) Sun Microsystems' Network.com Delivers Immediate Access to Online Applications with "Click and Run" Ease. Sun press release, 13 March 2007. http://www.sun.com/aboutsun/pr/2007-03/sunflash.20070313.1.xml. Accessed: 25 June 2009

Sun (2009a) A Guide to Getting Started with Cloud Computing. Sun white paper. https://www.sun.com/offers/docs/cloud_computing_primer.pdf. Accessed: 10 June 2009

Sun (2009b) Sun Microsystems Unveils Open Cloud Platform. Sun press release, 18 March 2009. http://www.sun.com/aboutsun/pr/2009-03/sunflash.20090318.2.xml. Accessed: 25 June 2009

Sun (2009c) Cloud Comptuing. http://www.sun.com/solutions/cloudcomputing/. Accessed: 25 June 2009

Sun (2009d) Network.com. http://network.com/. Accessed: 26 January 2009

Sun (2009e) Customer Success Stories for "Sun Grid Utility Computing". http://www.sun.com/customers/index.xml?s=c6f88d64-8fb5-4f7f-ac04-ef23401600b6. Accessed 15 August 2009

Sun (2009f) Customer Snapshot: Technology, Virtual Compute Corporation. http://www.sun.com/customers/service/virtual_compute.xml. Accessed 14 July 2009

Sun (2009g) gridengine Project home. SunSource.net. http://gridengine.sunsource.net/. Accessed 14 July 2009

Sun (2009h) Sun Grid Engine 6.2 Update 3. http://www.sun.com/software/sge/index.xml. Accessed 14 July

Tabscott D, Ticoll D, Lowy A (2000) Digital Capital – Harnessing the Power of Business Webs. Harvard Business School Press, Boston

Takashima H (2008) PC GRID use cases and requirements. Presentation in Enterprise Grid Requirement (EGR)-RG (EGR-RG) session of the 22nd Open Grid Forum (OGF22). http://www.ogf.org/OGF22/materials/1091/OGF22_egr-rg_novartis.pdf. Accessed 20 August 2009

Talia D (2002) The Open Grid Services Architecture: Where the Grid Meets the Web. IEEE Internet Computing 6(6):67-71. doi:10.1109/MIC.2002.1067739

Thanos GA, Courcoubetis C, Stamoulis GD (2007) Adopting the Grid for Business Purposes: The Main Objectives and the Associated Economic Issues. In: Proceedings of the 4th International Workshop on Grid Economics and Business Models (GECON 2007), pp. 1-15, Lecture Notes in Computer Science (LNCS 4685). Springer, Heidelberg

The Economist (2008) Where the cloud meets the ground. Special Report: Corporate IT. http://www.economist.com/specialreports/displaystory.cfm?story_id=12411920. Accessed 30 August 2009

Total Telecom Magazine (2009) Media & Entertainment: Online gaming: Multi tasking. Total Telecom Magazine, July 2009

Toyota MMK (2006) Toyota Production System Terms. Toyota Motor Manufacturing Kentucky. http://toyotageorgetown.com/terms.asp. Accessed 14th April 2009

TraceTracker (2009) TraceTracker. http://www.tracetracker.com. Accessed 26 June 2009

UDDI (2004) OASIS UDDI v3 Specification TC, Dated 20041019. http://uddi.org/pubs/uddi-v3.0.2-20041019.htm Accessed 1 July 2009

van Oosterhout M, Waarts E, van Heck E, van Hillegersberg (2007) Business Agility: Need, Readiness and Alignment with IT Strategies. In: Desouza KC (ed) Agile Information Systems: Conceptualization, Construction, and Management, pp. 52-69. Elsevier Butterworth-Heinemann

Vaquero LM, Rodero-Merino L, Caceres J, Lindner M (2008) A break in the clouds: towards a cloud definition. SIGCOMM Comput. Commun. Rev. 39(1):50-55. doi:10.1145/1496091.1496100

Volk E, Jacob A, Mueller M, Racz P, Waldburger M, Bjerke J (2009a) AgroGrid – Composition and Monitoring of Dynamic Supply Chains. In: Proceedings of the Cracow Grid Workshop 2008 (CGW'08), pp. 373-381

Volk E, Mueller M, Jacob A, Racz P, Waldburger M (2009b) Increasing Capacity Exploitation in Food Supply Chains Using Grid Concepts. In: Proceedings of the 6th International Workshop on Grid Economics and Business Models (GECON 2009), pp. 88-101, Lecture Notes in Computer Science (LNCS 5745). Springer, Heidelberg

Wadhwa S, Rao KS (2003) Flexibility and agility for enterprise synchronization: knowledge and innovation management towards flexagility. SIC Journal 12(2):111-128

Wall Street & Technology (2009) Energy Stars: Wall Street Firms' Sustainable IT Efforts. Wall Street & Technology, 17 June 2009. http://www.wallstreetandtech.com/showArticle.jhtml?articleID=218000171. Accessed 31 July 2009

Wang FF (2008) Obstacles and Solutions to Internet Jurisdiction: A Comparative Analysis of the EU and US Laws. J. Int'l Comm. Law Tech 3(4):233-241

Weill P, Vitale MR (2001) Place to Space: Migrating to eBusiness Models. Harvard Business School Press, Boston

Weisbecker A, Pfreundt F, Linden J, Unger U (2008) Einleitung. In: Weisbecker A, Pfreundt F, Linden J, Unger U (eds) Fraunhofer Enterprise Grids: Business Cases. Fraunhofer IRB, Stuttgart. http://www.epg.fraunhofer.de/fhg/Images/Enterprise_Grids_Band2_Screen_tcm267-133305.pdf. Accessed 20 August 2009

Weishäupl T, Donno F, Schikuta E, Stockinger H, Wanek H (2005) Business In the Grid: The BIG Project. In: Proceedings of the 2nd International Workshop on Grid Economics and Business Models (GECON 2005). http://hst.home.cern.ch/hst/publications/gecon-2005-BIGproject.pdf. Accessed 20 August 2009

Wijnands J, van der Meulen B, Poppe KJ (eds) (2006) Competitiveness of the European Food
    Industry – An economic and legal assessment. Technical report, European Commission. http://
    ec.europa.eu/enterprise/sectors/food/files/competitiveness_study_en.pdf
Wikipedia (2009a) Business plan. Wikipedia, the free encyclopedia. http://en.wikipedia.org/wiki/
    Business_plan. Accessed 15 March 2009
Wikipedia (2009b) Sun Cloud. Wikipedia, the free encyclopedia. http://en.wikipedia.org/wiki/
    Sun_Cloud. Accessed 14 July 2009
Wikipedia (2009c) Software as a service. Wikipedia, the free encyclopedia. http://en.wikipedia.
    org/wiki/Software_as_a_service. Accessed: 16 June 2008
Wikipedia (2009d) Total cost of ownership. Wikipedia, the free encyclopedia. http://en.wikipedia.
    org/wiki/Total_cost_of_ownership. Accessed: 30 July 2009
Wohl A (2008) Succeeding at SaaS: Computing in the Cloud. Wohl Associates
WS-Agreement (2007) Web Services Agreement Specification, Grid Resource Allocation
    Agreement Protocol (GRAAP) WG, Open Grid Forum, 14 March 2007
Xu H, Seltsikas P (2002) Evolving the ASP Business Model: Web Service Provision in the Grid
    Era. In: Proceedings of the 2nd International Conference on Peer-to-Peer Computing (P2P'02).
    doi:10.1109/PTP.2002.1046325
Youseff L, Butrico M, Da Silva D (2008) Towards a Unified Ontology of Cloud Computing. In:
    Grid Computing Environments Workshop (GCE'08). doi:10.1109/GCE.2008.4738443
ZDNet UK (2009) BT moves infrastructure into the cloud. ZDNet UK, 18 June 2009. http://news.
    zdnet.co.uk/communications/0,1000000085,39665232,00.htm. Accessed 31 July 2009

List of Abbreviations

=mcminstitute	Institute for Media and Communications Management
3D	three-dimensional
3G	3rd Generation
AAA	Authentication, Authorization, and Accounting
ACC Cyfronet	Academic Computer Centre CYFRONET AGH
ACM	Association for Computing Machinery
ADO	ActiveX Data Objects
ADR	Alternative Dispute Resolution
AG	Aktiengesellschaft
AGP	Andago Game Platform
AgroGrid	Agriculture and Grid
Akogrimo	Access to Knowledge through the Grid in a Mobile World
Amazon EC2	Amazon Elastic Compute Cloud
Amazon S3	Amazon Simple Storage Service
AMIES	Automotive Multi-company Integrated Engineering System
ANSYS	ANalysis SYStem
API	Application Programming Interface
Art.	Article
asbl	Association sans but lucratif
ASP	Application Service Provisioning and Application Service Provider
AssessGrid	Advanced Risk Assessment & Management for Trustable Grids
AUEB	Athens University of Economics and Business
AuthZ	Authorisation
B2B	Business-to-Business
B2C	Business to consumer
BE	Business Experiment
BEinEIMRT	Business Experiment in Enhanced IMRT planning using Grid services on-demand with SLAS
BEinGRID	Business Experiments in GRID
BEng	Bachelor of Engineering
BM	business model
Bn	billion
BREIN	Business objective driven REliable and Intelligent grids for real busiNess
BSc	Bachelor of Science
C	Celsius
ca.	circa
CaaS	Composition as a Service

Calif.	California
CC	common capabilities
CD	Compact Disc
CE	Conformité Européene (English: European Conformity)
CERN	Conseil Européen pour la Recherche Nucléaire (English: European Organization for Nuclear Research)
CESGA	Centro de Supercomputación de Galicia
CFD	Computation Fluid Dynamics
CHUS	Complexo Hospitalario de la Universidad de Santiago
CISSP	Certified Information Systems Security Professional
CMT	Center of Maritime Technologies e.V.
CobIT	Control Objectives for Information and related Technology
Contract C/R	Contract between Consolidator and Retailer
Contract C/T	Contract between Consolidator and Transport Company
Contract P/C	Contract between Producer and Consolidator
COSO	Committee of Sponsoring Organizations of Treadway Commission
COTS	Commercial, off-the-shelf
CPU	Central Processing Unit
CRM	Customer Relationship Management
CRMPA	Centro di Ricerca in Matematica Pura ed Applicata (English: Centre of Research in Pure and Applied Mathematics)
Crossgrid	Development of Grid Environment for Interactive Applications
CROSSWORK	Cross-Organisational Workflow Formation and Enactment
CRT	Conformal Radiotherapy
CSG	Communication Systems Group
CSR	Corporate Social Responsibility
DB	Database
DEISA	Distributed European Infrastructure For Supercomputing Applications
DICOM	Digital Imaging and Communications in Medicine
DICOM-RTPLAN	Digital Imaging and Communications in Medicine extension for Radiotherapy External/Brachy plan
Dipl.-Inform.	Diplom-Informatiker
DIRAC	Directory of Radiotherapy Centers
DISRUPT-IT	Disruptive Innovation
DLR	Deutsches Zentrum für Luft- und Raumfahrt (English: German Aerospace Center)
DOE	Department of Energy
Dr.	Doctor
DRMAA	Distributed Resource Management Application API
DVD	Digital Versatile Disc
e.g.	exempli gratia (English: for example)

e.V.	eingetragener Verein
ebXML	Electronic Business XML
EC	European Community
EC	European Communities / European Commission
EC2	Elastic Compute Cloud
e-Canned	Electronic commerce in the cannery industry
EGEE	Enabling Grids for E-siencE
EGF	Enterprise Grid Forum
e-IMRT	Advanced Systems For Radiotherapy Planning Using Distributed Computation project
ELeGI	European Learning Grid Infrastructure
EMANICS	European Network of Excellence for the Management of Internet Technologies and Complex Services
e-MINDER	Electronic CoMmerce Leveraging Network for Developing European Regions
eMMEDIATE	electronic Managing of product Manufacturing, Engineering, Design and Investment Applying information Technology for SMEs
ERP	Enterprise Resource Planning
ESU	European Size Units
et al.	et alii (English: and others)
etc	et cetera
ETH Zürich	Eidgenössische Technische Hochschule Zürich
EU	European Union
FDA	Food and Drug Administration
FDS	Fire Dynamics Simulator
FEM	Finite Element Method
fig.	figure
FP5	Framework Programme 5
FP6	Framework Programme 6
FP7	Framework Programme 7
FSG	Flensburger Schiffbau-Gesellschaft mbH und Co. KG
GAP	Good Agricultural Practices
GB	Gigabyte
GDPdU	Grundsätze zum Datenzugriff und zur Prüfbarkeit digitaler Unterlagen
GLOBECOM	Global Communications Conference
GmbH	Gesellschaft mit beschränkter Haftung
GMD	German National Institute for Research in Information Technology
GP2PC	Global and Peer-to-Peer Computing
GR	Game Ratings
GRASP	Grid Application Service Provision
GrASP	Grid-based Application Service Provision

GS	Game Servers
GT4	Globus Toolkit 4.0
GTK4	Globus Toolkit 4
GTNet®	Global Traceability Network
GUI	Graphical User Interface
GW-SLA	GridWay pluging for negotiating resources using SLA
HaaS	Hardware-as-a-Service
HL	high level
HL-QoS	high-level QoS
HLRS	High Performance Computing Center Stuttgart
HOSP	Hospitals
HPC	High-Performance Computing
HR	Human resources
HTML	Hypertext Markup Language
HTTPS	Hypertext Transfer Protocol Secure
i.e.	id est (English: that is)
I/O	Input/Output
IaaS	Infrastructure as a Service
IAEA	International Atomic Energy Agency
ICHEC	Institut Catholique des Hautes Etudes Commerciales
ICRI	Interdisciplinair Centrum voor Recht en Informatica
ICT	Information and Communication Technologies
IDCHUS	Fundación para la Investigación, Desarrollo e Innovación del Complejo Hospitalario Universitario de Santiago de Compostela
IEEE	The Institute of Electrical and Electronics Engineers
IFI	Institut für Informatik (English: Department of Informatics)
IFIP	International Federation for Information Processing
IGRT	Image Guide Radiotherapy
INES	Iniciativa Española de Software y Servicios
INFRAWEBS	Intelligent Framework for Generating Open (Adaptable) Development Platforms for Web-Service Enabled Applications Using Semantic Web Technologies, Distributed Decision Support Units and Multi-Agent-Systems
IP	Internet Protocol
ISIS	Intelligent Service Infrastructures
ISO	International Organization for Standardization
ISP	Internet Service Provider
IST	Information Society Technologies
ISV	Independent Software Vendor
IT	Information Technology
IT Food Trace	IT supported food traceability in food supply chains

ITC	International Teletraffic Congress
ITIL	Information Technology Infrastructure Library
KFKI	Central Research Institute for Physics
KPI	Key performance indicators
L&D	Location & Discovery
Lab	Laboratory
LHC	Large Hadron Collider
LL	low level
LLM	Master of Laws
LL-QoS	lower-level QoS
LOHAS	Lifestyle On Health And Sustainability
Ltd	Limited
M&E	Monitoring & Evaluation
MB	Megabyte
METACAMPUS	MetaCampus for life-long learning
METACAMPUS REAL	MetaCampus, Raising European Awareness on e-Learning
Metafor	Distance Learning by Satellite
Mgmt	Management
MMOG	massive multiplayer online games
MRT	Modulated Radiation Therapy
MSc	Master of Science
MSP	Managed Service Provider
N. CPUs	Number of CPUs
NATO	North Atlantic Treaty Organization
NESSI	Networked European Software & Services Initiative
NextGRID	Architecture for Next Generation Grids
No.	number
NYT	New York Times
OASIS	Organization for the Advancement of Structured Information Standards
ODBC	Open Database Connectivity
OECD	Organization for Economic Cooperation and Development
OGF	Open Grid Forum
OGSA	Open Grid Service Architecture
OGSI	Open Grid Service Infrastructure
OLG	Online gaming
Org.	Organisation
OSGi™	The Dynamic Module System for Java™
P2P	Peer-to-peer
P2P	Point to Point

PaaS	Platform as a Service
PAYG	Pay-as-you-go
PBS	Portable Batch System
PC	Personal Computer
PDF	Portable Document Format
PDP	Policy Decision Point
PEP	Policy Enforcement Point
PhD	Doctor of Philosophy
PPARC	Particle Physics and Astronomy Research Council
PROMINENCE	PROMoting Inter European Networks of Collaborating Extended Enterprises
QoS	Quality of Service
R&D	Research & Development
R&D&I	Research & Development & Innovation
RACI	Responsible, Accountable, Consulted, and Informed
RAM	Random-Access Memory
RCE	Reconfigurable Computing Environment
RFID	Radio Frequency Identification
RIA	Rich Internet Application
RMI	Remote Method Invocation
RoI	Return on Investment
RSS	Really Simple Syndication
RWTH	Rheinisch-Westfälische Technische Hochschule Aachen
s.t.	such that
S3	Simple Storage Service
SA	Société Anonyme
SaaP	Software-as-a-Product
SaaS	Software-as-a-Service
SAML	Security Assertion Markup Language
SC	Supply Chain
SCAI	Fraunhofer-Institute for Algorithms and Scientific Computing (German: Fraunhofer Institut für Algorithmen und Wissenschaftliches Rechnen)
SCM	Supply Chain Management
SESIS	Ship Design and Simulation Environment (German: SchiffEntwurfs- und SImulationsSystem)
SIIA	Software & Information Industry Association
SISTEC	Simulation and Software Technology devision
SLA	Service Level Agreement
SLAs&SLGs	Service Level Agreements and Guarantees
SLO	Service Level Objectives

SmartLM	Grid-friendly software licensing for location independent application execution IST FP7 Project
SMARTMAN	Supply Chain Management Tools for Machinery Manufacturer SMEs
SME	Small and medium-sized enterprise
SMS	Short Message Service
SOA	Service Oriented Architecture
SOA4All	Service Oriented Architectures for All
SOAP	Single Object Access Protocol
SoftWEAR	Software for Wearable Computer
SOI	Service-Oriented Infrastructure
SOI-AuthZ-PDP	SOI Authorisation Service
SOI-GGW	SOI Governance Gateway
SOI-SMG	SOI Secure Messaging Gateway
SOI-STS	SOI Security Token Service
SOX	Sarbanes Oxley Act
SP	service provider
SPU	Sun Power Unit
STS	Security Token Service
TB	terabyte
TH	Technische Hochschule
TIFF	Tagged Image File Format
TIME	Telecommunication, IT/Internet, Media and Entertainment
TIX	Traceability Information Exchange
TPS	Treatment Planning System
TrustCoM	Trust and Contract Management
T-Systems SfR	T-Systems Solutions for Research GmbH
TUHH	Technische Universität Hamburg-Harburg (English: Hamburg University of Technology)
UCL	Université Catholique de Louvain
UDDI	Universal Description, Discovery and Integration
UK	United Kingdom
UMIST	University of Manchester Institute of Science and Technology
UMTS	Universal Mobile Telecommunications System
UNICORE	Uniform Interface to Computing Resources
URJC	University of Rey Juan Carlos
US	United States
USA	United States of America
USD	United States Dollar
UZH	Universität Zürich (English: University of Zurich)
VAS	Value-added-Services

VHE	Virtual Hosting Environment
VIP-DATA	Virtual Input Pan for Data
VO	Virtual Organization
VoIP	Voice over IP
VOM	VO Management
VOMS	Virtual Organization Management Service
W3C	World Wide Web Consortium
WebDAV	Web-based Distributed Authoring and Versioning
WP	Work Package
WRG	White Rose Grid
WS	Web Services
WSDL	Web Services Description Language
WSDM	Web Services Distributed Management
WSRF	Web Service Resource Framework
XACML	eXtensible Access Control Markup Language
XML	eXtensible Markup Language

List of Authors

Eleni Agiatzidou is a member of the Network Economics Group at the Athens University of Economics and Business in the department of Informatics. Mrs Agiatzidou received her BSc degree in Informatics and her MSc in Information Systems, both from the Athens University of Economics and Business where now she is a PhD Candidate in the area of "Incentive mechanisms for the enhancement of locality in the Internet". Other research activity focuses on Grid technology, economic network mechanisms and dynamic spectrum management.

David Brossard received his MEng from the Institut National des Sciences Appliquées in Lyon, France. He is currently a senior researcher in the security architectures group of BT's Centre for Information Systems & Security Research, where his interests centre on SOA security and governance. David is a Sun-certified enterprise architect, an affiliate of the Institute of Information Security Professionals, a member of the IEEE and is working towards achieving CISSP accreditation. He has been actively involved in European Union research projects including TrustCoM and BEinGRID, where he leads the security theme. Prior to joining BT, David worked as architect/designer at Portugalmail, a Portuguese ISP, working on the company's blogging platform. He also worked for leading defence company, Thales, in various programming roles.

Prof. Costas Courcoubetis is heading the Network Economics and Services Group and the Theory, Economics and Systems Lab at the Athens University of Economics and Business. He received his Diploma (1977) from the National Technical University of Athens, Greece, in Electrical and Mechanical Engineering, his MSc (1980) and PhD (1982) from the University of California, Berkeley, in Electrical Engineering and Computer Science. He is currently a Professor in the Computer Science Department at the Athens University of Economics and Business.

His current research interests are economics of networks with emphasis in the development of pricing schemes that reduce congestion and enhance stability and robustness, quality of service and management of integrated services, performance and traffic analysis of large systems, applied probability models. Other interests include the combination of e-commerce technologies with telecommunications, and formal methods for software verification.

He has published over 100 papers in scientific journals and refereed conferences. His work has over 3000 citations according to the CiteSeer citation index. He is a co-author with Richard Weber of "Pricing Communication Networks: Economics, Technology and Modelling" (Wiley, 2003).

Juan Carlos Cuesta holds a Telecommunication Engineering degree from Universidad Politécnica de Madrid and works at Telefónica I+D as Project Manager. He has been involved for nearly 15 years in many automated and operator-based services that Telefónica provides to its customers (e.g. 118XY services, incoming and outcoming national and international access, commercial services, support for broadband users) and several innovation projects mainly related to the remote management of equipment at customer premises. He is currently member of the Services for Enterprises unit and participates in the BEinGRID project as business consultant.

Francesco D'Andria works as Project Manager in Atos Origin. He has obtained a Master's degree in Electronic Engineering from the "Università Degli Studi Di Salerno," Salerno, Italy (2002). His research activities concern the study of Grid technologies and he is interested in the application of these technologies in the business world. He is investigating the use of Commodity Technologies in order to implement Grid Services and their integration with COTS components. He has a significant expertise in SLA management architecture for use in Grid environments focusing on resource negotiation, monitoring and policing. Some of the European Union R&D projects in which he has participated in FP5 and FP6 and FP7 related to Grid technologies are: GRASP, Akogrimo, ELeGI, BEinGRID, and SmartLM. Afterwards he has designed and implemented a .NET monolithic infrastructure (C#, ADO) for Eni ICT in Bologna.

Theo Dimitrakos graduated from the University of Crete in 1993 and gained a PhD from Imperial College, London, in 1998. With fifteen years experience in a wide range of topics relating to information security and software and systems engineering, he now leads the SOA Security Research Group in BT's centre for information and security systems research. Theo also has a strong academic background in the areas of security risk analysis, formal modelling and applications of semantics and logic in computer science. He was the scientific coordinator of the European Union's BEinGRID and TrustCoM research projects and contributed to a UK Department of Trade & Industry Foresight project on cyber trust and crime prevention. The author of more than fifty scientific papers and (co-)editor of five books and two special editions of technical journals relevant to his interests, Theo serves as vice-chair of an International Federation for Information Processing (IFIP) working group on trust management and a member of the IFIP special interest group on enterprise interoperability.

Angelo Gaeta took the Laurea degree in Electronic Engineering cum laude from the University of Salerno in January 2002 with a thesis concerning the distributed simulation and next generation architectures to support wide scale distributed simulation. Current interests are related to investigations in Grid and SOA for e-business and e-science. He is co-author of several scientific papers related to the Web and Grid technologies. He has been involved in research activities in several EU co-funded projects. Currently, he collaborates with the CRMPA and he is mainly involved in the European Union project BEinGRID where he leads the activities of the WP related to VO Management.

Andrés Gómez is the Projects & Applications manager at CESGA and received his PhD in Physics from the University of Santiago de Compostela. From 1992 to 2001, he was working for several industrial and IT companies as CESATEL or UNISYS Spain, mainly in distributed systems. Since 2001, he is working in CESGA as Projects and Applications manager, where he has participated in several IST European projects as e-MINDER, e-Canned, Crossgrid, Metafor, EGEE, and int.eu.grid. He has knowledge and experience in design of distributed systems, performance engineering and application development. He has published more than 15 papers in scientific journals and has presented at more than 20 conferences.

Dr. Ulrich Heindl studied agriculture, specialized in nutrition, at the Technical University of Munich. He obtained his PhD in 1993 from the Institute of Nutrition Physiology. From 1993 to 1996 he worked as an assistant at the same institute. From 1996 to 1997 he had taken on responsibility in applied research for feed additives in the industry. Since April 1997 he has been employed by BASF and was responsible for global technical marketing of feed enzymes. His function there was developing existing and new feed enzymes, biological research in the field of enzymes and strategic marketing for enzymes. From October 1st, 2000 onwards he took over the responsibility as senior regional marketing manager for Asia/Pacific. Since July 2006, Dr. Heindl is the Vice President Business Development for TraceTracker developing concepts for traceability and information management in the feed and food values chain.

Volker Hoyer holds a diploma degree on Business Information Systems of the University of Hamburg, Germany. He also studied Business Administration at the Bordeaux Business School, France. Before joining SAP he gained experience in management consulting (LogicaCMG) at industrial projects in the utilities sector as well as in enterprise Web software development for strategic outsourcing projects (IBM e-Business Innovation Center). He currently works as a Research Associate and doctoral student at the Institute for Media and Communications Management (=mcm*institute*, University of St. Gallen) and at the SAP Research CEC St. Gallen, Switzerland. His research so far led to approximately 30 journal papers, conference papers, and book chapters. It includes, among others, Enterprise Mashups, Cloud Computing, Internet of Services, Cross-Organizational Business Processes, Enterprise Service-Oriented Architectures, and Business Cases.

Ansger Jacob studied Industrial Engineering at the University of Karlsruhe (TH), Germany, and received his diploma degree Diplom-Wirtschaftsingenieur (Industrial Engineering) in 2002. For some years he worked as a consultant in business process and IT optimization in the financial sector. Currently, he is doctoral candidate and assistant at Information Systems 2 at the University of Hohenheim. In his research, he addresses the use of context and situation technologies in distributed supply chain information systems. He has been involved in research projects as for example IT FoodTrace, SoftWEAR and BEinGRID Business Experiment 22- AgroGrid, bringing in his knowledge in supply chain technologies.

Ottmar Krämer-Fuhrmann, Dipl.-Inform., has received his diploma in Computer Science at the University of Bonn in 1984. He is working at the Fraunhofer Institute for Algorithms and Scientific Computing SCAI in Sankt Augustin. He is currently heading the group for high performance computing and distributed systems where he supervises about 10 researchers. He has long years experience in software development for scientific applications. He was involved in several projects where an integration platform for distributed systems called Reconfigurable Computing Environment (RCE) was developed. Recent projects in which Ottmar Krämer-Fuhrmann is involved mainly dealt with Grid Computing in the engineering sector. Prior to working at Fraunhofer he worked at German National Institute for Research in Information Technology (GMD).

Karita Luokkanen-Rabetino works as business consultant in the department of Research and Innovation in Atos Origin (Spain). She is Exploitation leader of the BEinGRID project (EU research project), and also participates in the exploitation activities in SmartLM (Licensing Management project). She has expertise in the analysis of enterprise competitive behaviour, strategic changes, and market dynamics. Karita Luokkanen-Rabetino received her master degree in marketing (MSc Econ) in 2002 from the University of Vaasa (Finland), and she participated in the European Doctoral Programme in Entrepreneurship and Small Business Management in 2003 in Universidad Autonoma de Barcelona (Spain) and the University of Växjö (Sweden). Prior working experience: Researcher and assistant at the University of Vaasa (2000-2005).

Marcus Mueller studied Economics at the University of Hohenheim, Germany. He received his diploma degree "Diplom Ökonom" in September 2007. During his studies he worked as a self-employed IT-consultant for the tax adviser sector. Currently, he is a PhD student and research assistant at the chair Information Systems 2 at University of Hohenheim. His work focuses on the use of distributed sensors in supply chains. Within BEinGRID, he works in the business experiment AgroGrid, and acts as a contributor of supply chain management and virtual organization knowledge.

Davide M. Parrilli obtained his Law degree at the University of Padova (Italy) in 2005 with a final thesis on International and Comparative Taxation ('The Regime of Transfer Pricing under Italian and Brazilian Law'). In 2006, he took his Master in Laws (LLM cum laude) in International and European Business Law at the University of Tilburg (The Netherlands) with a final dissertation in the area of company law ('The Defensive Measures in Case of Takeover Bids: The Italian Perspective'). In 2007, he obtained a specialization degree in Labour Law ('The Labour Law under Transformation') at the University of Padova (Italy). Actually he works as legal researcher at the Interdisciplinary Center for Law and ICT (ICRI) of the Catholic University of Leuven (Belgium) where he conducts research on business, including taxation, contracts and intellectual property rights, in the area of Grid and Cloud computing and, in more general terms, in the Information and

Communication Technology sector. He gained also extensive experience in the legal and business aspects related to clusters of small and medium-sized enterprises. He also practices as a lawyer at the Brussels bar.

Peter Racz received his MSc Degree in Computer Science from Budapest University of Technology and Economics in 2000 and his Doctoral Degree in Computer Science from University of Zurich in 2008. He was with the Department of Mobile Networks at Siemens AG, Germany from 2000 until end of 2002, working on next generation mobile networks and QoS provisioning in 3G networks. In 2003 he joined the University of Federal Armed Forces Munich as a research assistant. Since 2005 he is with the Communication Systems Group at University of Zurich. His areas of expertise include AAA architectures, accounting for IP-based services, QoS and mobility provisioning in IP networks, mobile telecommunication systems, and security architectures.

Yona Raekow, MSc, has been working at the Fraunhofer Institute for Algorithms and Scientific Computing SCAI since 2006. Her current research focuses on various aspects of Grid and Cloud Computing, Software Licence Management in distributed environments, Grid middlewares, Service Oriented Computing (SOA), web services. She has experience in various national and international research projects. Currently, she is working in the BEinGRID project, the largest collaborative research investment in Europe on IT for Business. Yona received her degree in Computer Science and Engineering at the University of Connecticut, USA in 2005. She is currently also pursuing her PhD degree at the University of Bonn where her research focuses on Computer Security and Cryptography.

Prof. Dr. George D. Stamoulis is a faculty member, currently Professor, in the Department of Informatics at Athens University of Economics and Business (AUEB). He received his Diploma in Electrical Engineering (1987, with highest honours) from the National Technical University of Athens, Greece, and the MSc (1988) and PhD (1991) degrees in Electrical Engineering from the Massachusetts Institute of Technology, Cambridge, Massachusetts, USA.

His main present research interests are in network economics and applications of economic mechanisms in management of Future Internet traffic and services, auction mechanisms for computation and communications resources with applications in Grid and Cloud computing, reputation mechanisms for electronic environments, and telecommunications regulation. He has published over 60 papers in scientific journals such as IEEE/ACM Transactions on Networks, Telecommunications Systems, Computer Communications, IEEE Transactions on Communications, Journal of the ACM, and IEEE Transactions on Information Theory, as well as in conferences such as INFOCOM, ITC, ACM SIGMETRICS, GLOBECOM and GP2PC.

Santi Ristol received a high degree in Telecommunication Engineering, from the Polytechnic University of Catalonia in Barcelona (1992) and a master degree in e-commerce by the Universitat Ramon Llull (2001).

He joined Atos Origin Spain in 1992 and he is currently Business Director leading the Services Area in Atos Research & Innovation. This area includes all R&D&I activities related to GRID & Cloud Computing technologies, Semantic Services, Software Engineering, Services Engineering, Open Source and Innovation Management, Green IT and eTourism.

He is President of the Spanish Technology Platform INES (National Initiative for Software & Services – www.ines.org.es) and Vice-Chair of the Steering Committee of the European Technology Platform NESSI (Networked European Software & Services Initiative - www.nessi-europe.com).

He has participated in many European R&D Projects primarily as Project Coordinator (SOA4All, BEinGRID, TrustCoM, CHALLENGERS, CROSSWORK, COREGRID, INFRAWEBS, EMMEDIATE, VIP-DATA, GRASP, DISRUPT-IT, PROMINENCE, METACAMPUS REAL, METACAMPUS, AMIES, SMART-MAN...).

A representative example is the project BEinGRID – Business Experiments in GRID; with nearly 100 partners and 25M€ budget, is not only the European Union's largest integrated project funded in ICT in FP6, but the reference initiative in Europe to establish effective routes to foster the adoption of Grid technologies.

Additionally he has worked as independent expert for the European Commission as evaluator and has acted as collaborator and speaker in many conferences and working groups around Europe.

Prof. Dr. Katarina Stanoevska-Slabeva is associate professor at the University of St. Gallen and vice-director of the Institute for Media and Communications Management (=mcm*institute*, University of St. Gallen). She is leading the research group "Digital Products and Communication" at the same institute. Prof. Stanoevska-Slabeva got her PhD and her habilitation from the University of St. Gallen. Her main research areas are analysis and development of product and market strategies as well as business models in converging and changing industries, in particular (Telecommunication, Information, Media and Entertainment)-TIME-industries. Another focus of her research is the empirical analysis of both acceptance by end and business users and social impact of innovative products based on emerging information and communication technologies. In this context a specific focus of her research was the adoption of grid and cloud technologies in companies, innovative business models related to grid and in the software industry as well as case studies of grid adoption. Prof. Dr. Stanoevska-Slabeva is an experienced manager of research and development projects and has been coordinating work packages and projects related to business aspects of innovative technologies in several international projects supported by the European Commission. She has furthermore published more than 120 articles at scientific conferences and journals and has edited four books.

Prof. Dr. Burkhard Stiller chairs as a full professor at Communication Systems Group CSG, Department of Informatics IFI at the University of Zurich UZH since 2004. He holds a Computer Science Diploma and a PhD degree of the University of Karlsruhe, Germany. During his research locations of the Computer Laboratory, University of Cambridge, UK, the Computer Engineering and Networks Laboratory, ETH Zürich, Switzerland, and the University of Federal Armed Forces, Munich, Germany his main research interests cover, including current CSG topics, charging and accounting of Internet services, economic management, systems with a fully decentralized control (P2P), telecommunication economics, and biometric management systems.

George Thanos is a member of the Network Economics and Services Group at the Athens University of Economics and Business in the department of Informatics where he is pursuing a PhD in the area of "Economics of the Next Generation of Internet". Mr. Thanos received his BEng degree in Computer Systems Engineering from the University of Manchester (former UMIST) and his MSc in Mobile and Satellite Communications from the University of Surrey, both in the UK.

In the past he has been working in the private sector (Motorola Ltd & Teletel SA) as a senior systems architect involved in the research and development of telecommunications systems for mobile networks, mainly based on UMTS/3G technologies. His current research focuses in the investigation of economic issues in Service Oriented Architectures (SOA), Grids and Next-Generation web repositories. He has also been working in the past in a number of European FP5, FP6 and currently FP7 projects in various technical and management positions.

Eugen Volk works as Research Assistant at the High Performance Computing Centre (HLRS) (Germany) and is a member of the Intelligent Service Infrastructures (ISIS) group. He has been working in large integrated grid projects since 2007, such as DEISA, BREIN and BEinGRID. He has been involved as technical manager of the Business Experiment AgroGrid of FP6 project BEinGRID and was responsible for architecture design and integration of grid components. His research interest rests on Service Oriented Architectures (SOA) and on automated service composition. Eugen Volk studied at the University of Stuttgart (Germany), where he obtained a diploma degree in Computer Sciences.

Martin Waldburger holds a Master of Science (MSc) degree which he received in 2004 from the University of Zurich. In the same year, he joined Prof. Dr. Burkhard Stiller's Communication Systems Group (CSG) at the University of Zurich in the position of an assistant and doctoral student. He participated in the European Union project "Access to Knowledge through the Grid in a Mobile World" (Akogrimo) and the "European Union Network of Excellence for the Management of Internet Technologies and Complex Services" (EMANICS). His research work is mainly focused on legal aspects of electronic service provisioning in multi-domain environments. In particular, he is focusing on research challenges in automated contract formation for value-added electronic services in an international context.

Thomas Wozniak works as Research Assistant and is doctoral student at the Institute for Media and Communications Management (=mcm*institute*, University of St. Gallen) in Switzerland. He has been involved in EU research projects in the fields of Grid computing and context-aware mobile services, thereby focusing on business aspects. He works on market analyses, business models, and provides business consultancy to project partners. Thomas Wozniak studied at University of Leipzig (Germany), Berlin University of the Arts (Germany), and Edith Cowan University Perth (Australia). He holds a diploma degree in Business Administration of the University of Leipzig and a diploma degree in Electronic Business of the Berlin University of the Arts.

Author (E-Mail)	Postal
Eleni Agiatzidou agiatzidou@aueb.gr	Network Economics and Services Group, Athens University of Business and Economics, 76 Patission Str. Athens,Greece
David Brossard david.brossard@bt.com	Centre for Information & Security Systems Research, BT Innovation & Design, Adastral Park, IP5 3RE Martlesham Heath, United Kingdom
Prof. Costas Courcoubetis courcou@aueb.gr	Network Economics and Services Group, Athens University of Business and Economics, 76 Patission Str. Athens,Greece
Juan Carlos Cuesta jcuesta@tid.es	Services for Enterprises, Telefónica Investigación y Desarrollo, Emilio Vargas 6, 28043 Madrid, Spain
Francesco D'Andria francesco.dandria@atosorigin.com	Atos Origin - Research and Innovation, Diagonal 200, Barcelona, 08018, Spain
Theo Dimitrakos theo.dimitrakos@bt.com	Centre for Information & Security Systems Research, BT Innovation & Design, Adastral Park, IP5 3RE Martlesham Heath, United Kingdom
Angelo Gaeta agaeta@crmpa.unisa.it	Centro di Ricerca in Matematica Pura ed Applicata (CRMPA), via ponte don Melillo, 84084 Fisciano (SA), Italy
Andrés Gómez agomez@cesga.es	Foundation CESGA, Avda. de Vigo S/N, 15705 Santiago de Compostela, Spain
Dr. Ulrich Heindl ulrich.heindl@tracetracker.com	TraceTracker AG, Robert-Bosch-Str. 9, D-68542 Heddesheim
Volker Hoyer volker.hoyer@sap.com	Institut for Media and Communications Management(=mcminstitute), University of St. Gallen, Blumenbergplatz 9, CH-9000 St. Gallen
Ansger Jacob ansger.jacob@uni-hohenheim.de	Universität Hohenheim, Information Systems 2, Schwerzstrasse 35, D-70599 Stuttgart
Ottmar Krämer-Fuhrmann ottmar.kraemer-fuhrmann@scai.fraunhofer.de	Fraunhofer-Institut für Algorithmen und Wissenschaftliches Rechnen SCAI, Schloss Birlinghoven, D-53754 Sankt Augustin
Karita Luokkanen-Rabetino karita.luokkanen@atosresearch.eu	Atos Origin - Research and Innovation, Diagonal 200, Barcelona, 08018, Spain
Marcus Mueller marcus.mueller@uni-hohenheim.de	Universität Hohenheim, Information Systems 2, Schwerzstrasse 35, D-70599 Stuttgart
Davide M. Parrilli davide.parrilli@law.kuleuven.be	Interdisciplinary Centre for Law and Technology (ICRI), K.U. Leuven, IBBT, Sint-Michielsstraat 6, 3000 Leuven, Belgium
Peter Racz racz@ifi.uzh.ch	University of Zurich, Department of Informatics (IFI), CSG, Binzmühlestrasse 14, CH-8050 Zürich

Yona Raekow
yona.raekow@scai.fraunhofer.de

Fraunhofer-Institut für Algorithmen und
Wissenschaftliches Rechnen SCAI, Schloss
Birlinghoven, D-53754 Sankt Augustin

Prof. Dr. George D. Stamoulis
gstamoul@aueb.gr

Network Economics and Services Group,
Athens University of Business and Economics,
76 Patission Str. Athens,Greece

Santi Ristol
santi.ristol@atosresearch.eu

Atos Origin - Research and Innovation,
Diagonal 200, Barcelona, 08018, Spain

Prof. Dr. Katarina Stanoevska-Slabeva
katarina.stanoevska@unisg.ch

Institut for Media and Communications
Management(=mcminstitute), University of St.
Gallen, Blumenbergplatz 9, CH-9000 St. Gallen

Prof. Dr. Burkhard Stiller
stiller@ifi.uzh.ch

University of Zurich, Department of Informatics
(IFI), CSG, Binzmühlestrasse 14, CH-8050
Zürich

George Thanos
gthanos@aueb.gr

Network Economics and Services Group,
Athens University of Business and Economics,
76 Patission Str. Athens,Greece

Eugen Volk
volk@hlrs.de

High Performance Computing Center Stuttgart
(HLRS), Nobelstrasse 19, D-70550 Stuttgart

Martin Waldburger
waldburger@ifi.uzh.ch

University of Zurich, Department of Informatics
(IFI), CSG, Binzmühlestrasse 14, CH-8050
Zürich

Thomas Wozniak
thomas.wozniak@unisg.ch

Institut for Media and Communications
Management(=mcminstitute), University of St.
Gallen, Blumenbergplatz 9, CH-9000 St. Gallen